To the I.I.U. Library

Best wishes,

Dr. Richard C. Lukas

February 11, 1971

EAGLES EAST

EAGLES EAST

The Army Air Forces and
the Soviet Union, 1941-1945

RICHARD C. LUKAS

FLORIDA STATE UNIVERSITY PRESS
Tallahassee, 1970

A Florida State University Press Book

COPYRIGHT © 1970 BY THE STATE OF FLORIDA
DEPARTMENT OF GENERAL SERVICES

LIBRARY OF CONGRESS CATALOG CARD NUMBER 78-126957

All rights reserved

PRINTED FOR THE PUBLISHER BY
E. O. PAINTER PRINTING COMPANY, INC., DE LAND, FLORIDA

To Frank,
whom we miss
and Elizabeth,
who carries on

Preface

THIS BOOK IS INTENDED to enlighten a crucial part of Russo-American relations during World War II. Using archival and published sources, this writer has sought to present a documented objective account of American air force relations with the Soviet Union.

Russo-American military relations during the Second World War essentially concerned aerial affairs. These relations involved allocating and delivering thousands of Lend-Lease aircraft, the item most in demand by the Russians, trying to establish AAF bases in southern Russia and Siberia and attempting to collaborate by the exchange of military information, establishing close liaison, and securing the release of interned American flyers from Soviet occupied territory. These military matters carried political overtones which the White House used in the hope of improving diplomatic relations between the two countries. This study explores these aspects of America's wartime relations with the Kremlin.

The records of the United States Army and the Department of State in the National Archives (Washington, D.C.) and those of the Army Air Forces in the United States Air Force Historical Archives (Maxwell Air Force Base, Alabama) proved a rich mine of material, as did relevant documents in the Library of Congress (Washington, D.C.), the Federal Records Center (Suitland, Maryland), and the Franklin D. Roosevelt Library (Hyde Park, New York).

I owe many groups and individuals gratitude for their assistance in completing this manuscript. I am grateful to the United States Army, the United States Air Force, and the Department of

viii PREFACE

State for their cooperation in arranging and extending security clearances for me to consult the massive amount of material still under classification. To the National Endowment for the Humanities which generously awarded me a grant for the summer of 1968 to complete my research, I am grateful. I also owe a debt to the Faculty Research Committee of Tennessee Technological University, and especially to its chairman, Dean Richard H. Fraser, for the release time during the academic year 1968-69 to complete this book.

My thanks goes to Dr. Earl R. Beck, Chairman of the Department of History at Florida State University, who guided me in my doctoral dissertation which is the basis of this book. I wish to mention, too, Dr. Maurer Maurer of the United States Air Force Historical Division for his special helpfulness. There are many other men and women who surely deserve fuller acknowledgement, especially Miss Marguerite Kennedy and Mr. Frank Myers of the United States Air Force Historical Archives and Mr. Thomas Hohmann and Mrs. Hazel Ward of the Modern Military Records Division of the National Archives, but space does not permit. Lastly and above all, to my wife goes my thanks for her patience and encouragement which sustained me through many trying moments. I, of course, assume responsibility for errors of fact and interpretation.

R.C.L.

Cookeville, Tennessee
June, 1970

Contents

I	The Impact of Barbarossa on the Soviet Air Force	1
II	Stopgap Commitments to Russia	14
III	Planning Long Range Aircraft Commitments: The Moscow Protocol	37
IV	The Problem of Delivery and North Russia	56
V	P-40's, Parts and Protests	69
VI	Iran: Corridor to Russia	80
VII	Alsib: Russo-American Link in the Pacific	95
VIII	The Washington Protocol	109
IX	The Bradley Mission to Moscow	125
X	The *Velvet* Project: Hope and Frustration	139
XI	The Passing of the Crisis: The Status of Aircraft Aid (July 1942–June 1944)	164
XII	The Elusive Bomb Line	181
XIII	Eastern Command: United States Strategic Air Forces, 1944-45	192
XIV	The Last Phase: Problems and Portents	215
	Appendixes	233
	Bibliography	239
	Index	249

CHAPTER I

The Impact of Barbarossa on the Soviet Air Force

O N JUNE 22, 1941, German armies plunged across the borders between an expanded Reich and a friendly Soviet Union. Accompanying these armies were Luftwaffe forces of 2,000 combat planes. The rapid advances of the German armies were matched by the devastating blows of the Luftwaffe. A Soviet air arm numerically superior but technically inferior to that of the German suffered drastic losses. While the rest of the world, in Hitler's words, "held its breath," the Soviet Union appeared to be at the point of collapse. Capitalist powers, hostile to the economic system of the Soviet Union and angered at its two-year support of their enemies, began to concert measures of military assistance which helped to forge the alliance that ultimately defeated the Nazis.

American military policy toward Russia consisted of three major objectives, the first of which was to supply Soviet armies against Germany. The principal means of doing this was to send Lend-Lease aircraft, which carried the highest priority in all Soviet requests for aid. Second, the United States sought to coordinate military operations with the Soviets. Since this involved two different groups of armies fighting on widely separated fronts, the major form of military collaboration during most of the war had to be the air forces, where continuity was unnecessary and American superiority in long distance planes was acknowledged. Third, the United States tried to bring the Russians into the Pacific war and to use Siberian bases for AAF attacks against the Japanese home islands. This study appraises these aspects of Russo-American military collaboration during World War II.

From the outbreak of World War II in September, 1939, until the summer of 1940, Germany had scored quick and easy victories against its weak opponents. In rapid succession, Poland, Denmark, Norway, the Low Countries, and France succumbed to the German panzers. Britain remained to be plucked. But this was a task more formidable than German leaders anticipated. Germany expected its Luftwaffe either to force Britain to surrender or at least to pave the way for an invasion. This stage of the war, known as the Battle of Britain, was a struggle fought entirely in the air. It began in the summer of 1940 and reached a climax during the fall of the year. The Luftwaffe failed to achieve its objectives: the Third Reich had received its first military setback.

During these critical months, the United States and Russia were non-belligerents. The United States nestled behind the alleged security of the neutrality legislation while Russia faithfully maintained its ties with Germany spawned in the Molotov-Ribbentrop Pact. By the time of the fall of France and the Battle of Britain, the United States had witnessed striking examples of Nazi success and ambition. Greater numbers of Americans saw that the threat to their nation's security was not quite so remote as it had once appeared. It was obviously in American interest to help Britain continue the fight while the country rearmed. However, public antipathy to involvement in the war continued. The consequence was that the measures under which the United States provided assistance to Great Britain were still depicted as only a modification of American neutrality. One of the major areas of assistance was in the provision of opportunities to purchase aircraft in the United States. This, however, posed the problem of allocation between the needs of the Royal Air Force (RAF) and those of the fledgling AAF, then called the Air Corps.

Prior to the fall of France and the Battle of Britain, when the threat to American security still seemed remote, the Air Corps had looked favorably upon foreign purchases of aircraft. It believed that these sales would stimulate aircraft production which would be available when the time came to serve the needs of American air power. In 1938 and 1939, Britain and France placed large orders. When the war broke out, the embargo provision of the neutrality laws was invoked, but Roosevelt, after debates in Congress, was able to have the cash and carry policy substituted.

The Impact of Barbarossa on the Soviet Air Force   3

This enabled Britain and France to resume purchases and shipments from the United States. Initially, the War Department approved the release of older model aircraft. By 1940, this policy had been liberalized, allowing the release of modern types. War Department planners believed that the advantages of an expanded aircraft industry, the delivery of the newest planes to the American air force, and the receipt of valuable combat data outweighed the inevitable delays of deliveries to the Air Corps.[1]

This relaxed approach to the buildup of American air power disappeared virtually overnight when France fell to the Nazi war machine. The full gravity of the European situation became apparent. Now military planners believed that the future might well see the end of neutrality and the involvement of the United States in the ever widening conflict. The country faced a great dilemma—how could it at the same time help to save Britain and prepare to cope with its own military problems?

If Air Corps needs became more urgent, RAF needs were more immediate. With the air battle over the island serving as dramatic proof of the immediacy of British requirements, the first chapter of the allocation problem, one of the most important in the history of the war, was resolved in Britain's favor. Representatives of the Air Corps, Navy Bureau of Aeronautics, and the British Purchasing Commission agreed on July 23, 1940, that Britain should receive approximately 14,375 aircraft by April, 1942. Over 8,500 planes, originally scheduled for the Air Corps, were transferred to the British. In September, 1940, the Joint Aircraft Committee was created to supervise allocations. Two months later, Roosevelt ordered "that planes coming off the production lines should be divided fifty-fifty with the British."[2]

Anglo-American strategy sessions early in 1941 confirmed the trends of the previous year. During the early months of 1941, military leaders met in Washington to chart Anglo-American strategy in the event the United States got involved in the war. An offensive posture in Europe and a defensive one in the Far East formed the basis of strategic planning. ABC-2, the report on air force collaboration which resulted from these conversations, urged

1. Wesley Frank Craven and James Lea Cate (eds.), *The Army Air Forces in World War II*, Vol. VI: *Men and Planes* (Chicago: The University of Chicago Press, 1955), pp. 302-3.
2. *Ibid.*, pp. 399-400.

EAGLES EAST

America to complete its 54 group program, not to mention projected increases. Aircraft would be delivered to services capable of using them effectively—in other words, British needs were favored over those of the Air Corps. Although not officially approved by the President, the policy served as a guideline.[3]

When Anglo-American military conversations ended in March, 1941, another important event occurred, presaging future competitors for American aircraft. That was the passage of the Lend-Lease Act. It firmly established the principle that the output of production would be available to nations whose defense the President considered vital to the United States. Although the opposition in Congress alluded critically to the then hypothetical question of Russia's inclusion under Lend-Lease,[4] few seriously believed then that the Soviet Union would be a major claimant on American production.

Under the impact of foreign purchases American aircraft production increased rapidly. It is probable that these sales "advanced by as much as a year the time within which American aircraft production would reach its peak."[5] For example, in the fourth quarter of 1940, American factories delivered 1,997 planes. In the first quarter of 1941, the figure advanced to 3,264. During the last six months of 1940 factories delivered 3,611 aircraft as opposed to 7,189 during the first six months of 1941. Given the policy governing allocations, the increase in production was not reflected in the number and quality of combat planes in the Air Corps. The following figures indicate United States factory deliveries of combat aircraft to the Air Corps and Britain in the period July, 1940—June, 1941:[6]

---

3. Wesley Frank Craven and James Lea Cate (eds.), *The Army Air Forces in World War II*, Vol. I: *Plans and Early Operations* (Chicago: The University of Chicago Press, 1948), pp. 130-31; Mark Skinner Watson, *Chief of Staff: Prewar Plans and Preparations* (Washington: Department of the Army, 1950), pp. 380-81.

4. For an interesting discussion of this subject see Raymond H. Dawson, *The Decision to Aid Russia, 1941: Foreign Policy and Domestic Politics* (Chapel Hill: The University of North Carolina Press, 1959), pp. 22-43.

5. Craven and Cate, *The Army Air Forces in World War II*, VI, 301.

6. U. S., Army Air Forces, *Army Air Forces Statistical Digest: World War II* (2nd Printing, Washington: Office of Statistical Control, 1945), pp. 127-28. It should be observed that the U. S. Navy received aircraft during this period.

1940	AIR CORPS	BRITAIN	1941	AIR CORPS	BRITAIN
July	38	219	January	8	296
August	53	157	February	89	292
September	99	109	March	192	220
October	45	169	April	237	246
November	6	218	May	56	296
December	15	288	June	99	219

Since most of the combat planes in this period did not go to the Air Corps, it is clear why shortages developed in meeting the defense needs of the United States and its possessions. In July, 1941, the Air Corps, now redesignated Army Air Forces and known as the AAF, had 149 combat planes, 31 of which were classified as "modern."[7] In the months preceding Pearl Harbor, suitable combat planes in the AAF flew to Hawaii and the Philippines to strengthen the unimpressive military position there. This left deficiencies of aircraft for continental defense. Out of approximately 3,000 combat planes available in the AAF on the eve of Pearl Harbor, General H. H. Arnold, Commanding General of the AAF, reported that less than 1,200 were suitable for combat. The attack found America, he said, "with plans but not with planes."[8]

American security was reasonably protected from German attack so long as Britain remained in the war. But there was no certainty that America could continue to remain aloof from the conflict. War clouds presaged its eventual involvement perhaps more from difficulties in the Pacific than from those in Europe. War planners stressed these factors in order to prepare the country for defensive and, if the need arose, offensive missions. In the case of the AAF, the argument that American needs were beginning to assume an urgency as great as those of Britain was a strong one.

America's entry into World War II was preceded by that of the Soviet Union and the problems of air force development were greatly complicated as a consequence. By operation "Barbarossa," Hitler dramatically ended the strained romance that began with the Molotov-Ribbentrop Pact and forced the Soviet Union into the anti-Axis camp. Although the world may not have held its

7. Memo, Arnold for Lovett, July 18, 1941 (File: 400.3295, AG, in WWIIRD/NA). See glossary at the end of this study for a full explanation of abbreviations used in the footnotes and text.
8. *The War Reports of General of the Army George C. Marshall, General of the Army H. H. Arnold, Fleet Admiral Ernest J. King* (Philadelphia: J. B. Lippincott Company, 1947), pp. 67, 69-70, 331.

breath when Hitler unleashed "Barbarossa," it had reason to gasp several times at the tremendous losses which Germany inflicted. American military planners expected Russian resistance to collapse in a matter of weeks. Therefore it appeared unlikely that Russia would become a serious claimant for American aircraft. Few, indeed, in June, 1941, would have predicted the important role which air power was soon to have in United States-Soviet relations.

Prior to the German attack, the Soviet Union had had the largest air force in the world and an equally large aircraft industry to sustain it. These were objectives upon which the Soviet government had concentrated since the end of the Bolshevik Revolution and Civil War. Russian aviation dated back to the tsarist period: Russian writers are fond of making the extravagant claim that Alexander F. Mozhaisky successfully flew a heavier-than-air flying machine a generation before the Wright brothers' feat at Kitty Hawk.[9]

The Russian aircraft industry had virtually ceased to exist when the Bolsheviks took over. In 1916, Russia manufactured 1,769 airframes and 660 aircraft; whereas in 1920, when the Bolsheviks were at war at home and abroad, none were produced.[10] But after the Bolsheviks consolidated their power, the Soviet government in the 1920's and 1930's devoted much of its energy to building aircraft and associated industries, developing research facilities, training pilots, technicians, and skilled personnel, and keeping abreast of aeronautical developments in the West. Andrei N. Tupolev and Nikolai Y. Zhukovsky laid the groundwork of Soviet aviation. They persuaded Lenin in 1918 to establish the Central-Aero-Hydro-Dynamic Institute, commonly known as TsAGI, and the Zhukovsky Air Academy which have dominated Soviet aviation to the present day.[11] In subsequent years, scores of laboratories, bureaus and schools involved in aeronautical work were

9. See the interesting article on this subject by Captain Glenn E. Wasson, "The Airplane, Another Soviet 'First'?" *The Airpower Historian*, IX (July, 1962), 151-56.

10. U. S., War Department, "Preliminary Report on the Soviet Air Force" (June, 1945), 8 A-1-3 (File: M-27613-S, in AUL).

11. Ramsay D. Potts, Jr., "The Foundations of Soviet Air Power: A Historical and Managerial Interpretation," *The Annals of the American Academy of Political and Social Science*, CCXCIX (May, 1955), 39-40. One graduate said of the Zhukovsky Air Academy that it was "a place which specialises [sic] in aeronautics just as European universities used to specialise in the humanities." Quoted in *ibid.*, p. 39.

The Impact of Barbarossa on the Soviet Air Force

established. By 1938, in addition to eleven military schools, there were 125 flying schools offering aeronautical training. The Society for Air and Chemical Defense was especially active in offering special courses, organizing advanced training clubs and encouraging study circles in all phases of aviation.[12]

Under the impact of the Five-Year Plans the Soviet aircraft industry showed a significant growth in production, and by 1941, there were approximately 100 plants active in the work, 25 of which were assembly plants.[13] The industry had modern equipment—much of it of western design—and a large force of skilled labor. But there were serious setbacks. Engine production did not show satisfactory results until 1935-1936. Moreover, the industry was too dependent upon foreign sources of aluminum, a situation aggravated by the lack of electric power essential for its operation.[14] Despite these problems the Soviet aircraft industry, primarily located in the western part of the state, impressed foreign observers who regarded it as the largest in the world.[15] Estimates of Soviet aircraft production for the period 1929-1940 confirmed their opinion:[16]

1929	500- 980	1935	5,500- 5,400
1930	850-1,100	1936	8,000- 7,000
1931	1,200-1,500	1937	9,000- 7,540
1932	1,500-1,920	1938	10,000-10,000
1933	1,700-2,800	1939	11,000-10,000
1934	3,100-4,000	1940	12,000-10,000

12. "Lyons War College Report" (January, 1938), pp. 2, 8 (File: 8000-9040, G-2, in WWIIRD/NA).

13. U. S., War Department, "Preliminary Report," 8A-1-3; the Lyons report cited above gives the following breakdown at the beginning of 1938: 28 airplane, 14 engine and 32 accessory factories.

14. "Lyons War College Report," pp. 6, 7; U. S., War Department, "Preliminary Report," 8A-1-3; Nikolai A. Voznesensky, *The Economy of the USSR during World War II* (Washington: Public Affairs Press, 1948), p. 40. The author, an official Soviet spokesman, points out that in the eastern regions, where hundreds of industrial centers were relocated, electric power needs were "practically overcome" in 1943. In other words, it can be assumed that at least until 1943, if not later, the aluminum industry suffered shortages.

15. "Lyons War College Report," p. 7.

16. Statistics relating to Soviet aircraft production are scarce and tentative at best. They are primarily based upon fragmentary references from Soviet sources and estimates made by observers. The figures in the first column are contained in U.S., War Department, "Preliminary Report," 8A-3; those in the second column are the estimates of the Institute for Research in Social Science, *The Soviet Aircraft Industry* (Chapel Hill: University of North Carolina, 1955), p. 90.

8   EAGLES EAST

Soviet aviation did not develop in a vacuum; it kept abreast of developments in leading western nations. After the Bolsheviks consolidated their power, scores of engineers and technicians from the West went to Russia. Many of them, especially from post-Versailles Germany, left their imprint on early Soviet aircraft design.[17] The magnitude of the orders placed in western nations for aircraft, parts, and tools revealed the prominent position of the Soviet Air Force in the budget and the sensitivity to non-Russian aircraft developments. In 1937, for example, the Russians concluded contracts totalling $1,000,000 for the delivery of two types of American aircraft. Additional orders for aircraft accessories totalled $1,250,000, an amount equal to the purchases of the War Department for experimental and service test aeronautical equipment including experimental aircraft.[18]

Despite warnings to Russia from the United States and Great Britain of an impending German attack, "Barbarossa" caught the Soviet Union by surprise.[19] On this occasion, declared Churchill, Stalin and his cronies were "the most completely outwitted bunglers of the Second World War."[20] And in the post-Stalin era, Soviet historians have come close to agreement with the capitalist critic.[21]

17. U. S., War Department, "Preliminary Report," 8A-1-2.
18. "Lyons War College Report," p. 2. During the era of the Stalin cult, aviation was labelled "Stalinist aviation" and pilots were often called "Stalinist falcons" since Stalin was allegedly responsible for the growth of the Soviet Air Force. For a rhapsodic account of the leader's role in the development of Red air power see V. P. Moskovskii, *Voenno-Vozdushnye Sily SSSR, 1918-1948: Kratkii Ocherk* (Moskva: Voennoe Izdatelstvo Ministerstva Vooruzhennykh Sil Soiuza SSR, 1948). Since the demise of the personality cult, Soviet historians conspicuously ignore references to Stalin's role in the development of Russian air power.
19. Msg., Hull to Steinhardt, March 4, 1941; memo of conversation by Welles, March 20, 1941 in U. S., Department of State, *Foreign Relations of the United States, Diplomatic Papers: 1941*, Vol. I: *General, The Soviet Union* (Washington: United States Government Printing Office, 1958), pp. 714, 723. (Hereinafter cited as *Foreign Relations*, 1941, I.) Welles notes an earlier American warning to Russia in January, 1941, but no record of it was found in State Department files. See memo of conversation by Welles, June 26, 1941, *ibid.*, I, 771-72. For an account of British warnings to Russia, see Winston S. Churchill, *The Grand Alliance* (Boston: Houghton Mifflin Co., 1950), pp. 358, 360.
20. Churchill, *The Grand Alliance*, p. 353.
21. B. S. Telpukhovskii, *Velikaia Otechestvennaia Voina Sovetskogo Soiuza, 1941-1945: Kratkii Ocherk* (Moskva: Gosudarstvennoe Izdatelstvo Politicheskoi Literatury, 1959), p. 39; Institut Marksizma-Leninizma, *Istoria Velikoi Otechestvennoi Voiny Sovetskogo Soiuza, 1941-1945 v Shesti Tomakh.* Vol. II: *Otrazhenie Sovetskim Narodom Verolomnogo Napadeniia Fashistskoi Germanii na SSSR. Sozdanie Uslovii Ilia Korennogo Pereloma v Voine, iiun 1941 g -*

The Impact of Barbarossa on the Soviet Air Force 9

Soviet lack of readiness was immediately apparent in the disorganization at the front and in the destruction of hundreds of planes on cramped fields in Poland and the Baltic states. Under these conditions, the Luftwaffe was able to inflict a gargantuan blow on Soviet air power during the early days of hostilities. The Luftwaffe executed "Barbarossa" with approximately 2,000 combat aircraft, including 880 bombers, 280 dive bombers, 60 ground attack planes, 60 twin-engine fighters, 600 single-engine fighters, 120 reconnaissance, and 230 air transport and liaison planes.[22] The Soviets had 6,000-7,500 aircraft in European Russia and 2,000-3,000 in the Far East.[23] Despite its numerical preponderance, the Soviet Air Force was no match for the technically superior Luftwaffe. Not more than 17 per cent of the planes on the airfields, for example, were modern types capable of meeting the enemy effectively.[24] The bulk of Soviet fighters was made up of obsolete I-15's and I-16's. These were no match for the ME-109 and ME-110. Even the first models of the MIG and YAK, rushed into service in 1941, were no competition in speed and firepower for Luftwaffe fighters. Soviet two-engine bombers, the PE-2 and DB-3, could not outperform their German equivalents. Of course,

---

noiabr 1942 g (Moskva: Voennoe Izdatelstvo Ministerstva Oborony SSSR, 1961), p. 10.

22. Generalleutnant a. D. Hermann Plocher, *The German Air Force Versus Russia, 1941* (USAF Historical Studies: No. 153, The Air University, 1965), p. 33; Karlsruhe Document Collection, "Verteilung Der Fliegerverbande Auf die Verschiedenen Kampffronten. Stand: 20. 6. 1941" (File: in USAF/HA).

23. The higher estimate is in Walter Schwabedissen, *The Russian Air Force in the Eyes of German Commanders* (USAF Historical Studies: No. 175, The Air University, 1960), pp. 17-18. The lower estimate is in U. S., Department of the Army, *The German Campaign in Russia: Planning and Operations, 1940-1942* (DA Pamphlet No. 20-261a, German Report Series, 1955), p. 24. Churchill says the Luftwaffe numbered 2,700 aircraft and were met by "at least five thousand aircraft" of the Soviet Union. See Churchill, *The Grand Alliance*, p. 378. Before Barbarossa the German radio intercept service estimated Russian aircraft strength at 13,000-14,000. See Schwabedissen, *The Russian Air Force*, p. 19. If German estimates of Soviet aircraft losses are accepted in connection with the strength figures of the Soviet Air Force which Stalin related to Harry Hopkins, President Roosevelt's troubleshooter, at the end of July, 1941, there is a strong suggestion that the Russians had as many planes as the Germans computed. In a study prepared in May, 1943, United States Army Intelligence placed Soviet strength in western Russia at 11,000 aircraft in June, 1941. See memo, with report entitled "U. S. S. R. Aircraft Strength and Production," Col. R. C. Jacobs, Jr. for Brig. Gen. A. C. Wedemeyer, May 7, 1943 (File: ABC 452.1, WPD, WDGS, in WWIIRD/NA).

24. Telpukhovskii, *Velikaia Otechestvennaia,* pp. 40-41.

neither country developed a strategic long-range bomber force, which ultimately proved to be disastrous for the Third Reich.

The extent of the losses suffered by the Soviet Air Force remains debatable. Estimates vary on both sides. Cyrille Kalinov, an officer who held a responsible position which granted him access to the General Staff, estimated that his compatriots lost 3,000 aircraft during the early hours of the invasion.[25] However, a recent Soviet study on World War II pointed out that losses on the first day of the conflict amounted to approximately 1,200 planes.[26] Soviet historians acknowledge the destruction of a large number of aircraft and agree, as Telpukhovskii puts it, that "enemy aviation seized command of the air."[27]

Nazi sources are in closer agreement on the losses. General Major Otto von Waldau, the brilliant Chief of the Luftwaffe Operations Staff, recorded that the Russians lost 1,800 planes on the first day of the war.[28] A study by the German Air Historical Branch estimated that by the second day of the invasion the Luftwaffe had destroyed 2,582 enemy aircraft.[29] "From the second day onwards," Field Marshal Albert Kesselring graphically wrote,

> I watched the battle with the Russian heavy bombers coming from the depth of Russia. It seemed almost a crime to allow these floundering aircraft to be attacked in tactically impossible formation. One flight after another came in innocently at regular intervals, an easy prey for our fighters. It was sheer 'infanticide.'[30]

The High Command placed the destruction at 3,630 aircraft for the period June 22-28, 1941.[31] Two weeks later, a German Armed Forces Communiqué put Soviet losses to that point at 6,233. The mustached leader in the Kremlin responded in typical fashion. He

---

25. Cyrille D. Kalinov, *Les Marechaux Sovietiques vous Parlent* (Paris: Stock, Delamain et Boutelleau, 1950), pp. 34-35.
26. Institut Marksizma - Leninizma, *Istoria Velikoi*, p. 16.
27. Telpukhovskii, *Velikaia Otechestvennaia*, p. 41.
28. Plocher, *The German Air Force*, p. 42.
29. Great Britain, Air Ministry (trans.), "A Survey of German Air Operations, 1939-1944" (prepared by the German Air Historical Branch, 8th Abteilung, September 21, 1944), p. 6 (File: 512.621/VII/28, in USAF/HA).
30. Maj. Gen. J. F. C. Fuller, *A Military History of the Western World*, Vol. III: *From the Seven Days Battle, 1862 to the Battle of Leyte Gulf, 1944* (New York: Funk and Wagnalls Co., 1956), p. 428.
31. Schwabedissen. *The Russian Air Force*, p. 55.

The Impact of Barbarossa on the Soviet Air Force   11

executed his air force commander on the northwestern front, General Rychagov, while another air officer, General Kopets, committed suicide for the same reason.[32]

The magnitude of the reduction of Soviet air power was made graver by the relatively minor punishment inflicted on the invaders. To be sure, the Moscow press maintained that the Luftwaffe lost more planes. This distortion is reflected in broadcasts immediately after the invasion. On June 25, 1941, the Moscow radio reported that in the period June 22-24, the Soviet Air Force lost 374 aircraft to the Luftwaffe's 431. On July 14, it claimed that the campaign had cost Germany 2,300 aircraft as opposed to 1,500 Soviet losses. After six weeks of war, the Moscow radio curiously reported that the Soviets had destroyed over 6,000 aircraft, three times the initial number of planes used by the Luftwaffe in the campaign. The cost to the Soviet Union, on the other hand, was placed at 4,000.[33] In striking contrast to this contention, figures based on German records put Luftwaffe losses for June at 460 and for July, at 695.[34]

While the Luftwaffe delivered its blows against the enemy air force, German armies plunged deeply into the Soviet heartland. The northern army group under Field Marshal Wilhelm Ritter von Leeb moved through the Baltic states toward Leningrad, its primary objective. Field Marshal Fedor von Bock's central army group ran into stubborn resistance at Smolensk, temporarily slowing its drive toward Moscow. The southern army group under Field Marshal Gerd von Rundstedt defeated the Russians in the tank battle at Zhitomir, bringing it to Kiev by the end of the month. The Luftwaffe, following the Barbarossa directive, supported the advances of the ground forces by bombing and strafing attacks on the front.

Although Soviet aircraft production increased from 1,000-1,250 in May and June to 1,500-2,000 in July and August,[35] the

---

32. U. S., Department of the Army, *The German Campaign in Russia*, p. 48; Robert Conquest, *The Great Terror: Stalin's Purge of the Thirties* (London: The Macmillan Company, 1968), p. 489.

33. Foreign Broadcast Intelligence Service, Transcripts of Monitored Foreign Broadcasts (File: RG 262, Boxes 426-27, in NA).

34. U. S. Army, "Air Staff Post Hostilities Intelligence: Requirements on German Air Force. Section II: Appendices. Appendix 17," p. 17 (File: 519.601 B-2, in USAF/HA).

35. U. S., War Department, "Preliminary Report," 8A-4.

12   EAGLES EAST

continuing German assault required an evacuation and relocation of armament industries from western Russia to the interior. As a consequence, the production gains of July and August were over-shadowed by the high rate of aircraft losses and the hegira of industries to the Urals, western Siberia, and Soviet Central Asia. Over 600 industrial centers were moved between the winter of 1941 and the end of 1942.[36] The extent of the disruption to the economy is revealed by the admission that between June and November, 1941, the gross industrial output of the Soviet Union declined by one-half.[37] By November, 1941, aircraft production had probably declined to 500-600 planes per month, or about one-half the level reached in June.[38]

The Soviet Union, unprepared for the German invasion, lost heavily in men and material. It possessed the capacity to produce most of its own equipment but required time, resources, and a stabilized front, none of which were in the offing during the summer and fall of 1941. As the most productive areas of the country fell rapidly under enemy control, the government moved industries eastward where they could later resume operation. Critical raw materials were needed to replace those lost to the enemy. Continued technical developments were necessary to close the gap which separated Russia from Germany. As a consequence, serious deficiencies confronted the Soviet armed forces. The most critical of these was the condition of the air force, an "Achilles heel"[39] after the German avalanche.

Little wonder, then, that the Soviet government placed the highest priority upon aircraft in its requests for aid from the United States and Great Britain. These requests posed serious problems for the United States, intensifying the existing problem of the allocation of aircraft. Now a three way division had to be made to the AAF, RAF, and SAF. This allocation could not be determined upon purely military considerations. Matters of political expediency were of equal significance. Even had it been possible to make decisions upon the basis of military considera-

36. Voznesensky, *The Economy of the USSR*, p. 22.
37. *Ibid.*, p. 25.
38. U. S., War Department, "Preliminary Report"; Asher Lee, *The Soviet Air Force* (2nd ed.; London: Gerald Duckworth & Co., Ltd., 1952), p. 89.
39. An apt term used by Ivan Krylov, *Soviet Staff Officer* (New York: Philosophical Library, 1951), p. 259.

The Impact of Barbarossa on the Soviet Air Force   13

tions alone, no easy conclusions could have been reached. The extent of the damage visited upon the Soviet Air Force was shrouded behind propaganda. To this day it remains so.[40]

40. Soviet historians have distorted the strength and quality of the Soviet Air Force on the eve of Russo-German hostilities. They suggest that the two air forces were evenly matched and point out that because of the surprise attack, the Luftwaffe was left with numerical superiority until the battle of Stalingrad. See Telpukhovskii, *Velikaia Otechestvennaia*, pp. 38-41, 550; Institut Marksizma-Leninizma, *Istoria Velikoi*, pp. 9ff.

CHAPTER II

Stopgap Commitments to Russia

THE GERMAN *Drang nach osten* had forced the Soviet government to seek material assistance from the West. Russian requests for American aircraft were gigantic, supporting the German claim that the Luftwaffe had rendered the Soviet Air Force virtually impotent.

These requests came at a critical time for the United States. By June, 1941, only nine months had elapsed since the nation began its rearmament program and only three months since the Lend-Lease Act was passed. The country was still divided over the question of even assisting Great Britain. And after "Barbarossa" the White House was confronted with a vociferous segment of public opinion that hoped Nazi Germany and Soviet Russia would destroy each other.

Although official American reactions to Soviet involvement in the war were cautious, the White House favored sending at least stopgap shipments of aircraft and other critical items to the new belligerent. The White House believed that such shipments might encourage resistance against Germany—a matter of grave concern in London and Washington. If the Soviet Union continued in the war, these shipments would have laid the basis for a later broadening of the American supply program. Then, too, the White House expected that as time passed the hostility toward Russia in large segments of American opinion would be mitigated to allow the implementation of a long-range program of aid. On the other hand, if the Soviet Union were either defeated or sued for peace, stopgap shipments lost in this essentially political maneuver would not loom large.

Stopgap Commitments to Russia

The War Department did not at first share this White House view. Since the fall of France, the AAF was more intent on satisfying the immediate needs of Britain, then battling for its very existence. Furthermore, the War Department was acutely sensitive to the critical shortages of combat aircraft that had developed in the AAF. Finally, the Department, conditioned by gloomy reports predicting Soviet defeat, believed that the communist state was near collapse. Diversions of critically needed planes under such conditions, these officials believed, were wasteful as well as injurious to the AAF.

As early as June 23 Acting Secretary of State Sumner Welles announced that Soviet resistance against Germany was to the benefit of American "defense and security."[1] President Roosevelt later confirmed this by offering aid to the Soviet Union if it would reveal its needs.[2] On June 26 Constantine Oumansky, Moscow's Ambassador, had his first interview with Welles since the outbreak of hostilities. Oumansky had been instructed not to raise the question of aid but to determine the attitude of the United States toward the new phase of the war. Welles dispelled any lingering Soviet doubts on the matter by stating that requests for assistance would receive prompt and favorable consideration. He also cited the friendly gestures by Washington in unfreezing Soviet assets in the United States and refusing to invoke a proclamation under the Neutrality Act.[3]

Four days after this clarification of policy, Oumansky presented Welles with a nine-point list of Soviet requests, which included huge quantities of military and industrial items.[4] The response was no doubt encouraging to American authorities since it reflected Soviet determination to remain in the war. The first two requests were especially significant. The Moscow government asked for 3,000 fighters and the same number of bombers.[5]

Oumansky was anxious that the United States dispatch some

1. Welles' statement is contained in msg., Welles to Steinhardt, June 23, 1941, *Foreign Relations*, 1941, I, 767-68; and in William L. Langer and S. Everett Gleason, *The Undeclared War, 1940-41* (New York: Harper & Brothers, 1953), p. 541.
2. Langer and Gleason, *The Undeclared War*, p. 541.
3. Memo of conversation by Welles, June 26, 1941; msg., Steinhardt to Hull, June 29, 1941, *Foreign Relations*, 1941, I, 769-70, 774.
4. Memo of conversation by Welles, June 30, 1941, *Foreign Relations*, 1941, I, 779-80.
5. Memo, Curtis for Welles, July 18, 1941 (File: 861.24/517 3/4, in DS/NA).

16 EAGLES EAST

planes as soon as possible and requested that a portion be flown via the Alaska-Siberia route, or Alsib as it was later known. Welles noted that:

> He [Oumansky] said he would like to mention, in the event the United States could make available some short-range bombers to Russia, the bombers could of course be flown from Alaska by way of the Aleutian Islands to Western Russia and that, . . . the airfields in Siberia from the Pacific to Western Russia were in excellent condition and amply capable of taking care of any transcontinental flight that might be arranged for any bombers sent from here.[6]

When the President received the Soviet Ambassador, it was clear that Roosevelt intended to follow through on formal assurances of support offered earlier. On July 10 he informed Oumansky that the United States would begin shipping supplies before October 1.[7]

Meanwhile, a temporary committee under the chairmanship of Charles P. Curtis, Jr., Special Assistant to Welles, processed Soviet requests.[8] They totaled almost $2,000,000,000, of which 95 per cent related to aircraft and ordnance.[9] The President then centered responsibility for obtaining immediate and substantial shipments of aid to Russia in the Division of Defense Aid Reports, headed by Major General James H. Burns.[10] He was assisted by Colonel Philip R. Faymonville, an ordnance officer who once served as military attaché in Moscow.[11] In appointing Burns to handle the aid, the President explained: "It is of the utmost importance that these shipments go forward in time to reach their destination before the

6. Memo of conversation by Welles, July 3, 1941, *Foreign Relations*, 1941, I, 786-87.
7. Memo of conversation by Welles, July 10, 1941, *Foreign Relations*, 1941, I, 788-89.
8. Memo, Curtis for Dean Acheson and Welles, June 30, 1941, with enclosed memo, same date (File: 861.24/516 1/2, in DS/NA).
9. U. S., Civilian Production Administration, *Industrial Mobilization for War: History of the War Production Board and Predecessor Agencies, 1940-1945*. Vol. I: *Program and Administration* (Washington: United States Government Printing Office, 1947), pp. 130-31.
10. Ltr., Roosevelt to Burns, July 21, 1941, *The Public Papers and Addresses of Franklin D. Roosevelt*. Vol. II: *The Call to Battle Stations*, comp. Samuel I. Rosenman (New York: Harper & Brothers, Publishers, 1950), p. 419.
11. Edward R. Stettinius, Jr., *Lend-Lease: Weapon for Victory* (New York: The Macmillan Co., 1944), p. 122.

Stopgap Commitments to Russia

winter makes ocean and land transportation difficult."[12] Roosevelt apparently believed that supplies sent to Russia by the winter might help to inspire continued resistance. He also directed Burns to review the Soviet requests with representatives from other agencies if necessary and submit within two days a list of items for quick delivery.[13]

In response to the President's instructions, members of the Division of Defense Aid Reports, the Army-Navy Munitions Board Priorities Committee, the Department of State, the Army, and the the Office of Production Management met and approved requests totalling $21,940,000 for various industrial items to be shipped on or before October 1.[14] All of these items could not be produced and sent by that date. Some of them, like aviation gasoline, were promptly found even though they were in short supply. By the end of August the Department of State, which played a major role in the search for the gasoline, announced that arrangements had been completed for the delivery of 52,000 tons, the amount requested by the Soviets for immediate shipment.[15] But some items, such as high octane gasoline and aviation lubrication plants, which constituted a major portion of Soviet requests, required two to three years before they could be produced, installed and placed in operation. This involved the delicate question of divulging new processes, many of them in the experimental state, that were vital to national defense and of compensating industrial firms which had failed, in pre-war negotiations with the Russians, to obtain satisfactory financial arrangements. According to an official of a leading firm engaged in these early negotiations, the Russians had made "proposals which would result in supplying them with a maximum of information for a minimum of actual payment

---

12. Ltr., Roosevelt to Burns, July 21, 1941, *The Public Papers*, p. 419.
13. *Ibid.*
14. Ltr., Burns to Roosevelt, July 23, 1941 (File: FW 861.24/517 2/4, in DS/NA).
15. Memo, Max Thornburg for Acheson, August 5, 1941 (File: 861.24/570 8/16, in DS/NA); American petroleum deliveries to Russia seriously strained Russo-Japanese relations. Japan considered these deliveries a challenge to its security and raised questions about the neutrality pact between the two countries. Japanese-American relations were also strained further but Tokyo suggested that they could be improved if the United States resumed shipments of top grade gasoline that had been stopped one year earlier. Memo, initialed SKH and JWB, August 27, 1941 (File: 861.24/657, in DS/NA); msg., Frank Lockhart to Secretary of State, August 23, 1941 (File: 861.24, in DS/NA); msg., Joseph Grew to Secretary of State, October 24, 1941 (File: 861.24/693, in DS/NA).

18   EAGLES EAST

to America."[16] Overriding these technical problems was the basic consideration of American foreign policy which was not yet prepared to move from immediate to long-range assistance: satisfaction of Soviet requests for heavy industrial plants and equipment would have implied such a shift.[17]

Aircraft and ordnance items received special attention. Burns told the President that "pursuit planes and bombers, which are considered by the Soviet Ambassador to be of prime urgency, are not included on the list, as these items are understood to be receiving the personal attention of Mr. Welles."[18] As the latter found out from the War Department, it was impossible for the United States to meet more than a small portion of the huge request for aircraft. Even the consideration of a token shipment—and the White House insisted upon some action—brought firm and unequivocal opposition from the War Department.

General George C. Marshall, the Chief of Staff, staunchly opposed sending planes in view of gaping security needs. He conveyed his views on the matter to Lieutenant General H. H. Arnold, Chief of the AAF. Marshall stated flatly that he was

> unalterably opposed to the release of any U. S. pursuit planes and light and medium bombers until we have first established units of these types in the Philippines for the security of the Fleet Anchorage, and the defense of the Islands. We have been trying for six months to meet the Navy's demands, and that of our Army Commander in the Philippines, that the obsolescent planes be replaced at the earliest possible moment with modern types. At the present moment, with Japan's known preparations to move South, the Philippines become of great strategic importance, as they constitute both a Naval and Air Base upon the immediate flank of the Japanese southern movement.[19]

16. Ltr., Johnson to Adolf Berle, September 5, 1941 (File: 861.24/746, in DS/NA); memo, Thornburg for Acheson, September 19, 1941 (File: 861.24/746, in DS/NA); note, Thornburg to Acheson, October 20, 1941, enclosing memo entitled "Draft memorandum on oil refining equipment requested by Soviet government" and memo, Berle for Thornburg, October 17, 1941 (File: 861.24/585 1/2, in DS/NA).
17. This is implied by Berle in his memo to Acheson on September 15, 1941 (File: 861.24/746, in DS/NA).
18. Ltr., Burns to Roosevelt, July 23, 1941.
19. Memo, Marshall for Arnold, July 16, 1941 (File: 400.3295, AG, in WWIIRD/NA).

Stopgap Commitments to Russia 19

But Marshall learned from Welles on the following day that the President had "ordered" a token release of P-40's and light bombers. The General promptly explained to the Assistant Secretary of War for Air, Robert A. Lovett, the reasons which prohibited a further drain of planes from the already weak AAF. He particularly emphasized the immediate need in the Philippines and in current maneuvers with the ground forces. In the latter case, he stated, "This is vitally important so far as the development of ground air teamwork is concerned, but it is possibly of even more pressing importance to meet the growing public pressure and criticism on this subject." He then pointed to the stress of allocating planes to Brazil and China. Marshall urged that the President receive "a complete picture of our present dilemma in this matter," and asked pointedly "Are we to risk the Philippine situation or the Brazilian situation, or the clamor of the press in this country or the purely military requirements of training our own field forces in this country?"[20]

Lovett took the matter of aircraft for the Soviet Union to Welles, pointing out that the United States was allocating half of its combat aircraft to Britain and China. The Assistant Secretary said that in July the British would receive more combat planes than the AAF. This, in fact, had been the general trend since the previous summer. Furthermore, he pointed out, there were other serious obstacles in the path of fulfilling the Soviet requests. He denied the feasibility of ferrying planes via Alaska and Siberia which Oumansky had earlier suggested to Welles. He noted that special intermediate fields would be needed due to the limited range of the fighters. He also called attention to the rugged territory which had to be traversed and the lack of meteorological and communication facilities along the route. By the time these planes arrived, Lovett told Welles, they would need a major overhaul and their value to the Russians would be extremely doubtful. Moreover, a token force would have "an effect exactly the

---

20. Memo, Marshall for Lovett, July 18, 1941 (File: 400.3295, AG, in WWIIRD/NA). Several types of planes will be mentioned in connection with the aid program to the Soviet Union. The planes can be divided into two categories—fighters, also known as pursuits, and bombers. The latter were modified by the words "light," "medium," and "heavy" which distinguished the aircraft according to weight, range, and altitude. The P-40 (fighter), A-20 (light bomber), and B-25 (medium bomber) were the main types of aircraft sent to the Soviets during World War II.

20 EAGLES EAST

reverse of what would be hoped for," since "the Russians might reasonably wonder why the greatest industrial country in the world could only deliver a mere handful of planes."[21]

The facts, Lovett implied, spoke for themselves, and he advised that the project in its existing form be abandoned. As an alternative, he suggested that the Russians get planes from the British who might release some Lockheed-Hudson bombers (A-29's) on contract in the United States. As for fighters, P-40's already in England could be sent directly to Archangel or via the Middle East. Since American aircraft resources "had been stretched to the breaking point," Lovett proposed that the British divert some of the planes which had been built for them in the United States. After hearing this analysis, Welles agreed to suggest to the President that a definite decision on aircraft requests be deferred until the problem could be discussed with the Soviet Military Mission, then on its way to Washington.[22]

To the President the question was not whether the planes came from British contract aircraft in the United States or from AAF sources. He simply wanted planes sent in order to substantiate verbal assurances of American support. In the days that followed, he overrode the opposition of his military advisers and ordered some immediate aid. These decisions were conveyed in broad terms to the Soviet Ambassador toward the end of July. During an interview with Welles on July 24 in which Oumansky complained "vehemently" and "in rather unmeasured terms" about the many delays in respect to the promised assistance, Welles revealed the President's decision that "a number" of Lockheed-Hudson bombers be made available to the Soviet Union. The planes were to be flown, as Oumansky had earlier suggested, via Alaska and Siberia. Welles went on to say that the President had also directed that at least a squadron of P-40's be made available. The problem, however, was to determine how the fighters were to be sent. Welles advised withholding this decision until the arrival of the Soviet Military Mission, which could resolve the question in meetings with American aviation experts.[23]

On July 31, Colonel General Philip I. Golikov, Chief of the

21. Memo, Lovett for Stimson, July 21, 1941 (File: 400.3295, AG, in WWIIRD/NA).
22. *Ibid.*
23. Memo of conversation by Welles, July 24, 1941, *Foreign Relations*, 1941, I, 797.

Stopgap Commitments to Russia

Soviet Military Mission; his assistant, Major General Alexander K. Repin; and Ambassador Oumansky saw the President.[24] Oumansky pointed out that he had not received a reply to the request for supplies which he had made almost one month earlier. The President, embarrassed by this revelation, promptly announced that 200 P-40's had been approved for the Soviets. He said that 50 of the planes in the United States on British contract could be diverted and the remainder, already in Britain, could be shipped from there.[25] Actually, Roosevelt's announcement was belated: Churchill had told Stalin a week earlier that Britain was sending these fighters.[26] Since the planes had been produced in the United States, the first shipment became something of a joint Anglo-American affair.

During his meeting with Golikov and Oumansky, the President also questioned the feasibility of ferrying fighters across Siberia where, he said, there were inadequate airfields. The Soviets promptly denied this and confidently assured him that the planes could make the trip. The President suggested the alternative that it might be more efficient if the 200 fighters were sent to Vladivostok. This would enable the Soviets to transfer 200 planes from the Far East to the German front. The visitors appeared to favor the idea. Before the interview was over, Roosevelt called attention to the shortage of spare parts in the United States but assured that every effort would be made to help in the matter.[27]

During an interview with Colonel Faymonville on the following day, Roosevelt pointed out that if the Soviets wanted the fighters sent via the Pacific, they would have to come from the United States. It was virtually impossible, he said, to ship the P-40's already in Britain back to the United States for reshipment; if other American sources were unavailable, then most of the planes would have to come from the AAF.[28] He reaffirmed this when

24. Golikov, a skillful military leader, commanded an army in the Battle of Moscow in the winter of 1941.
25. Memo, Brig. Gen. Sherman Miles for Marshall, August 1, 1941, containing the report of Capt. T. L. Crystal who was present at the meeting (File: 19776 to 20150, OCS, in WWIIRD/NA).
26. Msg., Churchill to Stalin, July 25, 1941, Churchill, *The Grand Alliance*, p. 386.
27. Memo, Miles for Marshall, August 1, 1941 (File: 19776 to 20150, OCS, in WWIIRD/NA).
28. Notes on Remarks of the President at Conference Held, August 1, 1941, signed Marshall (File: 19776 to 20150, OCS, in WWIIRD/NA). During a cabinet

22   EAGLES EAST

Wayne Coy was appointed to expedite the Soviet supply program: "It is ridiculous to bring any [fighters] back from England by stealing through the submarine zone, but we should expedite two hundred of them from here."[29]

As was to be expected, the President's pronouncement did not please the War Department. Sending 200 fighters to the Soviet Union would strip the continental United States of serviceable planes. Marshall informed the President that 59 P-40's in the United States on British order were being prepared for delivery to Alaska where Soviet pilots and mechanics would be trained and then ferry the planes to Siberia. Marshall implied that if the balance of 141 P-40's were to come from those in service in the country in order to meet the President's pledge of 200 fighters, this would leave only 8 serviceable P-40's in the United States.[30] Roosevelt's solution was obviously unrealistic and, as subsequent events revealed, this drastic measure was to prove unnecessary.

During his interview with Faymonville on August 1 the President also expressed his desire that a token shipment of heavy bombers, either B-17's or B-24's, be supplied to the Russians. He suggested 10 per month—5 from the United States and 5 from Britain.[31] When Marshall heard of this, he promptly informed Secretary Stimson of the critical situation with respect to heavy bombers, explaining that of the two types there were only 40 B-17's in service and possibly only one B-24. Of the B-17's, 9 were to go to Hawaii to replace an equivalent number leaving for Manila. This left 31 heavy bombers in commission to train 150 crews then in ranks or due to report by the end of the following month. Even if a greater number had been available, Marshall pointed out that it would take at least two to three months to train the crews. The situation with respect to medium bombers was somewhat more promising—50 B-25's and 12 B-26's were in service. The problem that plagued other types of aircraft was

---

meeting on the same day, Roosevelt expressed his concern to Stimson over the delay in sending supplies to Russia. After Stimson remarked that all he knew about Russian supplies was a request for planes, Roosevelt snapped: "Get 'em, even if it is necessary to take them from [U. S.] troops." Quoted in Langer and Gleason, *The Undeclared War*, pp. 560-61.

29. Memo, Roosevelt for Coy, August 2, 1941, quoted in Langer and Gleason, *The Undeclared War*, p. 561.

30. Memo, Marshall for Roosevelt, August 2, 1941 (File: 091 Russia, ASWA, in WWIIRD/NA).

31. Notes on Remarks of the President at Conference Held, August 1, 1941.

Stopgap Commitments to Russia

true of the mediums—the shortage of spare parts.[32] In the face of these revelations, the President dropped the idea of sending heavies and instead reverted to his original suggestion of sending another type. It was decided to send five B-25's along with the P-40's to Soviet crews due to arrive in Alaska.[33]

As these arrangements were set in motion, the War Department still lacked information that London had definitely agreed as mentioned earlier to divert to the Soviets the P-40's on British order in the United States. Of greater significance was the fact that these fighters had been wired for British radios which would have normally been installed there. Now with the impending transfer of planes in Alaska, the radios would have to be immediately dispatched to the United States for installation.[34] Prompt action was necessary since Soviet pilots were expected at Fairbanks about August 11.[35]

No sooner were plans initiated to transfer the planes in Alaska than Oumansky said that his government had revised the schedule. The Ambassador announced on August 5 that the P-40's should be crated and shipped to Archangel. Moreover, Soviet bomber pilots would now come to the United States by way of the Atlantic and, after training, would fly the B-25's via Newfoundland and Iceland. Stimson and Oumansky confirmed the new arrangements by an exchange of letters.[36] Commenting upon the use of the Alaska-Siberia route that Oumansky had originally suggested, Stimson wrote to him:

> It is further understood that in order to anticipate the possibility of future movements by air through Siberia, that you would undertake to secure and present to the War Department full information on all airports, including weather and communication facilities, across Siberia.[37]

32. Memo, Marshall for Stimson, August 1, 1941 (File: 19776 to 20150, OCS, in WWIIRD/NA).
33. Meeting in Marshall's Office, August 1, 1941 (File: 091 Russia, ASWA, in WWIIRD/NA); msg., AG to CG, 4th Army, August 2, 1941 (File: 580.7, AG, in WWIIRD/NA).
34. Memo, Marshall for Roosevelt, August 2, 1941.
35. Ltr., Stimson to Oumansky, August 4, 1941 (File: 19776 to 20150, OCS, in WWIIRD/NA).
36. Ltr., Stimson to Oumansky, August 5, 1941 (File: 21276 to 21350, OCS, in WWIIRD/NA); ltr., Oumansky to Stimson, August 11, 1941 (File: 452, AG, in WWIIRD/NA). In reply, Oumansky referred to Stimson's letter of August 8 which appears to be a later draft of the message of August 5.
37. Ltr., Stimson to Oumansky, August 5, 1941.

24 EAGLES EAST

This was the first serious American effort to secure information about Siberian facilities in order to plan for future aircraft deliveries via Alaska. Stimson's effort would fail however.

But the first shipment of planes to Russia required still further negotiations. The War Department learned that Moscow had reverted to its earlier plan of sending air crews to the United States via Siberia and Alaska for training in the bombers.[38] The progress of two aircraft carrying the thirty-eight member group across Siberia and Alaska was carefully reported to Washington. Finally, on August 31 the crews arrived at Nome,[39] thus completing the first flight during the war across the route which was used a year later to ferry Lend-Lease aircraft.

The Soviet contingent underwent two weeks of training at Spokane, Washington, where AAF instructors had been directed to extend every courtesy and "do their utmost, to the best of their ability, to further the training of their students." Originally, extensive classroom work had been planned but since the interpreters knew little technical information, the idea was abandoned in favor of practical work and demonstration. The Russians were eager to learn and got along well with Americans except when they criticized the aircraft they were to fly home.[40]

General Michael Gromov, the commander of the group, dubbed by Oumansky as "the number one airman of the Soviet government," lost little time in conveying his criticisms to Arnold and presenting demands for better aircraft. He told Arnold that the B-25 did not meet Soviet criteria because it lacked necessary armor, had no gun turrets or bombsights, lacked the range of the Lockheed-Hudson, and was not the latest model in the series. Although he would take the B-25's "which would do their small part," Gromov said the quality of his men demanded a much better plane, such as the B-17. Arnold patiently explained to the importunate Soviet general that it was impossible to find planes, built for American requirements, exactly suitable for Soviet ones.

38. Memo, Lt. Col. George McDonald for Lovett, August 29, 1941 (File: 400.336 Russia, ASWA, in WWIIRD/NA); paraphrase of radiogram, Moscow, No. 16, from Maj. Ivan Yeaton (File: 4557 to 49 Russia, WPD, WDGS, in WWIIRD/NA).
39. Msg., AG to CG, Alaskan Defense Command, August 27, 1941; msg., Maj. Gen. S. B. Buckner to AG, September 3, 1941 (File: 580.7, AG, in WWIIRD/NA).
40. Ltr., Brig. Gen. John B. Brooks to Chief, AAF, with enclosures A and B, October 1, 1941 (File: 145.95, Western Russia, BK.1, in USAF/HA).

Stopgap Commitments to Russia 25

He noted Gromov's inaccuracy concerning the range of the B-25 and explained that bombsights for the B-25 had not yet been released. As to Gromov's request for the B-17, Arnold said he would pursue the matter within the War Department.[41] The next day Stimson informed Oumansky that it was not possible to meet the request for B-17's in lieu of B-25's. He explained:

> My decision is purely one of circumstance in that previous commitments to the government of Great Britain, and the requirements of the U. S. Air Forces, which as a result of external demands have been reduced to an absolute minimum, leave me no choice in the matter.[42]

Stimson's reply reflected the position which Marshall had taken earlier when the President toyed with the idea of sending heavy bombers to the Soviet Union.

Factory deliveries of heavy bombers were inadequate to meet the demands of the AAF, not to mention those of Britain. The AAF received 8 in June, 2 in July, none in August, 5 in September, 11 in October, and 29 in November. In December, when the country was at war, the AAF received the largest number since production began—84.[43] The AAF had 109 B-17's on hand in August 1941, and 148 three months later.[44] Arnold argued convincingly that if every heavy bomber produced up to June, 1942, went to the AAF, there would still be a shortage in meeting minimum defense requirements of the United States and its possessions.[45] On these grounds alone, the American refusal of the Soviet Union's request for heavies was justified. Moreover, Russia's conception of air power militated against deliveries of this type of plane. The primary mission of the Soviet Air Force was to support ground forces by concentrating fighter and close support aircraft

41. Memo, (unkn.) for Arnold, September 9, 1941 (File: 167.6-39, Russia, in USAF/HA).
42. Ltr., Stimson to Oumansky, September 10, 1941 (File: 167.6-39, Russia, in USAF/HA).
43. U. S., Army Air Forces, *Army Air Forces Statistical Digest: World War II*, pp. 128-29.
44. U. S., Congress, Joint Committee on the Investigation of the Pearl Harbor Attack, *Hearings Pursuant to S. Con. Res. 27 and 49, Authorizing an Investigation of the Attack on Pearl Harbor on December 7, 1941 and Events and Circumstances Thereto*, 79th Cong., 1st and 2nd Sess., 1946, pp. 90, 102. Hereinafter cited as *Pearl Harbor Attack*.
45. Memo, Arnold for Marshall, September 9, 1941 (File 145.82-2, in USAF/HA).

26 EAGLES EAST

upon a point in the front. If a breakthrough were effected, the air force exploited it for the benefit of the ground troops. Although the Soviets had a strategic air arm, it was small and played an extremely limited role in contrast to its British and American counterparts. In other words, the Soviet Air Force was primarily a defensive-offensive arm of direct support for ground forces. Heavy bombers were not for this type of warfare.

After receiving Stimson's reply concerning the heavies, Gromov claimed that the B-25A, in which his men were training, was unsuitable.[46] The War Department made arrangements to have two different models of a medium bomber available for Russian scrutiny. On September 16, a B-25B and a B-26 were placed at the disposal of Gromov and a few other Russian officials at Bolling Field. Even Secretary Stimson personally appeared to help accommodate the Russians.[47] A few days later, Andrei Gromyko, the Soviet Chargé d'Affaires, advised Colonel B. E. Meyers of the AAF's Materiel Division that the Soviet Union would accept 3 B-26's and 2 B-25B's which, he said, should be ready for flight by October 5.[48] Thereupon, AAF transports carried the Soviet officers from Spokane, Washington, to Patterson Field, Ohio, for familiarization training. Colonel Meyers wrote that "By an almost superhuman effort, with the greatest cooperation on the part of the Martin, North American and Sperry Companies, these airplanes have been prepared for flight to Russia."[49]

Then, on October 1, Gromyko suddenly informed Meyers that the B-26 was unsuitable for combat, and since the Russians doubted the B-25 could make the trip by air, recommended that the medium bombers be sent by water. Now the Russians wanted the planes to be all B-25A's or B-25B's. Two days later, the Russians conveyed another change. They wanted all of the planes to have full de-icing equipment, which had not been insisted upon earlier.[50] The repeated changes were almost too much for Lovett who requested in desperation that Stettinius intervene. Gromyko's

46. Oumansky and Golikov decided on August 5, 1941 to accept the five B-25A's, and the arrangement had been confirmed in letters between Oumansky and Stimson.
47. Memo, Col. B. E. Meyers for Lovett, October 6, 1941 (File: 400.3295, ASWA, in WWIIRD/NA).
48. Ltr., Gromyko to Meyers, September 19, 1941 (File: AAF, Central Decimal Files, Box No. 950, in WWIRB/NA).
49. Memo, Meyers for Lovett, October 6, 1941.
50. *Ibid.*

Stopgap Commitments to Russia

earlier request for 3 B-26's and 2 B-25B's, Lovett complained, had "literally disrupted the routine of three factories to rush through these five planes, with special equipment, 11 days ahead of the promise we made them." The new request for 5 B-25's with full de-icing equipment, meant that the planes could not be ready before December.[51] A compromise was eventually reached with respect to Soviet requirements, and 5 B-25's eventually departed by water for northern Russia.[52]

One aspect of the initial shipment of planes caused particular and continuous concern. That was the inadequacy of spare parts. On various occasions the Soviets had been informed of the critical shortage of these. But their representatives complained to the President who promptly instructed Stimson to take corrective action:

> In my opinion, failure to make this shipment complete, in such a way as to be immediately serviceable and effective for combat operations abroad would entirely defeat the purpose for which this shipment is being made.
>
> In view of this situation, it is my desire that every consideration be given to sending with the airplanes the requisite supplies and equipment from existing stocks in amounts approaching as nearly as possible those which would be required for our own forces operating under similar conditions.[53]

Stimson conveyed the President's remarks to Arnold who explained that available spare parts and tools had been or were in the process of being shipped. "All of the facilities of the War Department," he said, "were placed at their [Soviet] disposal to assist them in every way possible."[54] Stimson related Arnold's analysis to the President, concluding with remarks which illustrated the critical nature of the problem:

> I trust that you will agree, after examining the above facts, that we have taken such steps as are possible at this time to

51. Ltr., Lovett to Stettinius, October 6, 1941 (File: 400.3295, ASWA, in WWIIRD/NA).
52. U. S., Department of State, "Report on War Aid Furnished by the United States to the USSR," November, 1945, p. 18.
53. Ltr., Roosevelt to Stimson, August 27, 1941 (File: 167.6-39, Russia, in USAF/HA).
54. Memo, Arnold for Stimson, August 28, 1941 (File: 167.6-39, Russia, in USAF/HA).

28   EAGLES EAST

meet the request from the Soviet Government, which has come at a time when, largely as a result of urgent British demands for Middle East use, there are no spares in existence.[55]

Marshall's reaction was less restrained. He told Stimson:

In the first place our entire Air Corps is suffering from a severe shortage in spare parts of *all* kinds. We have planes on the ground because we cannot repair them. As a matter of fact, we have been forced for the time being to take about one-fifth of the new planes to provide parts for older planes that we are keeping in the air.

He cited the earlier meetings during which the Soviets had been informed of the shortage and left no doubt about his irritation. "If any criticism is to be made in this matter," he stated, "in my opinion it is that we have been too generous, to our own disadvantage." Marshall added that he questioned the release of the planes themselves "even more when it only results in criticism. The President should have it clearly pointed out to him," the Chief of Staff advised, "that Mr. Oumansky will take everything we own if we submit to his criticisms."[56]

The first shipment of aircraft to Russia revealed some of the problems which would appear in magnified form when the United States committed itself to make substantial aircraft shipments to the Soviet Union. From the standpoint of United States policy trends, the President's intention to find planes, even if it meant taking them from AAF units, reflected his keen determination to make good on American pledges to assist Russia. The significant point to the White House was not the military value of a handful of planes but rather the psychological effect on Soviet resistance.

This concern, which troubled Washington and London during the early years of the war, prompted the suddenly conceived and quickly executed trip which Harry Hopkins, the President's enigmatic adviser, made to Moscow late in July. While in London conferring with Churchill and other British authorities, Hopkins himself appears to have originated the idea of going to Russia. In a message to the President on July 25, Hopkins gave his reasons for the visit:

55. Ltr., Stimson to Roosevelt, undated (File: 167.6-39, Russia, in USAF/HA).
56. Memo, Marshall for Stimson, August 29, 1941 (File: 21276 to 21350, OCS, in WWIIRD/NA).

Stopgap Commitments to Russia

I have a feeling that everything possible should be done to make certain the Russians maintain a permanent front even though they be defeated in this immediate battle. If Stalin could in any way be influenced at a critical time I think it would be worth doing by a direct communication from you through a personal envoy. I think the stakes are so great that it should be done. Stalin would then know in an unmistakable way that we mean business on a long term supply job.[57]

The President approved the idea and sent Hopkins a message, explaining the reasons for his visit, for presentation to Stalin. The message convincingly explained that Hopkins was to secure a clarification of Stalin's "most urgent requirements" which the United States might be able to meet within the next few months. Hopkins was also to get an idea of Stalin's "individual problems" on which the United States might be able to help.[58] These matters did not require a Presidential envoy to Moscow: they could have been effectively handled by the Soviet Military Mission which had arrived in Washington. But what could not be fully determined in Washington was a realistic picture of the Soviet military situation. If Russia were not at the point of imminent collapse, a long-range program of American aid could be justified.

Brigadier General Joseph T. McNarney, an AAF officer who served as Chief of Staff of the Special Observer Group (SPOBS) in Britain, accompanied Hopkins on the PBY which left Invergordon, Scotland, on July 28 for Moscow. John R. Alison, a P-40 expert, was also in the group.[59] Since most of the planes in the first shipment were P-40's, it was expected that Alison would remain in Russia and assist in assembling and testing operations.[60]

After a long and dangerous flight which skirted enemy held territory, the mission arrived at Archangel. Russian hospitality overwhelmed Hopkins: he had a "monumental" dinner characterized by numerous courses of food and the ever present vodka which favorably impressed him. After a four-hour repast, Hopkins and the remainder of the party flew to Moscow. Hopkins met the

---

57. Msg., Hopkins to Roosevelt, July 25, 1941, quoted in Robert E. Sherwood, *Roosevelt and Hopkins: An Intimate History* (New York: Harper & Brothers, 1948), pp. 317-18.
58. *Ibid.*, pp. 318, 321-22.
59. *Ibid.*, p. 323.
60. For a discussion of Lt. Alison's work in Russia, see Chapter V.

30   EAGLES EAST

American Ambassador, Laurence Steinhardt, and informed him
that he was there to see if the situation was as grim as depicted by
the War Department. Steinhardt explained that Soviet suspicion
and secretiveness obscured a clear understanding of the situation.
Hopkins was confident that he would bridge the virtually im-
passable wall of Russian distrust.[61]

Hopkins had two conferences with Stalin. The Soviet leader
impressed Hopkins by his clarity and frankness. Stalin conveyed
the definite impression that his country was in the war until
Germany was defeated. His comments on the military situation
on the eastern front revealed gravity but not hopelessness. In
retrospect, it is strange that General McNarney, a competent military observer, was not invited to participate in the Hopkins-Stalin
discussions which primarily involved military matters. Hopkins
appears to have felt that the purpose of his mission would be best
served if he dealt with Stalin alone. Nevertheless, it was revealing
that America's first official contact during the war with the shrewd
chieftain of the Soviet Union had been made by a man who had
little experience in international or military affairs.

During the first meeting on July 30, Stalin pointed out that
his first category needs included anti-aircraft guns which, if provided, would release some 2,000 fighters from defense work to
active operations at the front. He also listed machine guns and
rifles in this category. His long range requirements emphasized
aluminum for aircraft, aviation gasoline, and other items on the
nine point list submitted by Oumansky. Stalin expressed a particular need for short-range bombers capable of operating within
a radius of 600 to 1,100 kilometers. In response to Stalin's aircraft
needs, Hopkins commented on the 200 P-40's en route from the
United States and Britain.[62]

Hopkins mentioned Lieutenant Alison's presence and pointed
out his qualifications in the P-40. He asked if Alison could remain
in Russia in an advisory role, and Stalin approved the idea.[63] This
was an opportunity for Alison not only to supervise the assembly
and testing of the P-40's but to observe the operation of American

61. Sherwood, *Roosevelt and Hopkins*, pp. 323-27. Sherwood gives a detailed
account of the trip.
62. Memo by Hopkins, Conference at the Kremlin on July 30, 1941, *Foreign
Relations*, 1941, I, 802-04.
63. *Ibid.*

Stopgap Commitments to Russia

as well as Soviet planes under combat conditions. The latter objective was particularly important: the United States could get valuable combat information on its own and foreign weapons mainly through observers in countries at war. It was essential that such information be provided in order to adapt weapons to the changing demands of combat. Soviet authorities, however, confined the activities of Alison and Lieutenant Hubert Zemke, who joined him later, to the supervision of the assembling and testing of the first group of P-40's which arrived in September. The Russians denied them access to the front.[64]

During his meeting with Hopkins, Stalin expansively invited the United States to send as many technicians as possible to train his airmen in the use of American planes.[65] This proved equally illusory since only a few days later Soviet representatives in Washington expressed a desire only for mechanics, not personnel to train their airmen in American planes.[66]

Later the same evening McNarney joined Hopkins in a meeting with Colonel General N. D. Yakovlev, Chief of the Main Technical Artillery Administration. The experience was unproductive in gaining any detailed information regarding Soviet requirements. But the meeting proved, as Hopkins wrote, that there was "literally no one in the whole Government who is willing to give any important information other than Mr. Stalin himself."[67] When asked what Russia needed most, Yakovlev replied crisply: aluminum, fighters and medium bombers. When Yakovlev implied that his country did not need other military equipment, Hopkins expressed surprise that he did not mention anti-tank guns and tanks. "I am not empowered to say whether we do or do not need tanks or anti-tank guns," Yakovlev replied calmly. The results of the discussion on Soviet aircraft needs were equally barren. Yakovlev

64. Zemke wrote "Neither John Alison or I were ever allowed to visit a front though we asked to do so several times." Ltr., Col. Hubert Zemke to writer, January 28, 1963. The Russians consistently refused visits of American officers to the front; the Military Attaché in Moscow believed that difficulties with the early shipments of American planes partially accounted for the Soviet attitude. For a fuller treatment, see Chapter V.

65. Memo by Hopkins, Conference at the Kremlin on July 30, 1941, *Foreign Relations*, 1941, I, 804.

66. Memo, McDonald for Lovett, August 5, 1941 (File: 19776 to 20150, OCS, in WWIIRD/NA).

67. Memo by Hopkins, Conference at the Kremlin on July 31, 1941, *Foreign Relations*, 1941, I, 813.

32   EAGLES EAST

dodged specific questions about the performance of Russian aircraft by saying, "I am an artillery man." It was obviously pointless to continue the discussion.[68]

The following evening Hopkins had another meeting with Stalin who revealed his great respect for the German military machine but was optimistic about Russia's ability and determination to withstand it. Stalin's analysis of the German and Soviet aircraft situation was interesting, but untrue.

In his resumé Stalin contradicted early Moscow broadcasts by admitting the loss of more planes than the Germans at the outset of the campaign. He now thought the advantage was "the other way," but conspicuously avoided bolstering his claim by providing figures on losses. Then he offered figures of Soviet air strength: 7,000-8,000 old fighters, 2,000 new ones, and 600 heavy bombers. He either gave no figures for medium bombers or if he did, Hopkins failed to record them. The striking feature about Stalin's information was that the Soviet Union had, after a month of heavy aircraft losses, a substantial number of planes to confront the enemy. It is known that the Luftwaffe began "Barbarossa" with slightly more than 2,000 aircraft of all types and rarely exceeded that figure during the war. Stalin was saying in effect that even after a month of disastrous losses, the Soviet Air Force still enjoyed numerical superiority over the Luftwaffe. Yet Stalin maintained that the Luftwaffe had more planes, artfully attributing his heavy aircraft losses to the numerical preponderance of the German air force rather than to the technical inferiority of his own.[69]

Perhaps Stalin's most candid remarks concerned the operational characteristics of his planes. But he exaggerated when he claimed his country produced 1,800 aircraft per month and expected it to reach 2,500 per month, exclusive of trainers, by January, 1942.[70] When Arnold later heard these figures, he quipped: "I think that we should ask them for help."[71] Since American factories produced a total of 5,156 planes for all recipients during

68. Report of Brig. Gen. Joseph T. McNarney on trip to Moscow, TAB B (File: 350.05, AG, WWIIRD/NA).
69. Memo by Hopkins, Conference at the Kremlin on July 31, 1941, *Foreign Relations*, 1941, I, 809-810.
70. *Ibid.*
71. Arnold's Notes at Argentia Conference (File: H. H. Arnold, Official Files, Conferences: Argentia through Casablanca, in MD/LC).

Stopgap Commitments to Russia 33

the third quarter of 1941,[72] or an average of 1,719 planes per month, one can appreciate the facts which prompted Arnold's facetious comment.

Stalin informed Hopkins that "the outcome of the war in Russia would largely depend on the ability to enter the spring campaign with adequate equipment, particularly in aircraft, tanks, and anti-aircraft guns." His desire that Britain send air force contingents later resulted in RAF operations in northern Russia. He also welcomed American troops to operate on Russian soil under their own commanders and expressed interest in training his pilots in the United States. As to avenues of supply, he suggested Archangel, Vladivostok and Iran, noting the difficulties of each, but admitted that all would have to be used at the outset.[73]

Hopkins informed Stalin that the United States and Britain would be unwilling to send heavy munitions such as anti-aircraft guns, tanks and planes until a conference between representatives of the three countries had met. The purpose of the meeting would be to survey the strategic needs of each country and combat theater. Aware that the conference should meet after the military situation had crystallized on the eastern front, Hopkins suggested that the conference convene after the current battle in Russia was over.[74]

Hopkins left Moscow the next day with the conviction, shared by McNarney, that Russia was far from collapse. Before he departed from Moscow, he sent the President a short message on August 1, expressing his confidence about the Soviet front and the morale of the Russian people. "There is unbounded determination to win," he said.[75] The Hopkins mission does not seem to have had "demonstrable bearing" on the policy decision which Welles announced to the Soviet Ambassador on August 2.[76] However, Hopkins' later report to the President confirmed the wisdom of the decision of the United States "to give all economic assistance practicable for the purpose of strengthening the Soviet Union in its struggle against armed aggression." This policy, Welles said in a note to Oumansky

72. U. S. Air Force, *United States Air Force Statistical Digest: 1947* (Washington: Director of Statistical Services, 1948), p. 121.
73. Memo by Hopkins, Conference at the Kremlin on July 31, 1941, *Foreign Relations*, 1941, I, 810-811, 814, 812.
74. *Ibid.*, pp. 812-13.
75. Msg., Hopkins to Roosevelt, August 1, 1941, *Foreign Relations*, 1941, I, 814.
76. Langer and Gleason, *The Undeclared War*, p. 563.

34 EAGLES EAST

on August 2, would be implemented by giving friendly consideration to Soviet requests, by issuing unlimited export licenses, and by extending available American shipping facilities to expedite deliveries.[77]

Hopkins returned to England where he joined Churchill and his advisors for a voyage aboard the *Prince of Wales* to a pre-arranged rendezvous with Roosevelt and his staff at Argentia Harbor in Newfoundland. The meetings of the Atlantic or Argentia Conference, as it was known, dealt primarily with the problem of Japan and the Atlantic Charter.[78] There was no debate regarding aid to Russia. Churchill and Roosevelt were firmly in agreement on that point; both approved the idea of a conference in Moscow. After the tryst in the Atlantic was over, they dispatched a joint message to Stalin, saying: "We are at the moment cooperating to provide you with the very maximum of supplies that you most urgently need. Already many shiploads have left our shores and more will leave in the immediate future." They formally proposed the now oft-talked about conference in Moscow regarding long-term aid and assured Stalin that before the conference met "we shall continue to send supplies and materials as rapidly as possible." The message concluded:

> We realize fully how vitally important to the defeat of Hitlerism is the brave and steadfast resistance of the Soviet Union and we feel therefore that we must not in any circumstances fail to act quickly and immediately in this matter of planning the program for the future allocation of our joint resources.[79]

Churchill appointed Lord William Beaverbrook, Minister of Supply, as his representative. It was assumed Hopkins would be the American envoy but due to the poor state of his health, Roosevelt chose Averell Harriman.[80]

An Anglo-American-Soviet alliance was in the making, a theme which the Soviet press used with effect. Each step in the procession of events after "Barbarossa" that brought Britain and the United States closer to the Soviet Union was depicted in the Russian press as evidence of the growth of a strong coalition against Germany.

77. Ltr., Welles to Oumansky, August 2, 1941, *Foreign Relations*, 1941, I, 816.
78. Documents on the Atlantic Conference can be found in *Foreign Relations*, 1941, I, 341-78.
79. Msg., Hull to Steinhardt, August 18, 1941, *Foreign Relations*, 1941, I, 822-23.
80. Sherwood, *Roosevelt and Hopkins*, p. 359.

Stopgap Commitments to Russia

The United States appeared prominently as an important part of the growing force against Fascism.[81] The Russian press gave unusual attention to the Hopkins mission which reflected the significance the government attached to it from the standpoint of future developments in United States-Soviet relations and, more immediately, from its effect upon Russian morale. Ambassador Steinhardt related his certainty "that the visit has been extremely gratifying to the Soviet government and that it will prove to have exercised a most beneficial effect upon Soviet-American relations in general and in particular to have greatly encouraged the Soviet war effort."[82]

The Hopkins mission and the exchange of notes between Welles and Oumansky on August 2 prompted *Pravda* to exaggerate that such evidence of cooperation, along with the Anglo-Soviet agreement, was "convincing proof that an invincible and powerful force has arisen which will annihilate Hitler forever."[83] Moscow radio said almost poetically:

> The freedom loving American people are among the adversaries of the Fascist barbarians . . . and for some time past the United States has been actively aiding Britain in her struggle against Hitler, and today, on the basis of common interest determined by the necessity of struggling against a common foe, the foundations have been laid for full cooperation between the Soviet Union and the United States of America.

It went on:

> The Soviet people and Soviet public opinion greeted with the greatest satisfaction the news that the way has been paved for fruitful collaboration between the Soviet Union and the United States. Collaboration based on common interest corresponding to those of the national defense of both countries and aimed at the destruction and smashing of the enemy who threatens the security and freedom of all nations.[84]

81. Steinhardt submitted summaries of articles in *Pravda* and *Izvestiya* to the Secretary of State. See msg., Steinhardt to Hull, August 7, 1941, *Foreign Relations*, 1941, I, 637-38.
82. Msg., Steinhardt to Hull, August 1, 1941, *Foreign Relations*, 1941, I, 815. For Moscow radio attention to the Hopkins visit, see Foreign Broadcast Intelligence Service, Box 427, in NA.
83. Quoted in msg., Steinhardt to Hull, August 7, 1941, *Foreign Relations*, 1941, I, 638.
84. Foreign Broadcast Intelligence Service, Box 427.

36   EAGLES EAST

Pravda regarded the message from Churchill and Roosevelt proposing a conference in Moscow as the beginning of a new stage in Anglo-American-Soviet cooperation. It described this stage as the recognition of the special role of the Soviet Union in the war against Germany and the initiation of practical measures by the three nations against the enemy.[85] Moscow radio reported that the practical collaboration between Russia, Britain and the United States already in existence and the proposals contained in the Churchill-Roosevelt message were "a blow of tremendous force, a major political retreat for Hitlerite Germany," which had failed to split its adversaries.[86] If the Soviet press is taken as a gauge of the ebb and flow in Russo-American wartime relations, then the period immediately following the Hopkins mission was, indeed, a high water mark of good will.

85. Msg., Steinhardt to Hull, August 17, 1941, *Foreign Relations*, 1941, I, 639.
86. Foreign Broadcast Intelligence Service, Box 428.

CHAPTER III

Planning Long Range Aircraft Commitments: The Moscow Protocol

THE MOSCOW CONFERENCE which convened at the end of September, 1941, was a significant milestone in Russo-American relations. It terminated the procession of events that had propelled American policy since June, 1941, toward a program of long-range aid to the Soviet Union and made the United States and Russia quasi-allies before Pearl Harbor. Through the protocol which they adopted, the United States and Great Britain agreed to provide large quantities of war materiel to the Soviet Union. One of the major problems that confronted the United States was the provision of military aircraft, the most critical item in demand by the Russians.

The preliminaries of the conference took place in an atmosphere of great concern for the survival of the Soviet Union. The President had proposed that American and British officials meet first in London, where a definite decision regarding western aid to the Soviet Union could be reached. This, of course, would enable the Anglo-American mission destined for Moscow to carry definite estimates of the amount of assistance which Britain and the United States planned to furnish. Roosevelt urged that the London talks begin about September 15 in order that the conference in Moscow could convene somewhat earlier than October 1, the date originally scheduled.[1] The President's desire to get the mission to Moscow sooner than planned was spurred by Prime Minister Churchill's recent revelation of an almost desperate message from Stalin which

1. Msg., Hopkins to John Winant, September 9, 1941, *Foreign Relations*, 1941, I, 829-30.

37

38   EAGLES EAST

had been delivered in menacing tones by the Soviet Ambassador to Britain, Ivan Maisky.

This was Stalin's second message to Churchill since the outbreak of Russo-German hostilities. Stalin painted a gloomy picture of the Soviet position and again pressed the Prime Minister for a British front "somewhere in the Balkans or in France." He also requested deliveries of aluminum and "a minimum monthly aid of 400 aeroplanes and 500 tanks." Without the second front and the supplies, he warned that "the Soviet Union will be either defeated or weakened to the extent that it will lose for a long time the ability to help its Allies by active operations at the front against Hitlerism."[2] Ambassador Maisky brought the message in person on the evening of September 4. He complained bitterly "how for the last eleven weeks Russia had been bearing the brunt of the German onslaught virtually alone."[3] Churchill retorted that Maisky should not reproach Britain, which had fought Hitler for a longer period of time than Russia. "We never thought," he added, "our survival was dependent on your action either way."[4]

Nevertheless the interview raised fears that the Soviet Union might negotiate a separate peace. Commenting on his exchange with Maisky, Churchill told Roosevelt that "although nothing in his language warranted the assumption, we could not exclude the impression that they might be thinking of separate terms."[5] This fear prompted the British Cabinet to approve a friendly reply in which Churchill patiently explained to Stalin the reasons why a second front was not yet possible. The reply also committed Britain to supply one half the monthly amount of planes and tanks that Stalin asked for. Churchill also suggested to Stalin the possibility that the United States might inform him before the Moscow Conference of the amount of supplies it would send.[6]

2. Msg., Stalin to Churchill, September 3, 1941, Ministry of Foreign Affairs of the U. S. S. R., *Stalin's Correspondence with Churchill, Attlee, Roosevelt and Truman, 1941-1945* (2 vols. in 1; London: Lawrence and Wishart, 1958), I, 20-21. Also in Churchill, *The Grand Alliance*, pp. 455-57. There is a slight difference in the date of the message in Churchill's book where it is listed as September 4, 1941. Such variations in diplomatic correspondence often exist. They can be explained largely in terms of the time difference from initial dispatch to ultimate receipt.
3. Churchill, *The Grand Alliance*, p. 457.
4. *Ibid.*
5. Msg., Churchill to Roosevelt, September 5, 1941, *The Grand Alliance*, p. 460.
6. Msg., Churchill to Stalin, September 4, 1941, *The Grand Alliance*, pp. 458-59.

The Moscow Protocol

Churchill hoped Roosevelt did not object to references to aid from the United States but, he explained, "the moment may be decisive."[7]

Stalin's reply to Churchill indicated that he was appropriately grateful for the commitment of supplies. But he still held hopes for direct military assistance also: he suggested that Britain send 25 to 30 divisions to Archangel or to southern Russia in order that "there could be established military collaboration between the Soviet and British troops on the territory of the U.S.S.R."[8] The appeal for direct military cooperation was taken under study,[9] and somewhat later Lord Beaverbrook conveyed to the Soviet chieftain the suggestion that the British might soon be able to provide direct military assistance: "If we can clear our own western flank in Libya of the enemy we shall have considerable forces, both air and army, to cooperate upon the southern flank of the Russian front."[10] But, meanwhile, Churchill was anxious to assure Stalin of the reality of assistance in the form of materiel. On September 17 he sketched out for the Soviet leader the progress of the conversations in London, informing him that the British and Americans were setting up a schedule of deliveries through June, 1942, but adding that this date was only for planning purposes—"Naturally we shall go on with you till victory."[11]

Although American military planners had come to endorse the policy of aiding Russia, they entertained many reservations in the field of aircraft allotments where critical domestic needs loomed so large. Since the armament program of the AAF was already depressed by the British priority on American aircraft production, Arnold continually pressed AAF needs when foreign demands threatened to cripple an already weak American establishment. He remarked that "there would never be a United States Air Force except on paper" if a realistic line were not drawn somewhere between helping our future allies "and giving everything away."[12]

---

7. Msg., Churchill to Roosevelt, September 5, 1941, *The Grand Alliance*, p. 460.
8. Msg., Stalin to Churchill, September 13, 1941, Ministry of Foreign Affairs of the U. S. S. R., *Stalin's Correspondence*, I, 24.
9. Msg., Churchill to Stalin, September 17, 1941, *The Grand Alliance*, pp. 463-64.
10. Ltr., Churchill to Stalin, September 21, 1941, *The Grand Alliance*, pp. 465-67.
11. Msg., Churchill to Stalin, Sept. 17, 1941, *The Grand Alliance*, pp. 463-64.
12. Henry H. Arnold, *Global Mission* (New York: Harper and Brothers, 1949), p. 184.

40 EAGLES EAST

Major General T. J. Hanley, Jr., former Assistant Chief of the Air Staff, Supply, commented: "We were generally against this aid to Russia because we needed the materiel ourselves. There was not any particular anti-Russian or any pro-Russian feeling. . . ."[13] Marshall shared this point of view and, as already seen, often took the initiative in pressing the case of the AAF. Stimson too consistently supported AAF claims to a larger share of aircraft production. This resulted in one of his few serious differences with the President.[14] The position of these men was clear. They wanted to safeguard the ability of the American air forces to undertake adequate defense of the United States and its possessions and to be ready, when the situation arose, to carry out its proper offensive mission.

The monumental task of preparation for actual involvement in war had been charted in a study called the Joint Board Estimate of United States Over-All Production Requirements. The section of the study dealing with air force matters was known as AWPD/1, prepared by the Air War Plans Division on August 12, 1941. In AWPD/1, the Air War Plans Division underscored the colossal number of planes which the AAF required before it could wage offensive war. It called for an "interim expedient" of 59,727 combat and training planes with a monthly replacement rate of 2,276 and an "ultimate requirement" of 63,467 combat and training planes with a monthly replacement rate of 2,133. Once potential enemies provoked war and became enemies in fact, the AAF's primary mission would be to undertake a sustained air offensive against Germany and to pursue a strategic-defensive posture in the Far East.[15] The AAF required 98 bombardment groups, 88 of which were to be equipped with heavy bombers.

It was obvious to the War Department that in order to build an air force capable of executing existing and potential missions, a valve had to be placed upon the pipe line of American aircraft production. But if AWPD/1 emphasized the needs of the AAF, then the strategy and policy sections of the Joint Board Estimate, endorsed by the Chiefs of Staff, emphasized the importance of the Soviet Union. The estimate stated:

13. Interview with Maj. Gen. T. J. Hanley, Jr., Retired, December 27, 1962.
14. Henry L. Stimson and McGeorge Bundy, *On Active Service in Peace and War* (New York: Harper and Brothers, 1947), p. 383.
15. AWPD/1, TAB 1, pp. 1-2 (File: 145.82-1, in USAF/HA).

The Moscow Protocol 41

The maintenance of an active front in Russia offers by far the best opportunity for a successful land offensive against Germany, because only Russia possesses adequate manpower, situated in favorable proximity to the center of German military power.[16]

Stressing the importance of ground and air forces to the Soviet Union, the Estimate went on to say that even if the Germans pushed the Soviets beyond the Urals, "there would always remain the hope of a final and complete defeat of Germany by land operations." Predictions as to the outcome of the existing conflict on the eastern front were premature, but the Estimate urged:

The effective arming of Russian forces, both by the supply of munitions from the outside and by providing industrial capacity in the Volga Basin, or to the east of the Ural Mountains, would be one of the most important moves that could be made by the Associated Powers.[17]

American military planners clearly emphasized the importance of the Soviet Union and the need to help its resistance. More optimistic in respect to the progress of the struggle in Russia than in the early summer, they now felt that resistance would probably continue at least for several months.[18] The need to ensure the continuance of Soviet participation in the war established the lock-step by which military leaders had to reconcile the needs of their own armed forces with those of another claimant on American production.

Thus the basic question concerning aircraft which confronted American and British representatives at the London talks involved the number and type of planes to be allocated to the United States, Great Britain, and the Soviet Union from American production through June, 1942. As for the British commitment of planes to Russia, this had already been set forth in Churchill's earlier message to Stalin.

Before the London talks began, Roosevelt directed the War

16. Quoted in Sherwood, *Roosevelt and Hopkins*, p. 417.
17. *Ibid.*
18. In September, 1941, military intelligence experts speculated that up to December Russia, although suffering reverses itself, would exact "a significant toll from the German armed forces." They went on to state that the destruction of the Russian armed forces "and overthrow of the Stalin regime within this period are possible but not yet probable." U. S., Congress, *Pearl Harbor Attack*, pp. 1349-50.

42 EAGLES EAST

Department to prepare a study of suggested distributions of aircraft through June, 1942, between the United States, Great Britain, and the Soviet Union. The President informed the Secretary of War, Henry L. Stimson:

> I deem it to be of paramount importance for the safety and security of America that all reasonable munitions help be provided for Russia, not only immediately but as long as she continues to fight the Axis Powers effectively. I am convinced that substantial and comprehensive commitments of such character must be made to Russia by Great Britain and the United States at the proposed [Moscow] conference.[19]

In response to this directive, the Air War Plans Division prepared a study, known as AWPD/2, which revealed the problems involved in arriving at an equitable division of aircraft from American production without injuring the basic defense requirements of the United States. AWPD/2 recommended that out of an estimated production of 14,802 tactical aircraft, the AAF receive 5,094. The remaining 9,708 aircraft were to be assigned to the anti-Axis pool. This meant that the anti-Axis pool would receive all aircraft produced under Defense Aid, all British and other contract production, and 15 per cent of combat types produced for the AAF. The War Department suggested a distribution of aircraft in the anti-Axis pool along these lines: 7,534 to Britain, 1,163 to the Soviet Union, and the remainder to other nations.[20]

After the talks in London began, Major General James E. Chaney, the ranking AAF member of the American delegation in London, presented figures which indicated a slight revision in Britain's favor and a reduction for the AAF. But this revision was not large, and British allocations were considerably less than expected. The British were frankly shocked. They had expected that their country would receive all the planes produced under the Defense Aid program and a large allocation of those from AAF orders.[21] The estimates now presented meant that they would receive approximately 1,800 fewer aircraft than had been expected,

19. Memo, Roosevelt for Stimson, August 30, 1941, *Foreign Relations*, 1941, I, 826.
20. AWPD/2 (File: 145.82-2, in USAF/HA).
21. "Report of Special Mission to U. S. S. R. on Allocation of Aircraft from U. K. and U. S. Production, September 16 to October 10, 1941." Tab A and B. This report, drafted by Maj. Gen. James E. Chaney, will be cited hereinafter as "The Chaney Report" (File: 178.104, in USAF/HA).

The Moscow Protocol

600 of which were in the heavy and medium bomber category. The latter was particularly alarming. In the words of the British official history of the event, "The loss of the heavy and medium bombers was regarded as likely to have a grave effect on the British air offensive against Germany."[22] Lord Beaverbrook remarked dolefully that American production figures were "much lower than anything we have had before and many of our minimum requirements cannot be met. It is imperative," he added, "that the Americans should organize immediately a rapid increase of their production."[23]

And, indeed, the British had real cause for concern. Their own production of bombers, particularly heavies, was lagging behind schedule, a natural consequence of the emphasis on fighters to defend the Isles during the Battle of Britain.[24] They were relying upon the United States for help in building a strong force of bombers, which they regarded as a logical counterweight to Nazi land power. As one British historian put it, "The bomber was still the only means of getting to grips with the enemy at home and ranked first among the offensive instruments available to this country."[25] It was natural that when British aircraft production failed to keep pace with planning, a greater premium was placed upon American deliveries.

The British pressed the Americans to reconsider their position, particularly to increase their share of heavy bombers. They stoutly opposed giving heavies to Russia, 30 of which were allocated under AWPD/2. They correctly argued that heavies could be used more effectively against German strategic targets from their bases than from Russia. The Russians, they pointed out, could only undertake strategic bombardment of the Romanian oil fields which, at the rate of the German advance, would probably soon be out of range.[26] On the other hand, the British proposed that the number of American aircraft allocated to Russia be increased from 1,163

22. H. Duncan Hall, *North American Supply* (London: Her Majesty's Stationery Office, 1955), pp. 332-33.
23. *Ibid.*, p. 333.
24. For a brief summary on the lag in British production of heavy bombers, see M. M. Postan, *British War Production* (London: Her Majesty's Stationery Office, 1952), pp. 124-26, 174.
25. *Ibid.*, p. 303.
26. An excellent summary of British objections to proposed American aircraft allocations can be found in "United States Proposals for Allocation of American Production," n. d. (File: 4557, WPD, WDGS, in WWIIRD/NA).

44 EAGLES EAST

to 1,800. The distribution of planes by type under AWPD/2 and the British proposal was as follows.

	AWPD/2	BRITISH PROPOSAL
Heavy bombers	30	None
Medium bombers	45	180
Light bombers	356	450
Pursuits	620	900
Observation	112	270
Total	1,163[27]	1,800[28]

The American mission accepted the increased allocation of planes to Russia, which represented a matching with British commitments. But there was a difference of opinion on the advisability of giving heavy bombers. Although Averell Harriman, head of the American mission, favored the British view, the ranking military members of his delegation favored the idea of giving heavy bombers to Russia. Generals James E. Chaney, James H. Burns, and Stanley D. Embick felt that the delivery of heavies would have a significant effect in bolstering Russian morale. General Embick, an experienced Army strategist, suggested that the heavies would have a deterrent effect upon Japanese designs on Siberia.[29] Chaney, therefore, drafted a suggested breakdown of deliveries, which continued to include a token number of heavy bombers. These figures, which Harriman forwarded to Washington, contemplated the following deliveries to Russia through June 1942:

Heavy bombers	27
Medium bombers	45
Light bombers	828
Pursuits	900
Total	1,800

Harriman also noted in his message to Washington that the American mission would offer 203 observation planes in the place of an equivalent number of light bombers or pursuits if the Russians could use them effectively.[30]

27. AWPD/2, Tab. 1. Also in AWPD/1 Scrap Book, Tab 79 (File: 145.82-1, pt. 3, in USAF/HA).
28. "The Chaney Report," Tab C.
29. Msg., Harriman to Roosevelt and Hopkins, September 18, 1941 (File: Russian Cables, ID, ASF, in WWIIRD/NA).
30. Msg., Harriman to Hopkins, September 18, 1941 [supplement to message cited above] (File: 091 Russia, ASWA, in WWIIRD/NA).

The Moscow Protocol 45

Roosevelt's reply to Harriman indicated that the problems disturbing the negotiations in London were also a matter of concern in Washington. He indicated that the United States would make every effort to go beyond scheduled production but that no decision had been reached yet concerning heavy bombers.[31] The question of heavies for Russia formed a part of the continuing problem of the relationships of aircraft exports to the needs of the AAF; the military advisers of the President continued to press the case of the American air force establishment as against foreign aid. The President followed up his message to Harriman with one to the Secretary of War, informing him that exports of aircraft, including heavies, should follow a "rule of thumb" of fifty per cent.[32] Stimson replied that American exports of various types of aircraft, excluding heavies, would exceed that figure. However, Stimson said that in view of AAF shortages the fifty per cent figure could not be applied to heavies.[33] The President did not feel that this was making the most effective use of the heavies. He told Stimson that it was far better, for example, to have heavies operating from Britain than Newfoundland. Stimson, on the other hand, continued to press the need to build the AAF. "It is better," he stated, "for her [Britain] to have in the world a potent, well-armed, friendly American air force than a few additional planes." He added: "The moment has now come when we should give our primary attention to the 'prompt' development of a well-armed, well-rounded, and well-trained American air force."[34] These words, of course, applied quite as cogently to aid to the Soviet Union as to Great Britain.

In the case of Russia, the White House inclined to favor at least token deliveries of heavy bombers, a view which the President advanced as early as August.[35] Presidential advisers continued to regard Army opposition to all-out aid coldly. During a conference

31. Msg., Roosevelt to Harriman, September 18, 1941 (File: 091 Russia, ASWA, in WWIIRD/NA).
32. Ltr., Roosevelt to Stimson, September 18, 1941 (File: 452.1, in WWIIRD/NA).
33. Ltr., Stimson to Roosevelt, September 22, 1941 (File: 452.1, in WWIIRD/NA).
34. Ltr., Roosevelt to Stimson, October 14, 1941; ltr., Stimson to Roosevelt, October 21, 1941 (File: 452.1, in WWIIRD/NA).
35. "Notes on Remarks of the President at Conference Held on August 1, 1941, signed Marshall." The conference was between Roosevelt and Col. Philip Faymonville (File: 19776 to 20150, OCS, in WWIIRD/NA).

46 EAGLES EAST

with a War Department representative, Lieutenant Colonel K. N. Walker, Presidential adviser Harry Hopkins said that he could not understand the opposition of Lovett and Arnold to the allocation of heavies to Russia. Hopkins noted that Generals Chaney, Embick, and Burns approved of them, especially from the standpoint of salubrious effects on Soviet morale. Walker, expressing the War Department position, agreed in principle, but he pointed out that as soon as the Soviet Union discovered the small number of planes scheduled for delivery the effects might be the opposite of those desired. He patiently explained that the character of Soviet air operations did not lend itself to the effective use of heavy bombers, which were sorely needed elsewhere.[36]

Finally, on September 25, Lovett offered a compromise solution to the problem. His proposal increased the number of medium bombers by the number of heavies in Chaney's suggested distribution. By taking away the allotment of heavy bombers from Russia, his proposal would pacify to some extent the British, who would receive the heavies scheduled for the Russians. Lovett's formula for delivery under the Moscow Protocol was 72 B-25's, 828 A-20's, and 900 P-40's.[37] Arnold agreed in part with the proposal but offered a somewhat different breakdown. In view of the difficulty in finding the number of A-20's for the Russians in Lovett's proposal, Arnold recommended that the United States allocate through June, 1942: 72 B-25's, 584 A-20's, 144 A-29's, 100 0-52's, and 900 P-40's. Arnold's recommendations were forwarded to Harriman and formed the basis of American discussions with the Russians in Moscow.[38]

This action officially increased the allocation of planes to the Soviet Union from 1,163 to 1,800. Left unsolved, however, was the basic question: Where were the additional planes to be obtained? The British, in offering their proposal, had suggested that they come from AAF allocations rather than from their share of Lend-Lease, to which the American mission with one exception, General Embick, agreed. Harriman urged Washington's approval of this decision. However, he also wanted a resolution of a second vital

36. AWPD/1 Scrap Book, Tab 76.
37. Ltr., Lovett to Hopkins, with suggested message for Harriman, September 25, 1941 (File: 091 Russia, ASWA, in WWIIRD/NA).
38. Memo, Arnold for Lovett, September 26, 1941; msg., Hopkins to Harriman, September 26, 1941 (File: 091 Russia, ASWA, in WWIIRD/NA).

The Moscow Protocol

issue— specifically, how were the munitions to be financed?[39]

Hopkins, speaking for the President, could do little to ease Harriman's apprehensions. Public opinion was improving with respect to Russia, he said, but he implied that no decision could be made as yet to include the Soviet Union under Lend-Lease.[40] The White House was waiting for Congressional action on the Second Supplemental National Defense Appropriations Bill, some of the funds of which the President intended to use for Russia. The President, who had been zealously fostering the creation of a better image of the Soviet Union, expected this bill to pass. However, there would be opposition, and efforts to create large-scale financial support specifically assigned to the Soviet Union might well have floundered. As a consequence, the bill which would provide support for the initial phases of the Russian aid program was being debated in Congress as Harriman reached Moscow. Thus, Harriman found himself in the curious position of leading a mission to commit the United States to a substantial program of aid without definite assurances of how it was to be financed.

After the London meetings the Anglo-American mission, composed of civilian and military officials, prepared for the trek to Moscow. Part of the delegation, including Harriman and Beaverbrook, proceeded to Russia aboard HMS *London,* the remainder went in two B-24's. The flight of the B-24's was a particularly dangerous one, since there was the possibility of attack not only by the enemy but also by the Russians themselves. For some reason the Russians failed to acknowledge the proper radio signals of the planes, causing many anxious moments for those involved. The group which arrived by ship at Archangel was transferred to a Soviet plane which flew it to Moscow. This group also received a strange but a more dramatic welcome—Russian batteries accidentally fired on the Soviet plane.[41]

Harriman and Beaverbrook met Stalin upon their arrival on September 28.[42] The other members of the American and British

39. Msg., Harriman to Roosevelt, 9/19/41 (File: 167.6-39, Russia, in USAF/HA).
40. Msg., Hopkins to Harriman, September 20, 1941 (File: Russian Cables, ID, ASF, in WWIIRD/NA).
41. U. S., Army Air Forces, Air Transport Command, "History of the Air Transport Command: Ferrying Command Operations, May 29-December 7, 1941," I, 63-64 (File: 300.1, in USAF/HA); Hastings L. Ismay, *The Memoirs of General Lord Ismay* (New York: The Viking Press, 1960), p. 230.
42. Msg., Steinhardt to Roosevelt and Hull, September 29, 1941, [No. 1726], *Foreign Relations,* 1941, I, 836.

48   EAGLES EAST

mission began their meetings on the following day. They served
on one of several committees established to deal with specific
areas of importance, one of which was the Air Supply Committee
under the chairmanship of Gen. Chaney. The other ranking members of this committee were the Undersecretary of State for Air,
H. H. Balfour, for Britain and Commissar for Aircraft Industries,
Shakurin, for the Soviet Union.[43]

In his meetings with Harriman and Beaverbrook, Stalin
stressed his need for aircraft, which constituted a "first priority"
in Russian munitions requests.[44] During the meetings of the Air
Supply Committee, which dealt with the details of these matters,
the Soviet request for bombers posed the most difficult problem.
Shakurin asked for a monthly total of 300 bombers and 100 fighters
from the United States and Britain, a reversal of the ratio which
Britain and the United States had previously agreed upon in
London. The Russian representative stated that his country was
producing 70 planes per day, including 40 fighters, 20 bombers,
and 10 Stormovik bombers. "This was not enough for the Soviet
Air Force," Shakurin said, "whose needs were particularly great
in the case of bombers."[45] The Soviets estimated that 1,000-1,200
bombers were produced monthly in the United States, and they
felt that this would allow the delivery to them of the 300 they
requested. Shakurin pressed for a medium bomber similar to the
Soviet PE-2 with a range of 15,000 kilometers, a bomb load of one
ton, and a maximum speed of 540 kilometers.

Chaney promptly corrected errors in Soviet estimates of
American bomber production. He pointed out that total aircraft
production for July and August 1941 was 1,500 and 1,800 respectively, a large percentage of which were trainers. Chaney explained
that light and medium bomber production was small, approximately 300 planes a month.[46] Chaney's estimates of American aircraft production were essentially correct. During the third quarter
of 1941, factory deliveries of all types reached 5,156, or an average
monthly rate of 1,719. During the same period deliveries of light
and medium bombers totaled 1,029, or an average monthly de-

43. "The Chaney Report," Inclosure 3. A brief summary of the committees and
the members who composed them can be found in msg., Steinhardt to Roosevelt and Hull, September 29, 1941, [No. 1732], *Foreign Relations*, 1941, I, 837-38.
44. Msg., Harriman to Hopkins, October 4, 1941, *Foreign Relations*, 1941, I, 842.
45. "The Chaney Report," Inclosure 3.
46. *Ibid.*

The Moscow Protocol   49

livery rate of 343.[47] Shakurin responded that if 300 bombers could not be delivered, the Soviet Union wanted at least 200 a month. The American and British representatives adhered to the "100 monthly" figure and suggested that the Soviet Air Force adapt Kittyhawks and Hurricanes for close-support bombardment work.[48] Chaney held out the possibility that a readjustment of the ratio of 300 fighters and 100 bombers per month could be considered in the next protocol period.[49]

Strangely, the Soviets now expressed a particular preference for the B-25, of which they had been so critical less than a month before.[50] They urged that the United States send as many of them as possible. When Chaney stated that these were still in the early stages of production and hence limited in availability, Shakurin indicated a choice for Boston 3's. For technical and military reasons, Shakurin argued that the planes should be of one type— a point of view that British and American representatives shared. However, due to existing production and the needs of others, it was doubtful, said Chaney, if more than 600 A-20's could be sent during the protocol period. Therefore the remainder might have to be made up with Lockheed-Hudsons or some smaller plane. Once again the Russians made a request for heavy bombers, but Chaney parried it by pointing out the limitations of American production.

The Russians preferred Spitfires and Kittyhawks. The British pointed out that production limitations made it impossible to meet their commitment of 200 fighters with Spitfires. Balfour added that Britain would try to send 100 of them a month toward the end of the protocol period; however, the bulk of the planes would have to be Hurricanes.[51]

Delivery problems also loomed large in the conversations. The Russians preferred that the planes be shipped to Archangel. They excluded delivery to Vladivostok as impractical[52] and opposed flight delivery via Alaska and Siberia—the so-called "Alsib" route— which Harriman had proposed in one of his conversations with Stalin. When Harriman suggested that the planes be flight-

47. U. S. Air Force, *United States Air Force Statistical Digest: 1947*, p. 121.
48. "The Chaney Report," Inclosure 3.
49. *Ibid.*, Tab G.
50. See Chapter II.
51. "The Chaney Report," Inclosure 3.
52. *Ibid.*

50   EAGLES EAST

delivered by AAF pilots over Alaska and Siberia, Stalin labeled
the route "too dangerous."[53]

However, Stalin had agreed to provide the Americans with
information about Siberian airports.[54] This soon proved to be an
unfulfilled promise. General Chaney had been led to believe that
the information about Siberian airdromes would come from a
certain General Golitov. But, Chaney complained, Golitov "indicated each time that the data was not ready and that I would hear
from him before my departure." Before he left Moscow, Chaney
received a map almost completely devoid of value for planning
ferrying operations from Nome to Siberia. No descriptive information was provided about airdromes on the portion of the route
from Nome to Vladivostok. The Russians explained that ample
facilities existed from Vladivostok to Moscow but that the route
from Nome across Siberia was inadvisable and would be especially
difficult during the winter. As a result of the Soviet attitude, Chaney
had no alternative but to recommend that if planes were to be
ferried to Russia the AAF would have to use the South Atlantic
route to the Middle East.[55]

The British did not fare any better than the Americans in
prying information from their hosts. Beaverbrook sought in vain
for data concerning a Soviet weapon—probably the "Katyusha"—
test-fired before a group of British and American observers some
time earlier. Likewise unavailing was his request that the Russians
send to Britain for examination one of the Stormoviks, which had
proved so effective on the Russo-German front.[56] Either to prevent
injury to Soviet sensibilities or to avoid arousing their suspicions,
these requests were not pressed in Moscow.[57] In other words, the
principle of *quid pro quo* was not applied, and the Anglo-Ameri-

53. Sherwood, *Roosevelt and Hopkins*, p. 388; William H. Standley and Arthur
A. Ageton, *Admiral Ambassador to Russia* (Chicago: Henry Regnery Co., 1955),
p. 66.
54. *Ibid.*
55. Memo, Chaney for Harriman, October 11, 1941 (File: 091 Russia, ASWA,
in WWIIRD/NA).
56. Msg., Chaney to AG, December 6, 1941 (File: 400.3295, AG, in WWIIRD/
NA). The Katyusha was a rocket mortar used with telling effect on the
Germans for the first time in significant numbers during the battle of Moscow.
57. Memo, Col. C. W. Bundy for Marshall, October 24, 1941, reveals Harriman's
instruction to the American members of the mission not to press the Russians
for military information (File: 4557 to 49 Russia, WPD, WDGS, in
WWIIRD/NA). This is confirmed in a note in reference to msg. from Yeaton
October 6, 1941 (File: 913410, G-2, in WWIIRD/NA).

The Moscow Protocol

can mission left Moscow with such insignificant information as the Russians chose to provide. Soviet historians have erroneously claimed that Harriman and Beaverbrook made western aid contingent upon the receipt of this information but when met by refusals they gave up their attempts. Soviet historians describe the information requested as allegedly "secret."[58] But the full extent of British-American inquiries concerned a weapon which had been publicly tested and observed by Russia's allies, a plane long in operation on the eastern front which would have been little in exchange for the various British and American types then in operation in Russia, and a knowledge of Siberian airdromes in order to initiate plans to ferry aircraft more speedily. It is an ironic commmentary upon the extent of mutual trust involved that American military planners knew more at this time about the Luftwaffe than they did about the Soviet Air Force.[59]

On October 1, 1941, Harriman, Beaverbrook, and Molotov signed the Moscow Protocol. The United States agreed to provide a monthly total of 100 fighters and 100 bombers. Britain agreed to provide 200 fighters per month. The combined commitment for a nine-month period totaled 3,600 planes. No statement of specific types and series of aircraft was included other than "fighters" and "bombers" since too many uncertainties existed to warrant such precision. The text of the agreement stated that the supplies

> . . . will be made available at British and U. S. A. centres of production, for the Soviet Union by Great Britain and the United States of America within the period beginning from October 1941, till the end of June 1942.

It went on to say that Great Britain and the United States "will give aid to the transportation of these materials to the Soviet Union and will help with the delivery."[60]

The results of the conference appeared to be as satisfactory to the Russians as they were to the Anglo-American mission. Harri-

58. V. L. Israelian, *Diplomatischeskaia Istoria Velikoi Otechestvennoi Voiny, 1941-1945* (Moskva: Izdatelstvo Instituta Mezhdunarodnykh Otnoshenii, 1959), p. 34; G. A. Deborin, *Vtoraia Mirovaia Voina* (Moskva: Voennoe Izdatelstvo Ministerstva Oborony SSSR, 1958), p. 148.
59. See the instructive remarks in memo with report, Jacobs for Wedemeyer, May 7, 1943 (File: ABC 452.1, WPD, WDGS, in WWIIRD/NA).
60. U. S., Department of State, *Soviet Supply Protocols* (Washington: United States Government Printing Office, n.d.), p. 3.

52   EAGLES EAST

man wrote to Roosevelt: "We have closed the conference today in an atmosphere of great enthusiasm by all who participated." He added, "Stalin personally is much gratified and sends you his personal thanks."[61] A few days later Harriman wrote that the results of the conferences "have been accepted with undisguised enthusiasm by Stalin and all others connected with the discussions."[62] Before the departure of the combined mission, a state dinner was held at the Kremlin. Thirty toasts were proposed, several of them by Stalin himself, who particularly praised American industry. Ambassador Steinhardt, who was present at the occasion, reported Stalin's observation that "the United States is giving more assistance as a non-belligerent than some countries in history had given as allies." He added the hope, soon to be realized, that the United States, Great Britain, and the Soviet Union would be fighting shoulder to shoulder.[63]

Harriman was most anxious that the United States initiate deliveries under the protocol without delay. On October 3 in a communication to Roosevelt, Harriman urged: "It is of the utmost importance that prompt action confirm the confidence the Russians now have in the sincerity of our aid."[64] In a message to Hopkins on the next day, Harriman declared that "In order to translate the spirit of our conference into actuality [it is] urgently desirable that a maximum amount [of] critically needed material be dispatched earliest possible. First priority is tanks and aircraft. . . ."[65] In a message to Stalin, Roosevelt expressed his "confidence that your armies will ultimately prevail over Hitler" and assured him "of our great determination to be of every possible material assistance."[66] Less than two weeks after the conference, Roosevelt announced that everything possible was being done to send material to the Russians to help them.[67]

61. Msg., Harriman to Roosevelt, October 1, 1941, *Foreign Relations*, 1941, I, 839-40.
62. Msg., Harriman to Roosevelt, October 3, 1941, *Foreign Relations*, 1941, I, 841-42.
63. Msg., Steinhardt to Hull, October 3, 1941, *Foreign Relations*, 1941, I, 840-41.
64. Msg., Harriman to Roosevelt, October 3, 1941, *Foreign Relations*, 1941, I, 841-42.
65. Msg., Harriman to Hopkins, October 4, 1941, *Foreign Relations*, 1941, I, 842.
66. U. S., Department of State, *The Department of State Bulletin*, October 11, 1941, p. 276.
67. *Ibid.*, October 18, 1941, p. 296.

The Moscow Protocol 53

After the departure of the American mission from Moscow, General Chaney submitted a report to Harriman containing the observations and recommendations of the members of the Air Supply Committee. In addition to the formal conferences with the Russians, members of the mission had had an opportunity to observe the work at Russian aircraft factories and to talk informally with other observers in the country. Chaney's report noted the soundness of Soviet principles of airplane and engine design and the efficiency of factory administration, production methods, and processes of inspection—all of which followed western patterns. The observers commented upon the skill of the workers who labored on production machinery and noted that although women and young boys worked in factories only men occupied key positions.[68]

The favorable commentary of General Chaney was reinforced by the reports of the two AAF officers at Archangel, Lieutenant Alison and Lieutenant Zemke, who remarked upon the skill and ingenuity of Soviet mechanics and technicians who worked "without shelter in sleet, rain, and wind on an average of 14 hours a day." These officers also commented on the ability of the Russian pilots—120 of whom qualified in non-Soviet types in the period September 10-29, with the loss of only one plane. The mission was provided an example of the ability of Soviet workers to execute decisions by constructing an airdrome at Archangel for the reception of planes. Construction began on September 3, and within a month it was completed. During that time 47 planes were assembled and tested.[69]

Such observations naturally inspired the committee to recommend sending only the best planes and equipment. As a result of its meetings, the committee concluded that 0-52's were not suitable for Soviet needs and A-29's were of doubtful value— types that had been considered for delivery during the discussions in Moscow.[70] The committee's final recommendations to Harriman, who communicated them to Roosevelt on October 9, stated that the 1,800 planes provided by the United States through June, 1942,

68. "The Chaney Report," Tab H.
69. *Ibid.*
70. *Ibid.*; also see p. 4 of the text of the report. The A-29, popularly known as the "Hudson," was an observation and patrol bomber. The 0-52, also known as the "Owl," was an observation plane. Neither of these met Soviet requirements with respect to speed or armament.

54 EAGLES EAST

should include 900 P-40's, 828 A-20's, and 72 B-25's.[71] In other words, the Air Supply Committee recommended the distribution of aircraft proposed earlier by Secretary Lovett.

In view of commitments to the Soviet Union and recent production estimates, AWPD/2's recommended allocations were substantially revised. On October 29, 1941, Arnold announced a new schedule among the claimants on American aircraft production through June 1942:[72]

U.S.A.	GREAT BRITAIN	U.S.S.R.	CHINA	OTHERS
4,189	6,634	1,835	407	109

The breakdown of planes approved for the Soviet Union included 77 B-25's, 828 A-20's, 900 P-40's, and 30 0-52's.[73] The 35 planes above protocol commitments included 5 B-25's, approved before the Moscow Conference began, and 30 0-52's already in the process of shipment.[74] To provide the increased number of planes above the original AWPD/2 allocation was not a simple matter of rearranging figures. Any change inevitably affected other claimants. The problem was temporarily resolved when the British agreed to defer 300 A-20's, originally scheduled for them under Lend-Lease and British contracts. This enabled the United States, by drawing 515 planes from Defense Aid contracts and 13 from AAF contracts, to meet its deliveries of light bombers within the protocol period. But the British action was a deferment, not a cancellation, which meant that the United States was obliged to make up the amount later. In order to meet the commitment for the delivery of fighters, 343 were transferred from Defense Aid contracts and the remainder from planes in or scheduled for the AAF. Medium bombers and observation planes were to come entirely from those scheduled for the AAF.[75]

71. *Ibid.*, pp. 4-5 of text. An official copy of the message can be found in 091 Russia, ASWA, in WWIIRD/NA.
72. Craven and Cate, *The Army Air Forces in World War II*, I, 134; memo, Arnold for distribution with Inclosure 1, October 29, 1941, in AWPD/2, gives different figures for the American and British share, listing 4,205 and 6,590 aircraft respectively.
73. Memo, Arnold for distribution, with Inclosure 1, October 29, 1941.
74. The extra 5 B-25's constituted part of America's first allocation of aircraft to Russia during the summer. Since they were available, 30 0-52's were scheduled for shipment to Russia in October. See msg., Hopkins to Harriman, October 3, 1941; ltr., Hopkins to Hull, with message to Harriman, October 13, 1941 (File: Russian Cables, ID, ASF, in WWIIRD/NA).
75. "Minutes of Conferences, October 21-22, 1941, held by the Chief of the Army Air Forces with following British Representatives: Captain Balfour,

The Moscow Protocol

It was not an easy matter to reach decisions concerning the number and type of aircraft which the United States approved for Russia, since this involved a reduction of the share which the AAF and Britain received from limited production. The existence of another claimant upon American aircraft production added pressing dimensions to the problem of allocation.

The aircraft as well as other supplies which the United States and Britain agreed to provide Russia during the Moscow Protocol period might not have loomed large when measured in terms of total production. However, when viewed in connection with the effects of these commitments on American and British requirements, the sacrifice was substantial. Churchill aptly summed this up to Hopkins when he said: "There is no disguising the fact . . . that they make grievous inroads into what is required by you for expanding your forces and by us for intensifying our war effort."[76]

Sir Henry Self, Air Marshal A. T. Harris, Air Commodore E. B. C. Batts, Mr. C. R. Fairey, and Mr. T. D. Weldon" (File: 452.1, Deliveries of planes to Russia, ID, ASF, in WWIIRD/NA).

76. Churchill, *The Grand Alliance*, p. 469.

CHAPTER IV

The Problem of Delivery and North Russia

THE PROBLEM OF ALLOCATION was matched in seriousness by that of determining how and where to deliver the aircraft to the Soviet Union. During the war, the United States delivered aircraft by four avenues, two of which were water routes: the run to Archangel and Murmansk and the route around the Cape of Good Hope to the Persian Corridor. The other two were air passages: the aircraft were piloted across the South Atlantic to Africa and Iran or across the arctic wastes of Alaska and Siberia. All of them posed technical and diplomatic problems which had to be overcome by long and patient effort.

During the period of the Moscow Protocol, the Russians preferred to have most war munitions, including aircraft, delivered at Archangel and Murmansk. One of the most serious factors which hampered deliveries to the Russians over this route was the limited shipping, a shortage which plagued other aspects of the Anglo-American war effort. Once this problem became less acute, German air and submarine attacks against Allied convoys making the north Russian run emerged as the major obstacle to the fulfillment of protocol commitments. This meant, of course, that aircraft deliveries to northern Russia were inevitably affected. To be sure, the Russians also had their share of problems, the most serious of which was their inability to clear the cargoes of Allied convoys.

The actual delivery of aid was not an obligation which the United States or Great Britain had assumed in the Moscow Protocol. Anglo-American supplies were to "be made available at British and U. S. A. centres of production." The Protocol was

Problem of Delivery and North Russia 57

explicit on the point of transportation. "Great Britain and the U. S. A.," it stated, "will give aid to the transportation of these materials to the Soviet Union and will help with the delivery."[1] In other words, British and American endeavors to transport supplies were voluntary and constituted, as Churchill put it, "a good-will effort."[2] Or, as Harriman observed in regard to the problem of transportation, "We made no commitment but offered to help."[3] The Soviet Union, on the other hand, regarded actual delivery of the promised material as a *de facto* obligation and considered supplies delivered only when they reached Russian points of acceptance. Many of the Anglo-American difficulties with the Russians, therefore, stemmed from Moscow's peculiar interpretation of the protocol.

Few American officials could have anticipated that the "good-will effort" would constitute so herculean a task. It involved meeting several difficult challenges, first and foremost of which was finding enough ships to transport the supplies. In order to clear the large volume of materiel under the protocol, the Soviet Union estimated its shipping requirements at 1,500,000 tons but admitted that it could provide only a small fraction of what was needed—117,000 tons.[4] Shortly after the Moscow Protocol had been concluded, it was increasingly apparent that shipping would be the limiting factor for some time in meeting deliveries. And the scale of Nazi operations against the Allied merchant fleet presaged increasing difficulties in meeting needs. The United States, Britain, and Canada produced 10.6 million deadweight tons of merchant shipping in 1942, "But even this large total was exceeded by sinkings; and the merchant fleet of the United Nations was smaller at the end of the year than at the beginning."[5]

Prior to Pearl Harbor the number of ships sailing for Russian ports did not meet expectations: 15 in October and 13 in November.[6] If the record of departures continued at that rate, it was

1. U. S., Department of State, *Soviet Supply Protocols*, p. 3.
2. Winston S. Churchill, *The Hinge of Fate* (Boston: Houghton Mifflin Company, 1950), p. 271.
3. Msg., Harriman to Roosevelt, October 1, 1941, *Foreign Relations*, 1941, I, 840.
4. Ltr., Harriman to Roosevelt, October 29, 1941, *Foreign Relations*, 1941, I. 850.
5. Hall, *North American Supply*, p. 398; memo, Lt. Col. A. S. Palmerlee for Wardlow, undated (File: RG 160, Box 21, ASF, in WWIRB/NA).
6. Foreign Economic Administration, "Status of the Soviet Aid Program as of March 31, 1944," April, 1944 (File: 194F, in USAF/HA).

58 EAGLES EAST

clear that only a small portion of aircraft would reach Russian ports. Harriman explained to Stalin that the lack of shipping was primarily responsible for the delay in sending supplies but assured him that the necessary ships would be found.[7] This assurance did not prevent the Soviet representative in the United States from describing the lack of ships for the Russian aid program "as catastrophic." In New York and Boston, the Soviets alleged, there was sufficient cargo, already a month overdue, to fill 18 ships.[8] General Arnold partially confirmed the Soviet contention by pointing out that almost 300 planes awaited shipment from New York and Boston.[9]

Soviet representatives complained that their repeated requests for ships had been ignored and claimed that they needed about 80 of them each month to carry merchandise. Acheson assured the Russians that the various agencies which were working on the matter were doing everything possible to provide shipping facilities.[10]

The course of events which followed threatened a drastic change for the worse. When the Japanese attacked Pearl Harbor, all available ships and munitions were frantically dispatched to stave off continued Japanese advances in the Pacific and to bolster American strength in other vital areas. A few days after the Japanese attack on Pearl Harbor, the AAF decided to divert planes from Russian and British allocations in order to strengthen combat groups in Hawaii, Panama, and the west coast of the United States. "We must," Arnold told his staff, "run a rake through the United States, gathering up every combat plane and fill up every pursuit group. . . ."[11] Emphasizing the importance of the diversions of aircraft to the security of the nation, Marshall assured the President, however, that they would only be temporary. Quoting a statement of Colonel Henry S. Aurand,

7. Msg., Harriman to Stalin, November 15, 1941, *Foreign Relations*, 1941, I, 860.
8. Memo of conversation by Loy Henderson, November 19, 1941, *Foreign Relations*, 1941, I, 862-63.
9. Ltr., Arnold to Burns, November 28, 1941; memo, Arnold for Marshall, December 2, 1941 (File: 167.6-39, Russia, in USAF/HA).
10. Memo of conversation by Henderson, November 19, 1941, *Foreign Relations*, 1941, I, 863.
11. Minutes of meeting in Arnold's Office on December 9, 1941 (File: 145.96.220, in USAF/HA).

Problem of Delivery and North Russia 59

Director of Defense Aid, the Chief of Staff reviewed the situation for the President:

> At the present time it would appear that February first, [sic] 1942, would be the approximate date of the full resumption of transfers under the protocol commitments. In the interim, there will be transferred according to the protocol, or as near to it as our situation allows, of all articles which the reinforcement referred to above will permit.[12]

The White House was especially anxious to dispel doubts regarding the effects of Pearl Harbor upon American aid. On December 8, the President assured the Soviet Ambassador of America's determination to continue aid to Russia.[13] The following day, in his Fireside Chat, Roosevelt made it clear that American production was not reserved solely for its armed forces. "It must," he said, "reinforce the other armies and navies and air forces fighting the Nazis and the war lords of Japan throughout the Americas and throughout the world."[14] A few days later, Hull repeated the President's assurances of support to Russia.[15]

The ban on shipments was brief. During a meeting on December 17 with Edward R. Stettinius, Lend-Lease Administrator, Colonel Aurand revealed that aircraft and munitions deliveries to Russia had been resumed and that deliveries of other items would soon follow.[16]

During these critical days the President again emphasized his determination that protocol deliveries be resumed promptly and the deficits be made up as soon as possible. He directed Stimson to make up existing deficits in the protocol "not later than April 1." The President understood that America's involvement in the war required certain amendments relating to the time of delivery of certain items in the protocol. But, when such changes were made, he wanted the War Department to seriously consider increasing

12. Draft memo, Marshall for Roosevelt, undated. The memo was taken to Marshall by Col. Thomas T. Handy of the Plans Group, War Plans Division, on December 13. (File: 4557 to 49 Russia, WPD, WDGS, in WWIIRD/NA).
13. U.S., Department of State, *The Department of State Bulletin*, December 13, 1941, p. 506.
14. Rosenman, *The Public Papers and Addresses of Franklin D. Roosevelt*, II, 526.
15. U. S., Department of State, *The Department of State Bulletin*, December 13, 1941, p. 506.
16. Minutes of meeting in the Office of Edward R. Stettinius, December 17, 1941 (File: RG 179, Box 785, WPB, in WWIRB/NA).

60 EAGLES EAST

the amounts of other articles in the protocol. Emphasizing the importance of the aid program to Russia, the President affirmed:

> The whole Russian program is so vital to our interests I know that only the gravest consideration will lead you to recommend our witholding longer the munitions our Government has promised the U.S.S.R.

He concluded with what constituted a Presidential directive: "I wish, therefore, that all items go forward promptly after January 1, unless I authorize the specific amendment."[17] Stimson keenly appreciated the significance of the aid program to Russia but he rightly believed that the emergency needs of the armed forces must prevail. To assuage the President's apprehensions, Stimson pointed out that the War Department planned in January to establish monthly deliveries of aircraft at the rate of 100 fighters and 100 light bombers. In view of approved plans to bolster the strength of the AAF, the War Department did not see how increases in plane deliveries to Russia were possible. Moreover, if production drops necessitated adjustment, reductions would have to be made in Lend-Lease deliveries. Although Stimson anticipated that deliveries would be increased rather than reduced, he warned: "I feel that I must, as a matter of caution, point out that exigencies may arise as a result of our entry into the war which preclude us from making any absolute commitments."[18]

In order to cope with the problem of supplies piling up due to a lack of shipping to export them, Stimson recommended that "Anything in excess of one month's accumulation of supplies awaiting transport may be diverted to the use of United States or other forces." Roosevelt realistically approved the recommendation subject to the condition that such diversions be replaced as soon as shipping became available.[19]

No sooner had the President taken this action than General Marshall proposed a plan to Roosevelt and Churchill during the *Arcadia* Conference which raised serious questions about the ability of the United States to implement its promises to Russia.

17. Ltr., Roosevelt to Stimson, December 28, 1941, *Foreign Relations*, 1941, I, 865.
18. Ltr., Stimson to Roosevelt, December 30, 1941 (File: 031.1 Protocol, vol. I, ID, ASF, in WWIIRD/NA).
19. *Ibid.*; ltr., Roosevelt to Stimson, January 4, 1941 (File: 031.1 Protocol, vol. I, ID, ASF, in WWIIRD/NA).

Problem of Delivery and North Russia

It appeared as though the coat of Anglo-American strategy had outgrown the cloth of shipping. During a meeting on January 12, Marshall presented his plan for the reinforcement of the so-called ABDA Area, the vast expanse of the South Pacific stretching from the shores of India to Australasia. In order to implement the plan, Marshall estimated that a 30 per cent cut of Lend-Lease to Russia for at least four months would be necessary. The leaders at this meeting were confronted with the problem of how to approve Marshall's plan without injury to the supply program to Russia, both of which were top priority. Hopkins, believing that the matter reduced itself to only seven ships, confidently predicted that the ships could be found without injury to Marshall's plan. The Chief of Staff won approval for his plan while Hopkins and Beaverbrook sought to find the seven ships for the supply program to Russia. In retrospect, it is perhaps difficult to understand how a few ships could dominate a meeting of one of the most important conferences between British and American leaders. It is clear that although both nations had tremendous resources at their command, they were available at this time in negligible amounts.[20]

Although a greater number of vessels sailed for the Soviet Union in December, 1941, and January, 1942, than in the first two months of the protocol period,[21] shipments of planes were disappointingly small. At the end of November, a total of 70 planes departed the United States. These included 39 P-40's, 26 0-52's, and 5 B-25's.[22] At the end of December, three months after the Moscow Protocol, total aircraft shipments from the United States reached 151, including 76 P-40's, 44 A-20's, 26 0-52's, and 5 B-25's.[23]

The situation was serious enough to warrant the intervention of the White House. The President felt it necessary personally to assure Stalin that more planes were on their way to Russia. On February 9, he itemized scheduled aircraft shipments for January and February—244 fighters, 24 B-25's, and 233 A-20's. He assured Stalin of "the importance of getting our supplies to you at the earliest possible date and every effort is being made to get ship-

20. Sherwood, *Roosevelt and Hopkins*, pp. 459-66.
21. Foreign Economic Administration, "Status of the Soviet Aid Program as of March 31, 1944."
22. "Status of Airplanes Shipped to the USSR as of February 17, 1942" (File: 452.1 Deliveries of Planes to Russia, ID, ASF, in WWIIRD/NA).
23. *Ibid.*

62 EAGLES EAST

ments off."[24] Stalin replied tersely. Verbal assurances were not enough. He emphasized that "the fulfillment of American deliveries, including tanks and aeroplanes, is of the utmost importance for our common cause, for our further successes."[25] The United States, he urged, should follow the same procedures as Britain in dispatching convoys—namely, organizing, loading and convoying them to Soviet ports.[26]

During these months the delivery of supplies to Russia was a cause of considerable friction between War Department officials and Russian representatives in Washington. The confusion in the aid program which inevitably followed in the wake of Pearl Harbor had been wrongly interpreted by the Russians as an intentional effort by the Department to withhold deliveries. Konstantin Lukashev, President of the Amtorg Trading Corporation, informed Stettinius that the delays in moving supplies out of American ports "were the result of misunderstandings and lack of cooperation on the part of the representatives of the War Department. . . ."[27]

Russian representatives failed to appreciate the serious problems, especially after Pearl Harbor, which accounted for the American delay in dispatching supplies. Early in 1942 twenty ships in Philadelphia awaited the reception of cargo which glutted the dock and freight cars. When the Russians asked that the cargo be loaded, officials replied that clearance documents were needed before the transfer could be made. One of the exasperated Russians, forgetting which country he was in, commented to an American official: "I would ask you to open the boxes with

24. Msg., Roosevelt to Stalin, February 9, 1942, U. S., Department of State, *Foreign Relations of the United States, Diplomatic Papers: 1942*, Vol. III: *Europe* (Washington: United States Government Printing Office, 1961), p. 690. Hereinafter cited as *Foreign Relations*, 1942, III; Churchill was equally concerned about delays in meeting British aircraft commitments to Russia. See Churchill's msg. to Secretary of State for Air in Churchill, *The Hinge of Fate*, p. 842.
25. Msg., Stalin to Roosevelt, February 19, 1942, *Foreign Relations*, 1942, III, 691.
26. Msg., Stalin to Roosevelt, February 20, 1942, *Foreign Relations*, 1942, III, 691-92.
27. Memo, Lukashev for Stettinius, February 2, 1942 (File: Russia Correspondence no. 2, February, ID, ASF, in WWIIRD/NA). Amtorg was the official Soviet purchasing agency in the United States. With offices on Madison Avenue, New York, the corporation had a staff of some 200 people, many of whom were skilled technicians and specialists.

Problem of Delivery and North Russia

machine guns if we knew in which cars they were in and to use them right here."[28]

Whenever there was some delay in sending a particular item, the Russians, in the words of John J. McCloy, Assistant Secretary of War, took the position that "The President promised us this by a certain time and it has not been delivered."[29] Major General T. J. Hanley, Jr., wryly observed: "On any protest we made [to the Russians], they would say 'your President has ordered you to send us these airplanes. Now, don't you tell me that you can change your President's orders because we know better. . . .' "[30] The Russians made it appear that they were in alliance with the White House against the War Department.

Soviet criticisms of delays in meeting the protocol spurred the President to take decisive action to expedite the delivery of supplies. He decided that the Soviet supply program should have top priority over all other aspects of the war effort. He announced his decision in strongly worded messages to Donald Nelson, Chairman of the War Production Board, and to Rear Admiral Emory S. Land, War Shipping Administrator. The President told Nelson: "I wish that all material promised under the Protocol be released for shipment at the earliest possible date regardless of the effect of these shipments on any other part of our war program." To Land, the President said: "The meeting of the Russian Protocol must have a first priority in shipping. I wish that you would take the additional ships required from the Caribbean and South Atlantic routes regardless of all other considerations."[31] The top priority on shipping for the Russian supply program brought significant results: a total of forty-three ships sailed for Russia in March, as many as had cleared American ports in January and February combined. In April, seventy-eight ships left, the largest number of vessels sailing to Russian acceptance points during a

28. Memo, Maj. Gen. Brehon Somervell for Deputy Chief of Staff, February 17, 1942; memo, Capt. Harry W. Coon for Col. N. M. Coe, February 14, 1942 (File: Russia Correspondence no. 2, February, ID, ASF, in WWIIRD/NA); memo of interview with Mr. Gousev, July 2, 1943, by George Fort Milton (File: Lend-Lease Records, Box 100, in FRC).
29. Note entitled "General Status of the Russian Protocol," McCloy for Stimson, February 12, 1942 (File: 400.336, Russia, ASW, in WWIIRD/NA). Also see memo, Brig. Gen. Raymond E. Lee for Marshall, February 16, 1942 (File: 336 Staff Study, ID, ASF, in WWIIRD/NA).
30. Interview with Maj. Gen. T. J. Hanley, Jr., Retired, December 27, 1962.
31. Quoted in Stettinius, *Lend-Lease*, p. 205.

64 EAGLES EAST

single month in 1941 and 1942. Out of these, sixty-two sailed for northern Russia, six for Iran, and ten for Vladivostok.[32] The effect of Roosevelt's directive on the movement of planes was equally dramatic. By the end of April, 411 bombers and 460 fighters had been exported from the United States.[33]

American difficulties in finding ships to carry protocol cargoes were matched by Soviet problems in clearing the supplies delivered at Archangel and Murmansk. The Russians estimated that Archangel could handle 270,000-300,000 tons per month.[34] These figures were far larger than those of the Americans and the British who placed Archangel's capacity at 90,000 and 60,000 tons, respectively.[35] The Soviets favored Archangel and its adjacent ports rather than Murmansk because the former had a larger capacity and was not so seriously threatened by German attack. Despite these assets, Archangel was ice-free only from June to November whereas Murmansk on the Kola Inlet enjoyed that benefit all year.[36] Nevertheless, the Russians confidently announced their intention to keep the port open throughout the winter by the use of ice-breakers.[37] American military intelligence doubted the Soviet contention: G-2 stated that "Archangel has never yet, so far as we know, been kept open through the winter by ice-breakers."[38] However, the United States and Britain accepted Moscow's assurances and advised that ships making the trip into the White Sea have their hulls reinforced against the severe ice conditions.[39]

32. Foreign Economic Administration, "Status of the Soviet Aid Program as of March 31, 1944."
33. Office of Lend-Lease Administration, "Schedule of Availability of Material and Shipping for U. S. S. R. as of April 30, 1942" (File: unmarked folder, ID, ASF, in WWIIRD/NA).
34. Ltr., Harriman to Roosevelt, October 29, 1941; msg., Brown to Hopkins, October 6, 1941, *Foreign Relations*, 1941, I, 850, 843.
35. Paraphrase of msg., from Michela, November 1, 1941, with G-2 comments. Soviet sources informed Michela that Archangel's capacity was 120,000 tons per month which was closer in agreement to American and British figures than previous Soviet estimates (File: Information Cables—Russia, ID, ASF, in WWIIRD/NA).
36. "Transportation Routes via North and East" (File: 800, Port Facilities, Russian, ID, ASF, in WWIIRD/NA).
37. Ltr., Harriman to Roosevelt, October 29, 1941; msg., Douglas Brown to Hopkins, October 6, 1941, *Foreign Relations*, 1941, I, 850, 843.
38. G-2 comment on msg., Brown to Hopkins, October 6, 1941, cited above (File: Russian Cables, ID, ASF, in WWIIRD/NA).
39. Msg., Faymonville to Brig. Gen. S. P. Spalding, October 26, 1941 (File: Russian Cables, ID, ASF, in WWIIRD/NA).

Problem of Delivery and North Russia 65

By the middle of November, there were indications that the Russians would be unable to keep Archangel open after all. Commander Samuel B. Frankel, Assistant Naval Attaché, reported that on a trip there he had been stranded aboard a Soviet vessel for four days due to severe ice conditions. The captain of the ship described the ice conditions "as [of the] worst kind."[40] British representatives in Russia tried to convince the Russians of the futility of continued use of the port during the winter and suggested Murmansk instead. But Alexei D. Krutikov, Assistant Commissar for Foreign Trade, rejected the British suggestion since, he alleged, it was impossible to predict ice conditions before the middle of December.[41]

By January, however, it was clear that Archangel could not be kept open. British and American vessels already there were having difficulty getting out. Frankel reported that it took almost two weeks for two icebreakers to escort 12 vessels through the ice barrier.[42] When one of the few Soviet icebreakers, the *Stalin*, was put out of action, a dozen British and American ships were locked in the ice of Archangel for the winter.[43] In addition to severe ice conditions, American military observers reported on the slowness in unloading convoys, much of which was due to inadequate port facilities and inexperienced laborers.[44] In one case, it took almost three weeks to unload 9 vessels averaging 4,000 tons.[45]

By the middle of January the Soviets made preparations to receive American and British vessels at Murmansk which, although ice-free, proved to have its share of problems. Technical facilities for unloading were poor, and congestion often developed. Air

---

40. Memo, OP-16-F-5 for Lt. Col. L. A. Guenther, November 24, 1941 (File: 800, Port Facilities, Russian, ID, ASF, in WWIIRD/NA).

41. Msg., Faymonville to Spalding, November 14, 1941 (File: 800, Port Facilities, Russian, ID, ASF, in WWIIRD/NA).

42. Memo, Felthaus for Guenther, January 12, 1942 (File: 800, Port Facilities, Russian, ID, ASF, in WWIIRD/NA).

43. Memo, unaddressed and unsigned, February 17, 1942; summary of Shipments to Russia, April 2, 1942 (File: 913401, G-2, in WWIIRD/NA). Also see memo, from Office of Chief of Naval Operations, January 24, 1942 (File: 800, Port Facilities, Russian, ID, ASF, in WWIIRD/NA).

44. "Informal Report from Capt. J. O. Boswell on his voyage to USSR and Conditions in Archangel," October 19, 1941 (File: 800, Port Facilities, Russian, ID, ASF, in WWIIRD/NA); military attaché report, USSR, no. 1997, November 1, 1941 (File: 452.1, Deliveries of planes to Russia, ID, ASF, in WWIIRD/NA).

45. Extracts of msg., from Michela, November 1, 1941 (File: 800, Port Facilities, Russian, ID, ASF, in WWIIRD/NA).

66   EAGLES EAST

attacks by the Luftwaffe made the area uninhabitable by the summer, and ships had to be routed back to Archangel.[46] Although Anglo-American deliveries to north Russia were not up to Soviet expectations, it is doubtful that the Russians could have handled more supplies than were sent.[47]

By the spring of 1942, enemy action along the northern route emerged as the major obstacle to the delivery of supplies, resulting in periods of curtailment and suspension of the convoys and with it, severe reactions from Moscow. Since the beginning of the campaign in Russia, the Germans expended a great deal of effort to seize the north, particularly Murmansk where the Luftwaffe carried out extensive destruction of rail communications and installations. According to one German writer, the Soviets

> expended every effort and employed all available labor to repair damage to the rails and the depots to maintain the flow of traffic, because once the ice had formed in the navigable channel through the White Sea to the Arkhangelsk [sic] rail route, the Murman [sic] rail route was the only route open for the movement of Anglo-American supplies, besides being the shortest and capable of carrying the most traffic.[48]

In March, 1942, Hitler changed the Luftwaffe's primary mission in the north to anti-convoy operations. By then, twelve of the PQ convoys made the run to northern Russia. Because of the lack of German attention to the convoys up to that time and the darkness of the Arctic in the winter months, the convoys got through unharmed.[49]

Hitler's March directive took dramatic effect in April when PQ 13, attacked by air and sea, lost four or five of its nineteen

46. Samuel E. Morison, *History of United States Naval Operations in World War II*, Vol. I: *The Battle of the Atlantic, September 1939-May 1943* (Boston: Little, Brown & Co., 1950), pp. 371-72; extracts of messages from Alusna, Murmansk, 1942 (File: 913410, G-2, in WWIIRD/NA).
47. For a survey of conditions in Russia's northern ports see C. B. A. Behrens, *Merchant Shipping and the Demands of War* (London: Her Majesty's Stationery Office, 1955), pp. 253-54.
48. Generalleutnant a.D. Hermann Plocher, "The German Air Force Versus Russia on the Eastern Front" (GAF Monograph Studies 153-55), Chapters 4-8, p. 643. This is an unedited version of a three volume study to be published by the Air University, Maxwell AFB, Alabama.
49. Earl F. Ziemke, *The German Northern Theater of Operations, 1940-1945* (Department of the Army Pamphlet No. 20-271, 1959), p. 237; Denis Richards and Hilary St. George Saunders, *Royal Air Force, 1939-1945*, Vol. II: *The Fight Avails* (London: Her Majesty's Stationery Office, 1954), p. 80.

Problem of Delivery and North Russia 67

vessels. Three more convoys sailed in April and May, and losses mounted. PQ 14 met with ice conditions and fourteen out of the twenty-three vessels returned; eight of the remaining ships reached their destination. PQ 15 and PQ 16 suffered severe losses, losing ten ships between them.[50]

Under the impact of the large losses of lives and ships, the British favored a new understanding concerning the amount of supplies to be sent. Roosevelt opposed the idea and urged Churchill on April 27 that every effort be made to send the supplies banking up in Iceland to the Russians. The British proposal raised once again the fear in the White House that Russia might leave the war. The President warned Churchill "that any word reaching Stalin at this time that our supplies were stopping for any reason would have a most unfortunate effect." The President frankly admitted his fears of "political repercussions" if supplies were diminished in any way.[51] He pressed the matter again in a cable to Churchill a few days later. Churchill pointed out to the President that the dispatch of a convoy to Russia was not a simple matter of adding more anti-submarine escorts. Surface ships were also required. These, Churchill said, the British simply could not spare without jeopardizing control of the Atlantic. He grimly told Roosevelt that "we are absolutely extended. . . ." The most the British could handle was to send three convoys every two months with twenty-five to thirty-five ships in each convoy.[52] Since the naval forces for the northern convoys were predominately British, Roosevelt had no choice but to acquiesce in Churchill's position. The President urged, however, that the convoys be kept at a strength of thirty-five ships.[53] Roosevelt then informed Stalin on May 4 that "Grave difficulties are being met in the northern convoy route" but, he added, "I want to assure you, however, that we shall omit no effort in sending off the greatest possible number of ships."[54]

50. Morison, *History of United States Naval Operations in World War II*, I, 166-79; Churchill, *The Hinge of Fate*, p. 257; Ziemke, *The German Northern Theater of Operations, 1940-1945*, p. 237.
51. Msg., Churchill to Hopkins, April 26, 1942; msg., Roosevelt to Churchill, April 27, 1942, Churchill, *The Hinge of Fate*, p. 258.
52. Msg., Roosevelt to Churchill, April 30, 1942; msg., Churchill to Roosevelt, May 2, 1942, Churchill, *The Hinge of Fate*, pp. 258-60.
53. Msg., Roosevelt to Churchill, May 3, 1942, Churchill, *The Hinge of Fate*, p. 260.
54. Msg., Roosevelt to Stalin, May 4, 1942, *Foreign Relations*, 1942, III, 553-54.

68   EAGLES EAST

The Soviets were displeased with the changes, suggesting that British fears rather than military factors prompted the decision. "I have been asked the direct question," wrote Brigadier General Faymonville, "whether we will escort convoys from Iceland to north Russia if the British are afraid to do so."[55] Stalin pressed Churchill to dispatch all ships banking up in Iceland. The Prime Minister again explained that "We shall continue to do our utmost," but frankly told Stalin that "the passage of every convoy has become a serious fleet operation."[56] Toward the end of May, Molotov explored the matter during his visit to London and Washington. Unable to convince the British to send a greater number of convoys, he tried to get the President to agree to send one convoy a month from the United States escorted by the American navy directly to the northern ports. In view of the deployment of naval resources elsewhere, the United States wisely avoided specific commitments and urged that the Soviet Union provide air support for the convoys.[57]

The truth of the matter was that the risks in sending large convoys without proper escort, which only Britain could provide, was out of proportion to the aid which the ships could give the Soviet Union.[58] This could be equally true, however, of convoys with a heavy escort as dramatically displayed by the tragic episode of PQ 17. The heavy losses sustained by it constituted one of the most serious Allied setbacks during the war, resulting in the suspension of the northern convoys and bringing severe rejoinders from the Kremlin. The terrifying Allied losses on this route had other significant results as well: Iran logically became increasingly important in Anglo-American plans for delivering supplies to the Russians. The AAF, indeed, regarded the route to Iran as the most feasible one to deliver aircraft. Before turning to this subject, the matter of technical difficulties attached to early aircraft shipments to northern Russia must first be explored.

55. Msg., Faymonville to Thomas B. McCabe, May 7, 1942, *Foreign Relations*, 1942, III, 701.
56. Msg., Stalin to Churchill, May 6, 1942; msg., Churchill to Stalin, May 9, 1942, Churchill, *The Hinge of Fate*, pp. 260-61.
57. Memo of conference at the White House, May 30, 1942, by Samuel H. Cross; memo, Burns for Hopkins, June 4, 1942, *Foreign Relations*, 1942, III, 577-78, 707.
58. *Foreign Relations*, 1942, III, 701, footnote 84.

CHAPTER V

P-40's, Parts and Protests

THE FIRST AMERICAN-MADE PLANES to arrive in Russia brought outcries of criticism and dismay from the Kremlin. Several of the aircraft had defective generators, making them unfit for combat, and lacked adequate spare parts. Although these difficulties initially affected the P-40's sent from Britain, the United States was equally anxious to solve them. After all, the initial shipment of P-40's had been sent as a joint Anglo-American affair without a clear delineation between British and American commitments. Even if a distinction had been made, the planes were of American design and manufacture. Moreover, subsequent American shipments revealed some of the problems which had plagued the first P-40's sent to the Russians.

On September 1, 1941, the first Allied convoy docked at Archangel. Aboard the ships were forty-eight fighters from the British commitment. Lieutenant Hubert Zemke, an AAF officer, and a group of British mechanics accompanied the shipment. A British fighter unit under the command of Wing Commander H. N. G. Ramsbottom-Isherwood also accompanied the convoy. The unit, equipped with Hurricanes, subsequently conducted air operations to protect Allied vessels making the run to north Russia.[1]

Lieutenant John R. Alison, who had been in Russia since the end of July, met Zemke, and the two officers began to supervise the assembly of the P-40's at Tenth Kilometer Airdrome, a short

1. Military Attaché Report, USSR, November 1, 1941 (File: 452.1, ID, ASF, in WWIIRD/NA); ltr., Zemke to writer, January 28, 1963; Richards and Saunders, *Royal Air Force*, II, 77-80.

distance from Archangel. Despite limited facilities, assembly work went smoothly. The first ten planes were put together by British mechanics, the remainder by the Russians. The competence of Soviet personnel favorably impressed Alison and Zemke. Sometimes, however, the workers were hasty and required the supervision of the AAF officers in order to assure proper operation of the planes.[2]

The deficiencies of the shipment soon became apparent. Both officers tested the planes in flight and found that the generators of several of them did not operate properly. In addition, there were shortages of spare parts and written instructions for the operation of the planes.[3] In the haste to deliver the aircraft, British authorities either failed to modify them as the AAF had done to those sent from the United States, or did so improperly.[4] Moreover, the British could not provide parts. It was suggested to the Russians that they cannibalize some of the aircraft for spares, a common practice in the West. This was the only realistic solution to the problem since American production could not provide them until the spring.[5]

From the point of view of the Russians, the defective nature of the generators and the shortage of spare parts did not inspire confidence in western efforts to assist them. Discussion of these problems bogged down in bureaucratic channels and, in Soviet eyes, neither country appeared to take corrective measures. The longer the problems dragged on without satisfactory solutions, the greater was the number of Soviet complaints. The whole matter assumed gigantic proportions when subsequent deliveries of P-40's revealed some of the same deficiencies. At the end of December, 1941, the Soviet Union claimed that 35 out of 228 P-40's were out of commission and that the remainder were operating without generators.[6]

2. Military Attaché Report, USSR, November 1, 1941.
3. *Ibid.*; msg., Michela to WD, November 6, 1941 (File: 452.1, ID, ASF, in WWIIRD/NA).
4. Military Attaché Report, USSR, November 1, 1941; msg., Arnold to Brig. Gen. Ralph Royce, October 8, 1941; msg., Arnold to Maj. Gen. George Brett, October 20, 1941 (File: 452, AG, in WWIIRD/NA).
5. "Minutes of Conferences October 21-22, 1941, held by the Chief of the Army Air Forces with British representatives;" msg., Chaney to McNarney, October 29, 1941 (File: 400.3295, AG, in WWIIRD/NA).
6. Msg., Michela to WD, December 27, 1941 (File: 635, ID, ASF, in WWIIRD/NA).

P-40's, Parts and Protests 71

American observers in Moscow warned that these difficulties injured relations and strongly urged that corrective actions be taken promptly. The difficulties with the planes formed an embarassing background for the negotiations of the Moscow Protocol. Harriman was naturally apprehensive that the Russians might reasonably assume that similar difficulties could be expected in future aircraft shipments. A few days after the Moscow Protocol had been signed, Harriman bluntly told officials in London that the problems with the P-40's reflected adversely not only upon the efficiency of Anglo-American technical staffs but also upon the good will which the United States tried to cultivate with the Russians.[7] This theme was repeated with minor variations by American officials in Moscow in later months.

Major Joseph A. Michela, the American Military Attaché in Moscow, who usually eyed Soviet claims critically, wrote that the Russians "are now about to consider [American planes] as unfit and unsafe for use at the front."[8] To Michela the situation approached the stage where it began to react unfavorably upon American prestige. Major General Chaney shared the same opinion and warned of serious political repercussions.[9]

The difficulties with the P-40's appear to have confirmed the reluctance of Soviet officials to allow American military observers free movement within Russia. This policy especially affected the office of the Military Attaché whose functions involved extensive observation and reporting. Michela, most anxious that the P-40 mess be resolved without delay, wrote to the War Department:

> In order to enjoy full Soviet confidence and to overcome the present attitude, I cannot recommend too strongly vigorous action to expedite immediately shipment of these vitally needed generator assemblies, lack of which is keeping the majority of American Tomahawks grounded. . . .[10]

Four days later, Michela reported that he was cooperating with

7. Msg., Harriman to Military Attaché, London, October 4, 1941 (File: 913410, ACS, G-2, in WWIIRD/NA).
8. Msg., Michela to WD, November 20, 1941 (File: 452.1, ID, ASF, in WWIIRD/NA).
9. Msg., Michela to WD, December 4, 1941 (File: 400.3295, ASWA, in WWIIRD/NA); msg., Chaney to Agwar, December 6, 1941 (File: 452, AG, in WWIIRD/NA).
10. Msg., Michela to WD, December 23, 1941 (File: Information Cables—Russia, ID, ASF, in WWIIRD/NA).

72 EAGLES EAST

Russian authorities to resolve these difficulties and urged again that solutions be found. Once they were, he confidently predicted that the Russians would no longer oppose the free movement of American military personnel.[11]

The P-40 fiasco represented an ideal issue that the Soviets could exploit in refusing to allow a group of American aircraft specialists—who the Kremlin explicitly requested during the summer of 1941—from entering their country. The United States sought to comply with the request by making arrangements to send a group of technicians from the Curtiss-Wright and Allison companies. But the critical situation in Russia made it very difficult to find volunteers for the project. As a precautionary measure, the Curtiss Company urged that the group have an official rather than a private status.[12] Negotiations between these companies and the Amtorg Trading Corporation, the official Soviet purchasing agency in the United States, dragged on throughout the summer. At the time the Moscow Protocol was concluded, no agreement had yet been reached. The delay seemed to disturb the White House more than the Kremlin. The President directed that military personnel supplement the group if an adequate number of civilians could not be found.[13] After the intervention of the White House, the project crystallized as a combined civilian-military operation. By the end of October, the group consisted of three officers, fifty enlisted men and twenty-five civilian mechanics.[14]

Subsequent events soon revealed that the Soviet government had reversed its position regarding the acceptance of the specialists. Toward the end of October, when the P-40 question loomed so large, the Soviet Chargé d' Affaires informed officials in Washington that no visas were available for the group. Convinced that a mis-

11. Msg., Michela to WD, December 27, 1941.
12. Ltr., Burns to Allison Engineering Co. (attn: Mr. O. T. Kreusser), September 6, 1941; ltr., Kreusser to Office of Chief of the Air Corps, September 13, 1941 (File: RG 18, Boxes 210, 949, AAF, in WWIRB/NA).
13. Memo, Marshall for Stimson, October 14, 1941 (File: 21276 to 21350, OCS, in WWIIRD/NA).
14. R & R, CAS for OCAC, October 14, 1941; memo, Brig. Gen. M. F. Scanlon for Director of Defense Aid, October 28, 1941 (File: H. H. Arnold, Decimal File, 320.2—Russia, in MD/LC); memo, Arnold for Marshall, October 27, 1941; memo, Brig. Gen. J. K. Cain for Defense Aid Director, October 27, 1941; memo, Maj. Gen. R. C. Moore for Marshall, October 28, 1941 (File: 400.3295, AG, in WWIIRD/NA). Similar plans were also underway to send a group, entirely civilian in composition, of ordnance experts.

P-40's, Parts and Protests 73

understanding existed, Hopkins believed the matter could be cleared up if the Soviet government instructed its embassy in Washington to issue the necessary visas.[15] Three days later, Steinhardt reported to Hopkins that the Soviet government had complied with the American request.[16] However, there was a dissonant echo in Washington: the Soviet Embassy contended that it had received no instructions to issue visas for the specialists.

As Washington sought to clear the matter up, discouraging reports from American officials in Russia questioned the wisdom of sending the group at all. Michela reported the experiences of Zemke and Alison who advised:

> Should Russians be allowed to do the work with foreign technicians assisting, as in our case, there will be errors, lack of proper coordination with our government because of restrictions and policies of the Soviet government which are forcibly invoked upon all Russian personnel.[17]

Reports from other Americans in Russia offered convincing reasons against sending the aircraft specialists. Douglas Brown, who asked to be relieved from his position as head of the American Permanent Supply Mission, complained that he was unable to do more than act "merely as transmitting agent" which, since his arrival in Russia a month earlier, "has consumed a total of less than one hour of my time. Playing poker with many of these people," Brown added, "has absorbed a large share of my time." He advised against sending technicians, experts or other personnel unless the Soviet government sincerely wanted them. "It is most unlikely," he glumly stated, "that they will be permitted to do anything or to see anything and they will, in my opinion, not be welcome." Brown was convinced that the Russians intended to use their own experts and planned to utilize the equipment sent by the United States and Britain in their own way.[18] Later events more than confirmed his estimate.

15. Msg., Hopkins to Faymonville and Steinhardt, October 28, 1941 (File: Russian Cables, ID, ASF, in WWIIRD/NA). Also in *Foreign Relations*, 1941, I, 848.
16. Msg., Steinhardt to Hopkins, October 31, 1941 (File: Russian Cables, ID, ASF, in WWIIRD/NA). Also in abbreviated form in *Foreign Relations*, 1941, I, 848, footnote 16.
17. Military Attaché Report, U.S.S.R., November 1, 1941.
18. Msg., Brown to Batt and Harriman, November 4, 1941 (File: Russian Cables, ID, ASF, in WWIIRD/NA).

74 EAGLES EAST

Faymonville appeared to be one of the few Americans in Russia who believed that his government should send the specialists. His opinion proved to be as naive as it was erroneous. He attributed part of the failure of the Soviet government to issue the visas to Russian pride in their own experts. Another reason Faymonville offered was that the Russians were apprehensive that existing accomodations would not suit the Americans. According to him, the Russians felt that the specialists would be too meticulous in their work, thus preventing immediate use of the planes at the front. However, there was a more significant reason for Soviet reluctance to allow the men to come—namely, suspicion concerning the alleged "mixed motives" of the personnel for going to Russia. Faymonville suggested that Soviet suspicions would be mitigated if the members of the group were carefully selected not only with respect to technical ability but also to character. For Hopkins' benefit Faymonville recited the pristine qualities the men should possess. His exaggerated criteria were more appropriate for Boy Scouts on a romp in the Adirondacks than for seasoned aircraft technicians who were prepared to risk their lives to go to a far off country fighting for its survival.[19]

It was all quite unnecessary. The Soviets soon made it clear that they did not want the Americans. On November 12, Dmitri S. Chuvakhin, First Secretary of the Soviet Embassy, informed Loy Henderson that the Soviet Union simply could not use them.[20] As a result of this decision, the future course of American policy was an obvious one: if the specialists were desired, they would be sent; but the United States had no intention of pressing the matter if the Soviet Union did not want the men.[21]

19. Msg., Faymonville to Hopkins, November 4, 1941 (File: Russian Cables, ID, ASF, in WWIIRD/NA).
20. Memo of conversation by Henderson, November 12, 1941, *Foreign Relations, 1941*, I, 859-60.
21. Ltr., Spalding to Hull, November 22, 1941 (File: Russian Cables, ID, ASF, in WWIIRD/NA). Faymonville was still chasing windmills in Russia. After he received Spalding's message, Faymonville replied that according to the Commissar of Defense, 66 visas for the aircraft specialists had been granted. His information again was wrong. The Soviet Embassy in Washington had no instructions to issue the visas. Msg., Faymonville to Spalding, December 5, 1941; ltr., Spalding to Hull, December 9, 1941 (File: Information Cables—Russia, ID, ASF, in WWIIRD/NA). Thus, the military personnel of the group who had awaited further orders at Bolling Field for over a month were relieved of their assignment. Ltr., Chief of the Air Corps to Chief of the AAF, November 27, 1941, 2d wrapper endorsement; memo, A-2 to Lt. Col. T. J.

P-40's, Parts and Protests 75

Since the American effort to send the group to the Soviet Union came at a time when the Russians were displeased with the shortage of spare parts and the difficulties with the early shipments of P-40's, possibly this was a way of serving notice that it lacked confidence in America's technical ability. If this is true, it was a curious method to solve some of the problems which the Russians experienced with the planes. If the aircraft technicians had been allowed to enter, many of these problems could have been either solved or at least mitigated. If the Americans had accomplished no more than to answer many of the technical questions which Soviet officials continually presented to Faymonville for forwarding to Washington, a valuable service would have been rendered. The episode was to be repeated later with the same pattern of American offers and Soviet rejections.

The political effects of the P-40 fiasco appeared to assume larger and graver proportions with the passage of time. Lieutenant Colonel Townsend Griffiss, who was on a special mission to secure Soviet cooperation in providing air route information, commented:

> It is evident that the Soviets are none too confident of our aid effort. This naturally affects American-Soviet relations. The Russians' secretive and suspicious outlook of many years cannot be broken down over night. Now the unfortunate fiasco of the P-40's at Archangel, the question of responsibility of furnishing spare parts, the method of shipment, and the slowness of delivery have all presented added obstacles to closer relations.

Griffiss strongly advised that Soviet confidence in its allies had to be regained. If it continued to deteriorate, he prophesied that subsequent Russian military reverses might lead to a peace with Germany.[22]

Griffiss' gloomy views were held to some extent by Michela[23] and by Walter Thurston, American Chargé d'Affaires in Moscow.

Kolnig, December 6, 1941; R & R, Chief of the Air Staff for Chief of the Air Corps, December 13, 1941 (File: H. H. Arnold, Decimal File, 320.2—Russia, in MD/LC).

22. Memo, Lt. Col. Griffiss for Thurston, January 3, 1942; report, found in the Griffiss papers, January 3, 1942 (File: 8000-9040 USSR Old Files, ACS, G-2, in WWIIRD/NA).

23. Msg., Michela to WD, January 27, 1942 (File: 913410, ACS, G-2, in WWIIRD/NA).

76   EAGLES EAST

On February 3, Thurston wrote the best summary of the impact of aircraft matters on Russo-American relations.

> I have read Michela's telegrams to the War Department. He says that the opinions as reported by him were based upon the attitude and statements of Soviet officials following (a) the shipment to Russia of defective Tomahawk planes, (b) the failure to expedite the supply of urgently requested spare parts for those planes, (c) the confusing and obstructive division of responsibility as between the British and ourselves with regard to those planes, (d) the failure to profit by experience as reflected in the later shipment of Aircobras without spare parts, and (e) the Kazvin question. While no statement or obvious insinuation was made that these deficiencies were the result of political considerations it is not improbable that such an interpretation may have been placed upon them by the Russians.[24]

The Chargé believed that Soviet distrust could be mitigated substantially enough so that normal, even close, relations could be established between the two nations. He pointed out that "It has been regarded as axiomatic in Soviet doctrine that the capitalist world desires the destruction of the Soviet state." This attitude, he said, had been expressed in some sections of American opinion. "It is, therefore," he went on,

> an easy assumption on the part of a Soviet official that the capitalist states finding themselves fortuitous associates of the Soviet Union in the war against Germany will supply only enough aid to keep the Soviet Union fighting Germany as long as possible.

He strongly advised that actions should be taken to help eliminate suspicions of the United States. This could be accomplished "by exerting convincing efforts to supply the war needs of the Soviet Union to the satisfaction of the Soviet military observers and purchasing agents in the United States." He also suggested that the desired objective could be achieved in another way: "by avoiding action which might be construed by the Russians to indicate that we are holding back, or are seeking some ulterior advantage."[25]

24. Msg., Thurston to Hull, February 3, 1942, *Foreign Relations*, 1942, III, 688. See Chapter VI on the Kazvin question.
25. *Ibid.*, pp. 688-89.

P-40's, Parts and Protests 77

Toward the middle of January, 1942, the most serious difficulties concerning the P-40's were well on their way to solution. With a sense of relief Colonel B. E. Meyers told Colonel H. S. Aurand,

> In regard to the generator situation this matter at long last, I hope, has been cleared up. We are getting special immediate delivery of three hundred generators, complete with installed equipment, which will be immediately forwarded to the theaters where P-40 airplanes are operating.[26]

No sooner had this action been taken than Michela reported that American 0-52's had arrived in Russia without spare parts or instructions for assembly. Apprehensive that the shortages in the shipments of 0-52's might explode into another P-40 fiasco, Arnold immediately directed that full corrective measures be taken to prevent a repetition of earlier difficulties.[27]

The shortage of spare parts in the initial deliveries of P-40's presaged a persistent problem with respect to aircraft matters in Russo-American relations. Although the failure of production to provide the spare parts was the most important reason for the deficits and delays in meeting commitments, there were other aspects of the problem which confused and complicated the search for solutions throughout the war.

On the American side, the problem was sometimes aggravated by oversights in monitoring, mistakes in marking crates, delays in sending shipments to debarkation points, and authorizations to send supplies to ports unable to handle them. On the other hand, Russian officials in the United States contributed their share of difficulties which immensely complicated the problem. They invariably claimed a greater number of shortages than AAF records indicated. Although these records were not always correct, Russian claims were suspect since they were based largely upon incomplete documents which American authorities provided them. Moreover, the Russians themselves cast doubt on many of their claims by complaining about not having certain records which governed shipments of spare parts to their country.

This situation often gave rise to some peculiar claims. Soviet

26. Ltr., Meyers to Col. H. S. Aurand, January 11, 1942 (File: Russia Correspondence—Lend-Lease No. 1, ID, ASF, in WWIIRD/NA).
27. R & R, AAF/A-4 for AAF/AAG, January 26, 1942 (File: H. H. Arnold, Decimal File, 452.1, Russia 1-299, in MD-LC).

78   EAGLES EAST

representatives in Washington frequently alleged deficits without allowing for the fluctuations in the movement of spare parts or for the absence of records at their disposal to account for the items. Perhaps the cause of much of the difficulty was Soviet insistence that they were to receive a rigid complement of parts without regard to the changes in production or to the contracts under which the parts were produced. Furthermore, the Russians jeopardized the validity of their legitimate complaints by citing shortages of items which were not ordinarily furnished with the aircraft.[28]

The spare parts problem continued to be a headache, particularly during the first and second protocols, with no ostensible effort on the part of the Soviet Union either to understand or alleviate the burden on the United States. Early in the spring of 1942, Russian representatives even proposed to delay shipments of planes until spare parts were available to accompany them.[29] Considering the limited shipping resources at the disposal of the United States, which required their constant and efficient use, the proposal was quite ridiculous. Needless to say this created suspicion about the veracity of Russian claims that they needed all of the aircraft and related items in the protocol. Even British efforts to ease the problem by showing the Russians how to economize on the use of spare parts met with coolness.[30]

The War Department was well aware of the need to meet the shortages of spare parts in the Soviet supply program. The importance of the question in War Department policy was reflected in an important memo sent by Brigadier General B. E. Meyers to Secretary Lovett on April 23, 1942. "All airplane commitments to the USSR (including spare engines and spare parts)," Meyers stated, "have first priority over all other assignments."[31] As a

28. The records of the Assistant Chief of Staff, Materiel and Services and the International Division, Army Service Forces, in the WWIIRD/NA are quite voluminous on the subject of spare parts to Russia. The preceding analysis is based primarily upon folders filed under: "USSR Spares" and "Russian Aid Miscellaneous" of the Assistant Chief of Air Staff, Materiel and Services; and "Russia Correspondence—Lend-Lease No. 1," and the 452.11 group of folders on spare parts for specific types of planes of the International Division, Army Service Forces.
29. Shipping Conferences in Office of Lend-Lease Administration, March 24, 1942 and April 2, 1942 (File: 337, ID, ASF, in WWIIRD/NA).
30. Msg., Faymonville to McCabe, April 17, 1942, *Foreign Relations*, 1942, III, 700-701.
31. Memo, Meyers for Lovett, April 23, 1942 (File: 452.11 Spare parts for A-20's for Russia, ID, ASF, in WWIIRD/NA).

result of this policy, substantial progress had been made to meet the deficits of spares by the end of the Moscow Protocol.

The following figures indicate the percentage of total requirements of spare parts delivered to Russia for Lend-Lease planes by June 15, 1942:[32]

	B-25	A-20	P-40
Airframe spares	81	62	86
Spare engines	104	93	83
Engine spares	76	99	66
Spare propellors	181	64	113
Propellor spares	86	85	40

Although this record is not perfect, it reveals that provision of many categories of spares was very close to that which had been promised. Above all, it reflects the serious efforts on the part of a country trying to meet the demanding and often frustrating imperatives of a wartime alliance.

32. Chart entitled: "Status of Spares," as of June 15, 1942, and September 15, 1942 (File: USSR Spares, ACAS/MS, in WWIIRD/NA).

CHAPTER VI

Iran: Corridor to Russia

EXCEPT [FOR] THE BRITISH ISLES, the Middle East is the most accessible of the important active theaters to us, and our lines of supply to it, though long, are the least vulnerable."[1] Thus was phrased the estimate by military intelligence in November, 1941, of the general problem of supplying Allied forces in the Middle East. The implications for the delivery of aircraft to the Russians were obvious. The AAF, therefore, officially approved the route to Iran as the most feasible avenue by which to fulfill aircraft commitments to the Soviet Union.

The AAF's decision, however, raised several serious technical and diplomatic questions, and before they were solved, differences of opinion had placed considerable strain on United States-Soviet relations. One of these was: How would the planes be sent to the Middle East? Use of this avenue would require the development and maintenance of both water and air routes. Since this would be an enterprise of no mean proportions, it was obvious that until these problems were resolved, the flow of aircraft via the Middle East would be negligible for some time. The AAF's decision to deliver aircraft to the Russians in Iran also posed a second question: At what point in or near Iran would the planes be delivered? This raised diplomatic issues which involved considerable negotiations with Great Britain and the Soviet Union.

Shortly after the Moscow Protocol had been concluded, Arnold received a study from the Chief of the Air Corps, analyzing three possible routes to Russia. The first of these provided for

1. Quoted in U. S., Congress, *Pearl Harbor Attack*, Part 14, 79th Cong., 1st Sess., 1946, p. 1371.

the delivery of aircraft over an air route which began at Spokane, Washington, and extended across Alaska to Siberia. The second provided for delivery by ship to Takoradi, Africa, and from there by air to Kazan in the Soviet Union. The third involved delivery by ship to Basra, Iraq, and from there by air to Kazan.[2]

The air route to Siberia had two principal advantages over the others under consideration—planes would reach the Soviet Union sooner and shipping resources would be confined to servicing depots. However, it was not recommended for immediate adoption because of the tremendous task of establishing an air service of 8,000 miles over arctic wastes, the anticipated ill effects upon planes and pilots making the long trek, and the general paucity of information available to the Americans regarding facilities in Siberia.

The route by ship to Takoradi and from there by air to Kazan had the chief advantage of requiring fewer ships than the others under consideration. However, the flight from Takoradi to Kazan was almost as long as the one across Alaska and Siberia. Moreover, it passed through an area where facilities were either inadequate or unknown, not to mention the poor climate, proximity to Axis bases in west Africa and anticipated supply and maintenance problems. Although these factors militated against the adoption of the route, later a modified version of it was used to ferry aircraft to Iran.

This left, then, the way by ship to Basra, Iraq, and from there by air to Kazan. Although this route would require a greater number of ships and consume the maximum delivery time of all routes under consideration, its many advantages led to its adoption. Relatively secure from Axis interference, the route passed through an area of good climate, and hence it was anticipated that there would be few technical and supply problems. Moreover, the difficulties of the air section, although substantial, were not so great as those of the one across Alaska and Siberia or the one from Africa to Russia. Accordingly, Arnold recommended to Stimson "that the route by boat to Basra is the only feasible route by which, at this time, airplanes can be delivered to Russia."[3]

2. Office, Chief of the Air Corps, "Plan for Delivery of Airplanes to Russia," November 2, 1941 (File: 167.6-39, in USAF/HA).
3. *Ibid.*; memo, Arnold for Stimson, November 4, 1941 (File: 167.6-39, in USAF/HA).

82   EAGLES EAST

Arnold stressed another factor which in the eyes of the AAF was vital—the Middle Eastern route would be of material aid in reducing the extent of American ferrying operations necessary. Arnold told Stimson that every effort should "be made to relieve this government of any obligation for ferrying airplanes within Russia or Siberia." But, he explained, the AAF would compromise its position to the extent of sending the planes to Basra and of having the Russians accept the planes "either at Baku or Ashkhabad."[4] Although these points were in the Soviet Union, they were substantially closer to Basra than Kazan, the oft-discussed terminal point in the study. On November 5, Stimson gave his approval.[5]

Now decisions had to be reached with respect to the location of an aircraft assembly depot and the point at which the Russians would accept the American planes. A General Staff meeting on November 12 explored these questions and recommended Basra as the site of the assembly depot and Tehran as the point of Soviet acceptance.[6] No definite decisions could be reached until they were discussed with the British and Soviet governments. There were obvious diplomatic reasons. The British controlled the area in Iraq where the AAF planned to establish its assembly plant. In addition, Russia and Britain occupied Iran where the AAF expected to deliver its aircraft to the Russians.[7]

The War Department intended to establish an assembly point in the suburbs of Basra and, in the event the Middle East became untenable, a similar one at Karachi. Stimson wanted the Russians to pick up the planes at "an adequately defended point in Iran, acceptable to the American government." He added that "our preference is to make delivery to the Russians at a point as near the unloading and assembly area (Basra) as may be suitably arranged.

4. Memo, Arnold for Stimson, November 4, 1941.
5. Pencil notation of Stimson's approval, *ibid.*
6. Memo, (initialed by Arnold) for Secretary of General Staff, November 12, 1941 (File: 4557, WPD, WDGS, in WWIIRD/NA). This, of course, did not exclude the continued use of the northern water route which was the way the Russians wanted fighters delivered. The AAF eventually planned to send 100 A-20's per month by water to Basra and also to ferry 12 B-25's per month over the South Atlantic and Africa. See msg. Arnold to Adler, December 18, 1941 (File: 400.3295, AG, in WWIIRD/NA).
7. Before the General Staff meeting of November 12, Arnold wanted some preliminary exploration of British and Russian attitudes. See msg., Arnold to Faymonville, October 31, 1941 (File: 400.3295, in WWIIRD/NA); msg., Faymonville to Spalding, November 5, 1941 (File: 167.6-39, in USAF/HA).

Iran: Corridor to Russia 83

This indicates," he said, "consideration of Basra and Tehran in preference to any point within Russia."[8]

The wheels of American diplomacy were immediately set in motion. Hull requested John G. Winant, the American Ambassador in London, to discuss these questions with British officials.[9] Winant's communications to the State Department revealed that the establishment of American assembly and delivery points in the Middle East raised serious technical and political issues which would require long and patient negotiation.

The proposals for assembly plants at Basra and Karachi met with British opposition. Both areas had limited facilities which could not accommodate the combined needs of Britain and the United States. Therefore, officials in London proposed two alternative sites: Khosrowabad in Iran and Umm Qasr in Iraq. Until an American plant was erected at one of these points, the British agreed to provide facilities at Basra for the assembly of aircraft earmarked for delivery to the Russians.[10] The British assured that their treaties with Iran and Iraq would provide diplomatic authorization for the establishment of an American depot in either country.[11] As these negotiations progressed in London, the matter of American assembly operations was also seriously explored by British and AAF officials in the Middle East. As a result of these discussions, British military authorities approved the establishment of an erection facility at Abadan in Iran.[12] Brigadier General Elmer E. Adler, Chief of the Air Section, U. S. Military North African Mission, and Brigadier General Raymond A. Wheeler, Chief of the U. S. Military Iranian Mission, reconnoitered the area and strongly recommended it.[13] A short time later, both Washington

8. Ltr., Stimson to Hull, November 24, 1941 (File: 4557, WPD, WDGS, in WWIIRD/NA). Also in U. S., Department of State, *Foreign Relations of the United States: Diplomatic Papers, 1941*, Vol. III: *The British Commonwealth: The Near East and Africa* (Washington: United States Government Printing Office, 1963), pp. 478-79.
9. Msg., Hull to Winant, November 25, 1941, *ibid.*, p. 479.
10. Msg., Winant to Hull, December 11, 1941, *Foreign Relations*, 1941, III, 480-81.
11. Msg., Winant to Hull, December 12, 1941, *Foreign Relations*, 1941, III, 482-83.
12. Msg., Brig. Gen. Wheeler to Maj. Gen. R. C. Moore, December 15, 1941 (File: 635, Airplane Assembly Bases, Aircraft for Russia, ID, ASF, in WWIIRD/NA). Hull wanted London to confirm this. See msg., Hull to Winant, December 30, 1941, *Foreign Relations*, 1941, III, 483-84.
13. Msg., Wheeler to Moore, December 10, 1941 (File: RG 18, Box 949, AAF, in

84 EAGLES EAST

and London granted official approval of Abadan as the site of the American assembly depot.[14]

The point where the Russians were to accept the planes still had to be determined. Although the Russians were apparently willing to accept American aircraft at Tehran,[15] the British anticipated political difficulties there and instead, suggested Kazvin in northwestern Iran.[16] This suggestion was prompted by their reluctance to allow SAF pilots to fly over southern Iran, the area under British occupation.

The State Department, anxious to respect London's views, informed the embassy in Russia to convey to the Kremlin that Abadan would be the American assembly depot but, as for the place of delivery to SAF pilots, Hull added: "a point in Iran is preferable to any in Russia and Kazvin has been mentioned."[17] No sooner had Thurston conveyed the proposal of Kazvin to the Russians than he learned that the British government had suddenly reversed its policy of opposition to the entrance of Soviet personnel in southern Iran and Iraq.[18] This, of course, meant that Britain would now allow Russian pilots to accept British planes at its assembly station of Basra. The change in policy was sudden since as late as December 30, the British Air Commission in Washington was unaware of it.[19] In view of the situation created by the new British policy, it was in American interest to adopt a similar one—to allow Russian pilots to accept planes at Abadan. However, before the contradiction could be harmonized, the Russians had already received Washington's proposal regarding Kazvin. The Soviets were frankly displeased and rejected it. But American efforts to harmonize its policy with that of Great

---

WWIRB/NA); msg., Adler to Arnold, December 11, 1941 (File 400.3295, AG, in WWIIRD/NA).

14. Msg., Hull to Steinhardt, December 30, 1941 (File: 635, Airplane Assembly Bases, Aircraft for Russia, ID, ASF, in WWIIRD/NA). Also in *Foreign Relations*, 1941, III, 484.

15. Memo, Maj. Gen. John N. Greely for Chief of Air Intelligence, December 12, 1941; Document entitled "Discussion at Conference in the Office of Brig. Gen. George R. Spalding," December 17, 1941 (File: 452.1, Deliveries of Planes to Russia, ID, ASF, in WWIIRD/NA).

16. Msg., Winant to Hull, December 12, 1941, *Foreign Relations*, 1941, III, 483.

17. Msg., Hull to Steinhardt, December 30, 1941.

18. Msg., Thurston to Hull, January 3, 1942 (File: 635, Airplane Assembly Bases, Aircraft for Russia, ID, ASF, in WWIIRD/NA).

19. Memo, Col. O. S. Ferson for Greely, December 30, 1941 (File: 635, Airplane Assembly Bases, Aircraft for Russia, ID, ASF, in WWIIRD/NA).

Iran: Corridor to Russia

Britain finally bore fruit. The British agreed to American aircraft deliveries to the Russians at Basra and, after the American assembly depot was completed, at Abadan. The Russians also agreed.[20]

Although these arrangements had been finally worked out to the satisfaction of all parties concerned, the original American proposal concerning Kazvin did not escape Soviet suspicions. The Russians interpreted the Kazvin proposal as an effort to keep them out of southern Iran and to establish an American foothold in the northern part of the country.[21] This theme of American wartime imperialism in the Middle East is one which Soviet historians have monotonously dwelled upon ever since.[22] The facts reveal no scheme on the part of the United States to develop any part of Iran as a satrap. More than anything else the Kazvin affair illustrated the State Department's somewhat fumbling attempts to coordinate its policy with that of Whitehall, an effort which failed because of a sudden shift in the position of Britain. The consequence was the curious and unfortunate situation of the United States proposing a delivery point in northern Iran while Britain was allowing Soviet acceptance of aircraft in the south.

The problem of determining how the planes would be sent to Iran involved the development and maintenance of water and air routes. In the case of aircraft deliveries by the water route, the most pressing problem was that of finding shipping resources. After the War Department approved of the plan to make deliveries to Iran, it hoped to expedite shipments to the Russians by using sea train vessels and, at least initially, an aircraft carrier.[23] The latter idea, particularly favored by the AAF and the White House,

20. Msg., Michela to WD, January 8, 1942 (File: 635, Airplane Assembly Bases, Aircraft for Russia, ID, ASF, in WWIIRD/NA); msg., Hq. AAF to Michela, January 17, 1942 (File: 400.3295, AG, in WWIIRD/NA); memo, Chief of the Air Corps for Chief of the AAF, January 27, 1942 (RG 18, Box 949, AAF, in WWIRB/Na); msg., Military Attaché (Iran) to G-2, February 6, 1942 (File: 452.1, Deliveries of Planes to Russia, ID, ASF, in WWIIRD/NA); msg., Wheeler to Moore, February 7, 1942 (File: 913410, ACS, G-2, in WWIIRD/NA); msg., Baker (Baghdad) to Milid, February 8, 1942 (File: 21276 to 21350, OCS, in WWIIRD/NA).
21. Msg., Thurston to Hull, February 3, 1942, *Foreign Relations*, 1942, III, 689.
22. For example, see G. A. Deborin, *Vtoraia Mirovaia Voina* (Moskva: Voennoe Izdatelstvo Ministerstva Oborony Soiuza, SSR, 1958), pp. 143-44; M. Popov, "Nachalo Agressii S Sh A v Gody Vtoroi Mirovoi Voiny," *Voprosy Istorii*, No. 11 (1949), 37-43, 64.
23. Ltr., Stimson to Secretary of Navy, November 5, 1941; ltr., Stimson to Chairman of Maritime Commission, November 5, 1941 (File: 400.3295, AG, in

86   EAGLES EAST

was unacceptable to the Navy.[24] Hopkins, who acted in this matter
for the White House, summarized for the President the Navy's
position:

> I gather that what is really behind this is that in the light
> of the whole strategic situation as it is in the world today,
> the Navy feels it would be unwise to send a carrier. Hence,
> unless you decide otherwise, we are going to move these
> planes at once by merchant ship, although, as I have told you,
> the Maritime Commission is having a good deal of difficulty
> getting enough ships.[25]

Roosevelt noted the message saying: "OK but say to them for
me: Hurry, Hurry, Hurry!"[26] Sherwood aptly described the reasons
for the Navy's reluctance to authorize the use of a carrier for the
shipment of planes. As he puts it,

> In view of the date of this memorandum it can be seen that
> the Navy had some reason for feeling that 'the whole strategic
> situation made it unwise to send a carrier' all the way around
> Africa to the Persian Gulf. The date was November 25, 1941,
> twelve days before Pearl Harbor.[27]

Although a larger number of planes was sent to Iran by ship
than by air during the war, a flight delivery route across the South
Atlantic had been developed in 1941 and became increasingly important in ferrying operations to Iran. Originally it was to be used
as an all-weather route to Great Britain when the North Atlantic
was unsuitable as well as an avenue to reinforce the Allied position
in the Middle East. In August, 1941, the United States negotiated
contracts with Pan American Airways which, through its sub-
sidiaries, agreed to establish ferry and transport operations in
Africa and the Middle East. The government took this approach
rather than develop the route itself because the volume of traffic
initially did not justify an elaborate military organization for
this purpose, and the prohibitions of the neutrality legislation

---

WWIIRD/NA); ltr., Stimson to Secretary of Navy, November 7, 1941 (File:
167.6-39, in USAF/HA).
24. Memo, (initialed Arnold), for Secretary of General Staff, November 12, 1941;
memo, Lt. Col. L. P. Whitten for Arnold, November 13, 1941 (File: 4557, WPD,
WDGS, in WWIIRD/NA).
25. The document is reproduced in Sherwood, *Roosevelt and Hopkins*, p. 399.
26. *Ibid.*
27. *Ibid.*, p. 398.

Iran: Corridor to Russia

prevented a commitment of military resources to the project. The initial route followed was Miami-Bathurst-Khartoum-Cairo. By the end of November the restrictions of the neutrality laws had been progressively removed, thereby allowing the AAF to begin ferrying to the British in the Middle East. AAF operations began with the "16 Liberator Project," a dramatic effort to bolster the Allied position with heavy bombers. However, Pearl Harbor aborted the project. The British received only a few of the planes while the remainder were re-routed to reinforce American strength in the Philippines.[28]

Although the pre-Pearl Harbor record of deliveries to the British over the South Atlantic only reached 29 transports and 5 Liberators, at least the groundwork of the ferry route had been laid. Airfields and other facilities appeared where swamp and jungle had once existed. The nation did not have to start from scratch in developing this vital lifeline when, after Pearl Harbor, American aircraft and supplies joined the increasing flow of Lend-Lease goods to the Middle East, to Russia, and the Far East.[29] Until the route was militarized entirely, the crews of Pan American continued to fly the planes during most of 1942.[30]

Flight deliveries over the South Atlantic route to the Russians began two months after the first group of A-20's arrived by ship in Iran. They originally consisted of B-25 C's which began to arrive in Florida in March, 1942, for the historic flight.[31] By the end of June, thirty-eight of the planes had been delivered to the Russians in Iran.[32] Basra and Tehran were initially used as the delivery point, but eventually all releases were concentrated at Abadan.[33]

28. Army Air Forces, Air Transport Command, "History of the Air Transport Command, Ferrying Command Operations, May 29-December 7, 1941," I, pp. 81-123 (File: 300.01, in USAF/HA).
29. *Ibid.*, pp. 129-30.
30. Wesley Frank Craven and James Lea Cate, *The Army Air Forces in World War II*, Vol. VII: *Services Around the World* (Chicago: The University of Chicago Press, 1958), p. 47.
31. Army Air Forces, Air Transport Command, "History of the Air Transport Command, Ferrying Command Operations, December 7, 1941 - June 30, 1942," II, 100 (File: 300.01, in USAF/HA).
32. Headquarters, Air Materiel Command, "Special One Time Report of Deliveries of AAF Aircraft to the USSR," 1947. Copy procured from the Military Personnel Records Center, St. Louis, Missouri.
33. Army Air Forces, Air Transport Command, "History of the Air Transport Command," II, 100; T. H. Vail Motter, *The Persian Corridor and Aid to Russia* (Washington: Department of the Army, 1952), pp. 129-30.

88 EAGLES EAST

In addition to the development of an air route to Iran for the purpose of ferrying aircraft, there was a desperate need to improve Russo-American air communications by the inauguration of a regular air service between Iran and the Soviet Union. A few days after the Moscow Conference, Harriman suggested to Hopkins that a shuttle service be developed on a bi-monthly basis between Khartoum and Moscow. In making this proposal, Harriman referred to the obvious importance of such a service with respect to supplying the Russians. But he was well aware of a more compelling reason for the air service—namely, the healthy effects of regular communications upon Russo-American diplomatic relations.[34]

Harriman's suggestion eventually found its way to the AAF's Ferry Command which was prepared to initiate operations by October 15. But the project hinged upon Soviet agreement. Toward the end of the month, the proposal was formally made to the Russians and rejected. The following month, the proposal was again made, but this time in modified form. The Lend-Lease Administration suggested to Russian officials in Washington that the proposed air service operate on a civilian rather than military basis. The Russians once again rejected the idea[35] because of their reluctance to allow either American military or civilian air operations within the Soviet Union. Despite Russian rejections, Brigadier General Carl Spaatz, Chief of the Air Staff, urged Pan American on December 5 to extend its air line from Khartoum to Basra from where a branch line might be eventually extended into the Soviet Union.[36] By the early part of 1942 Pan American operated an air service to Basra and, on a less regular basis, to Tehran.[37] Russian opposition prevented the extension of a branch line into the Soviet Union.

The need to place air communications between Russia and Iran on a regular basis continued to nag Washington. Personnel and mail going to and coming from Russia were unduly delayed.

34. Msg., Harriman to Hopkins, October 3, 1941 (File: Russian Cables, ID, ASF, in WWIIRD/NA). The British also hoped to develop an air service from the Middle East to Russia. See memo, Chaney for Harriman, October 11, 1941.
35. Ltr., Robert P. Patterson to Hull, May 5, 1942 (File: 580.51, AG, in WWIIRD/NA).
36. Ltr., Spaatz to M. M. Bixby, December 5, 1941 (File: H. H. Arnold, 360.01, in MD/LC).
37. Ltr., Patterson to Hull, May 5, 1942.

Iran: Corridor to Russia

The inefficiency of the air service to Iran was dramatically revealed during the early months of 1942: from January 29 to March 9, no Russian plane with accomodations for American personnel departed from the Soviet Union for Iran. The aircraft which left Kuibyshev on March 9 returned on March 14, bringing the first mail to reach American officials in the Soviet Union since December 24.[38] It was apparent that the lack of efficient communications had a deteriorating effect on the alliance, depriving both countries of efficient and regular contact, which was a vital need for Allies who ostensibly waged a common cause. The Soviet Union apparently preferred to remain virtually isolated.

Since the Russians opposed the operation of an American air service within their country, representatives of the War, Navy and State Departments, along with members of the Lend-Lease Administration and Civil Aeronautics Board, proposed on March 18, 1942, that a Russo-American air service be developed on a weekly basis between Iran and the Soviet Union. The proposal involved American operation of the air services only to Iran. From there, the Soviet portion of the service would extend into Russia. In order to make the idea especially attractive to the Russians, the representatives at this meeting suggested that two transports be given out of AAF allocations for the Russian segment of the route. The War Department favored the project but believed that the planes should be taken from Lend-Lease allocations to Russia.[39]

American pressure to establish regular air services between the Middle East and the Soviet Union was resumed later by the American Ambassador in Moscow. On April 23, Admiral Standley emphasized to Stalin the importance of regular air traffic connecting Moscow or Kuibyshev with Basra. He illustrated this by pointing to the delays in preparing a number of bombers for the Russians at Basra for want of certain parts which could have been dispatched over a shuttle line from the Soviet Union. But Stalin showed no particular interest in the idea. A few days later, Standley took up the matter with Molotov but with similar results.[40]

A few months later, however, the Russians suddenly reversed their position. This change occurred at a time when the Soviet

38. Ltr., Welles to Stimson, March 26, 1942 (File: 580.81, AG, in WWIIRD/NA).
39. *Ibid.*; ltr., Patterson to Hull, May 5, 1942.
40. Msg., Standley to Roosevelt and Hull, April 24, 1942; msg., Standley to Hull, April 26, 1942, *Foreign Relations*, 1942, III, 546, 549.

90   EAGLES EAST

Union was especially anxious for an Anglo-American invasion of Europe. The Soviet desire for the second front was pressed by Molotov during his visit to Washington in May and June. This was, indeed, an opportune moment to confront the Russians once again with the question of an efficient air service between the two nations via Iran. During one of his conferences with Molotov on June 1, the President remarked upon the "slow and difficult" connections between Washington and Kuibyshev via Iran and suggested that the Russian and American services meet weekly at Tehran. Molotov replied without hesitation that his country would initiate a Kuibyshev-Tehran air link but, at the outset, only once every two weeks.[41] By the summer of 1942, air communications between Russia and the United States by way of Iran had improved, but they were still a far cry from the efficient operations urged by Washington.

While grappling with the problems of a supply and communication route to the Russians via Iran, the War Department decided that a special military mission might be the answer to the mounting number of supply, maintenance and training problems involved in the aid program to the Soviet Union. Stimson established the United States Military Mission to the U. S. S. R., similar to the one that the United States already had in Britain, under the command of Major General John N. Greely. Among its specific functions, Greely's mission was competent to deal with problems involving the maintenance and operation of Lend-Lease aircraft in the Soviet Union. Greely's sphere of operations which caused so much difficulty later included "the territory controlled by the U. S. S. R. and such other areas as may be necessary to carry out . . . [his] functions."[42]

The status of Greely's group became so confused that it never was able to do anything. The establishment of the mission at a time when the Russians complained about the P-40's and refused to accept the group of aircraft technicians did not augur well for its success. The failure to send the aircraft specialists influenced the curious policies which the War and State Departments followed with respect to Greely's team. No formal diplomatic request

41. Memo of conference at the White House, June 1, 1942 by Samuel H. Cross, *Foreign Relations*, 1942, III, 579.
42. Ltr., Stimson to Greely, November 5, 1941 (File: 21276 to 21350, OCS, in WWIIRD/NA).

Iran: Corridor to Russia

for his group to enter Russia was made. Greely expected the mission to operate first in Iran and to have visas to enter Russia "for some or all" of the group issued "when it appeared desirable."[43] After supplies moved "smoothly from the south [Iran]," he planned "to take up the question of whether my mission can be usefully employed in the U. S. S. R. proper."[44]

When he arrived in Iran, Greely saw that the functions of the U. S. Military Iranian Mission under the command of Brigadier General Raymond A. Wheeler would overlap those of his group. Greely then decided to procure visas for the entire mission to enter Russia. But only three visas came. The Russians, with some justification, were annoyed at the unorthodox way that the matter was handled. To the suspicious Russians this was an underhanded technique to force a foreign military group through their back door. The Soviet attitude, Loy Henderson wrote, was "not open to criticism."[45]

Not only were the Russians chary about allowing another mission into their country but American officials in Moscow seriously questioned what Greely could accomplish there even if he got in. The State Department, understandably embarrassed by the situation, asked Standley to determine whether or not to press the issue with the Kremlin.[46]

Standley advised not to pursue the matter because, even if the Russians cleared the group, the Greely mission would overlap the activities of Faymonville's supply agency which was already in Moscow. Standley had enough problems with Faymonville who enjoyed a quasi-independent status in Moscow with direct access to Hopkins. He often provoked Standley's anger by involving himself in matters which did not relate to his mission. Standley justifiably complained later that his position was undermined "by a pulling and hauling in different directions by our State Department and other agencies of our government, notably the Lend-Lease Administration. . . ." The proposed entry of the Greely

43. Quoted in Motter, *The Persian Corridor*, pp. 69-70.
44. Memo, Greely for Moore, January 12, 1942 (File: 334.8, U. S. Military Mission to the USSR, ID, ASF, in WWIIRD/NA).
45. "Final Report—USSR" (Report and Supporting Documents dealing with the U. S. Military Mission to the U.S.S.R.) (File: 334.8 in WWIIRD/NA); memo by Henderson, March 26, 1942, *Foreign Relations*, 1942, III, 535, footnote 71.
46. Ltr., Stimson to Hull, March 30, 1942; ltr., Welles to Stimson, April 3, 1942, with enclosed msg., Welles to Standley, same date (File: 334.8, U. S. Military Mission to the U.S.S.R., ID, ASF, in WWIIRD/NA).

92 EAGLES EAST

mission into Russia raised the specter that it might absorb the functions of the Military Attaché and act independently of the Embassy. This was too much for Standley who complained about the individuals and groups who ignored him in their dealings with the Russians and left him "an innocent bystander."[47] After receiving Standley's advice, Stimson dissolved the mission which[48] the historian of the Persian Corridor aptly described as "conceived in logic" but "doomed to the functionlessness of a fifth wheel on a cart."[49]

While Greely sought to get his mission into Russia, early shipments of aircraft had arrived in Iran. The margin between arrivals and acceptances by the Russians proved to be substantial. This was due to a host of difficulties which plagued the early months of aircraft operations. During most of the last six months of the Moscow Protocol in the Middle East, American aircraft were assembled by RAF personnel at or near Basra. The assembly depot at Abadan was not ready for operations until April, and most of the Douglas Aircraft personnel, who were under contract until March, 1943, to operate the facilities there, did not arrive until May, 1942. Only a handful of AAF and civilian personnel of Douglas were on hand during these months to assist the British in assembling and testing American aircraft. The shortage of personnel was so great that when Adler learned that B-25's would be ferried to Basra, he requested that even ferry crews be held in the area to test planes and assist in maintenance work.[50]

There were other difficulties which delayed aircraft deliveries. Many of the A-20's and Bostons arrived without the necessary parts to assemble and modify them. This was partially due to the lack of available parts at the time the planes were shipped. But

47. Ltr., Welles to Stimson, April 22, 1942, with enclosed msg., Standley to Hull, April 18, 1942 (File: 334.8, U. S. Military Mission to the U.S.S.R., ID, ASF, in WWIIRD/NA). The latter message from Standley can be found in edited form in *Foreign Relations*, 1942, III, 544; msg., Standley to Hull, April 18, 1942, unedited copy; Standley, *Admiral Ambassador*, pp. 360, 236-38, 246, 119.
48. Ltr., Welles to Stimson, April 22, 1942.
49. Motter, *The Persian Corridor*, p. 65.
50. Msg., Wheeler to Moore, February 22, 1942 (File: 400.3295, AG, in WWIIRD/NA); msg., Adler to Arnold, Brig. Gen. Robert Olds, and Maj. Gen. O. P. Echols, March 18, 1942 (File: 452.1, Deliveries of Planes to Russia, ID, ASF, in WWIIRD/NA); ltr., Col. D. G. Shingler to CG, Services of Supply, April 10, 1942; weekly report, No. 10, April 21, 1942 (File: 319.1, ID, ASF, in WWIIRD/NA).

Iran: Corridor to Russia

the situation was also aggravated by errors in shipping them. As a consequence, the number of A-20's and Bostons delivered in Iran during the early months of American aircraft operations was unimpressive—only 210 by the end of June, 1942. The situation with respect to B-25 deliveries was not better—only 38 of the mediums arrived at the end of the same period. These planes had been delayed originally in the United States because of shortages in equipment. When the B-25's began to come to Iran, the turrets of several of them were inoperable.[51]

Soviet representatives in Iran did little to ease the problems for the Americans. They refused imperfect aircraft and sometimes requested items not ordinarily furnished. Before accepting a plane, Russian representatives wanted each item checked and its operation demonstrated. Even after a machine was accepted, its departure was delayed until a Soviet pilot arrived to fly it away. Due to a lack of pilots the Russians trained their personnel for ferrying operations in the area, a procedure which considerably delayed the progress of acceptances and sometimes resulted in damage to the aircraft. Moreover, it nullified a basic reason for the British and American decision to allow the Russians to accept the planes at Basra and Abadan rather than at a point further in Iran or in Russia.[52]

The strain and tension of operations during these early months reacted on all parties concerned, resulting in a clash between Commissar Ivan S. Karmilitsin and an American officer of the United States Military Iranian Mission, Lieutenant Colonel John A. Gillies. Faymonville reported that the poor relations be-

51. Msg., Adler to Arnold, February 18, 1942; msg., Arnold to Adler, February 18, 1942 (File: RG 18, Box 949, AAF, in WWIRB/NA); msg., Adler to Arnold, February 28, 1942 (File 400.3295, AG, in WWIIRD/NA); msg., Adler to Arnold, March 21, 1942; msg., Arnold to Adler, March, 1942 [sic]; msg., WD to Defense Aid Director, April 6, 1942 (File: 452.1, Deliveries of Planes to Russia, ID, ASF, in WWIIRD/NA); ltr., W. O. Hart to Lt. Col. W. J. Baird, May 28, 1942 (File: Russian Aid Miscellaneous, ACAS/MS, in WWIIRD/NA); ltr., Arnold to L. A. Razin, April 7, 1942 (File: 452.1, Deliveries of Planes to Russia, ID, ASF, in WWIIRD/NA); msg., Col. J. A. Wilson to Col. Kane, April 8, 1942 (File: USSR-Old File Cables, ACAS/MS in WWIIRD/NA); ltr., John A. Steele to Baird, with report, April 15, 1942 (File: 452, Reports on B-25 bombers by Ferrying Command, ID, ASF, in WWIIRD/NA).
52. Ltr., Shingler to CG, Services of Supply, April 10, 1942; report on reconnaissance to Basra and Andimeshk by Col. J. B. Luscombe, April, 1942 (File: 319.1 Reports, ID, ASF, in WWIIRD/NA); ltr., Gillespie to Arnold, April 22, 1942 (File: Russian Aid Miscellaneous, ACAS/MS, in WWIIRD/NA).

94 EAGLES EAST

tween Gillies and Karmilitsin allegedly stemmed from the former's stubborn refusal to honor legitimate Soviet requests. Faymonville believed that in view of the "tragic failure" to correct the generators of the P-40's delivered to northern Russia, the Soviet desire to have the planes tested on the ground and in the air—a bone of contention between the two men—was justified.[53] Greely was authorized to investigate the unsatisfactory situation and to smooth out the difficulties.

Colonel John N. Hauser, appointed inspector by Greely, conducted his investigations during the second week of March. By then, the two principals in the dispute, failing to return from a reconnaissance flight sometime earlier, were presumed dead. During the course of his investigations, Hauser found that some of the Soviet requests were reasonable and were not always met in a manner conducive to smooth relations. The cause of the dispute, however, was not quite so one-sided as Faymonville had reported. Hauser remarked that Karmilitsin's belligerent attitude aggravated relations with the Americans:

> On the part of the American witnesses I sensed belief that the Russian viewpoint was generally unreasonable. I sensed also, on the part of both American and Russian witnesses, a feeling that Mr. Karmilitsin contributed his share to the controversy, and a sentiment of relief at his absence. Analysis of statements made indicate a certain amount of unreasonableness on the part of Mr. Karmilitsin, with the vaguely indicated ulterior motive of placing the Americans in the wrong.

Hauser concluded that the Soviet request for an improved assembly and delivery establishment was justified,[54] a point of view which most American officials on the scene and in Washington shared.

53. Msg., Faymonville to Stettinius, March 5, 1942; Faymonville had earlier advised Stettinius of the matter but in less detail in a message on February 28, the substance of which is contained in ltr., Hazard to Baird, March 2, 1942 (File: Outgoing Cablegrams to U.S.S.R., ID, ASF, in WWIIRD/NA).
54. "Report to Chief, U. S. Military Mission to U.S.S.R., from Col. John N. Hauser, Special Inspector," March, 1942 (File: 333, Case of Col. Gillies and Commissar Ivan Karmilitsin, Investigation and Report, ID, ASF, in WWIIRD/NA).

CHAPTER VII

Alsib: Russo-American Link in the Pacific

A LLIED SUCCESS in World War II depended largely on opening and maintaining air, sea, and land routes to the embattled zones of Europe and Asia. The Alaska-Siberia air passage—commonly known as Alsib—was one of these vital supply arteries for delivering Lend-Lease planes to the Russians. Alsib was also potentially significant in the war against Japan if the Soviet Union could be persuaded to agree to the establishment of American air bases in Siberia. Officials in the AAF pressed the White House early in the war to obtain Russian agreement to open Alsib for logistical and strategic reasons. Through AAF initiative, the United States succeeded in securing Russian agreement to open Alsib for the purpose of delivering Lend-Lease planes. But the use of the route for operations against Japan ran counter to Soviet intentions of remaining neutral in the Pacific war and to prevailing American military strategy which established Europe as the principal combat theater.

The Joint Board Estimate, a comprehensive study of American military strategy, contained the clearest statement of the two-pronged significance of Alsib. Prepared two months before Pearl Harbor, the Estimate warned that Japan intended to include Siberia in her Co-Prosperity Sphere. Emphasizing the importance of the area and calling attention to deliveries of aircraft by air, the Estimate stated:

> Retention of Eastern Siberia by Russia is necessary if Japan is to be checked. Only material assistance can be provided by the United States to Siberia. No materials can be sent to Siberia by water when Japan is at war with Russia, but deliveries of aircraft could continue by air.[1]

1. Sherwood, *Roosevelt and Hopkins*, pp. 414-15, 418.

95

96 EAGLES EAST

According to the Joint Board Estimate, B-29's or B-32's operating from Alaska, with a refuelling area in Russia, could bomb vital points in Japan. It further urged giving serious thought to conversations with the Soviet Union concerning the use of a refuelling area in Siberia when B-29 or B-32 airplanes became available.[2] The idea was not a new one. In 1933, that controversial exponent of airpower, Billy Mitchell, pointed to the strategic values of air force operations from bases in Siberia in case of a war against Japan.[3]

Prior to the attack on Pearl Harbor, the AAF stressed the value of Alsib as a supply artery to the hard-pressed Russians and urged that a mission be sent to Siberia for the purpose of surveying air routes and facilities. If the project proved to be feasible, the AAF planned to deliver Lend-Lease aircraft to the Russians in Alaska.[4]

These projected plans hinged upon the acquisition of basic information concerning Siberian facilities in order to determine the feasibility of ferrying the planes. The most recent American effort to gather this information, made by Major General James E. Chaney during the Moscow Conference had been a failure.[5] But this did not deter the AAF. General Arnold directed Brigadier General McNarney to send a courier to Moscow to secure information concerning three air routes—two of these began at Nome and ended at a point within the Soviet Union. Lieutenant Colonel Townsend Griffiss was selected for the mission.[6] Before Griffiss' departure, Arnold requested that the Military Attaché, Lieutenant Colonel Joseph Michela, and the head of the American Supply Mission in Russia, Brigadier General Faymonville, exploit their contacts and gather whatever data they could.[7] The War Depart-

2. AWPD/1, Tab 7, (File: 145.82-1, in USAF/HA).
3. "Billy Mitchell on Alaska," *Washington Times Herald,* June 16, 1942, quoted in U. S., Senate, *Hearings Before a Subcommittee of the Committee on Foreign Relations,* 77th Cong., 2nd Sess., 1942, p. 87.
4. R & R, AWPD for CAS, October 30, 1941 (File: 145.96-172, IV-G, in USAF/HA).
5. Memo, Chaney for Harriman, October 11, 1941 (File: 091, Russia, ASWA, in WWIIRD/NA).
6. Msg., Arnold to McNarney, October 28, 1941; msg., McNarney to Arnold, October 29, 1941 (File: 400.3295, AG, in WWIIRD/NA).
7. R & R, AWPD for AAG, November 7, 1941 (File: 145.96-172, IV-G, in USAF/HA); msg., Arnold to Faymonville, October 31, 1941 (File: 400.3295, AG, in WWIIRD/NA).

Alsib: Russo-American Link in the Pacific

ment even enlisted the assistance of American diplomacy in order to cover all possibilities.[8]

Soon it was evident, however, that the AAF wanted the information to plan for possible use of the air route to, and bases within, Siberia in the event of war between Japan and the United States. If Japan attacked, Arnold hoped to have the bases in order to implement shuttle bombing operations in route to and from the Philippines. Since the AAF knew virtually nothing about facilities in the Soviet Far East, Arnold advised that the White House initiate diplomatic negotiations in order to permit an American survey of installations. In a proposed message from the President to Stalin, Arnold urged that Stalin should be told the survey was required not only for the delivery of Lend-Lease aircraft but also for future AAF operations from Siberian bases.[9]

But Arnold's proposed message from the President to Stalin was not regarded favorably by the General Staff. There was a risk that the message would leak out and be misunderstood at a time when the nation was conducting delicate negotiations with the Japanese. The General Staff, moreover, had serious doubts about Stalin himself: Could he be trusted in a matter of such delicacy? Some feared that he might even expose the message in order to involve the United States in a war with Japan. Indeed, Stalin had a good motive: a conflict between the United States and Japan would conveniently remove Japanese pressures on Siberia.[10] In view of these unacceptable risks, the General Staff opposed this approach to the problem and advised that the request for information and for the survey be framed purely in terms of facilitating delivery of Lend-Lease planes to the Soviet Union.[11]

This approach to the problem did not bring the desired results. A Soviet official told Michela that his government saw no reason to provide the information to the United States. "This answer," Michela blurted in amazement, "astounds me."[12] On the

8. Ltr., Stimson to Hull, October 31, 1941 (File: 4557 to 49 Russia, WPD, WDGS, in WWIIRD/NA).
9. Ltr., Arnold to Hopkins, November 6, 1941; ltr. Stimson to Roosevelt, November 14, 1941 with suggested message to Stalin (File: 145.95, Bk.1, in USAF/HA).
10. Memo, Gerow for Arnold, November 24, 1941 (File: 145.95, Bk.1, in USAF/HA).
11. *Ibid.*
12. Msg., Michela to Milid, November 30, 1941 (File: 635, ID, ASF in WWIIRD/NA). The tense relations between the United States and Japan

98 EAGLES EAST

following day, Michela reported with concern that "Unless some means can be found to break [the] present Soviet attitude this office is helpless."[13] After his arrival in Russia, Griffiss made the request on two different occasions and, like Michela, learned that the Soviet Union was not interested in having aircraft flown over Alsib. The Russians stubbornly maintained that the route was impracticable for ferrying operations. But there was more to the Soviet position than that. The Russians apparently suspected that the request was not strictly related to the question of ferrying planes but also involved matters of American military strategy against Japan.[14]

Suspicions about American intentions were a logical consequence of post-Pearl Harbor trends in United States policy which sought Soviet involvement in the Pacific war. While American requests for the information were pending in Moscow, the Secretary of State raised the question of bases for the AAF with the polished and precise Soviet Ambassador to the United States, Maxime Litvinov. This was on December 8, 1941.[15] A few days later, Hull informed him that the United States wanted two air bases, one on the Kamchatka Peninsula and one around Vladivostok. "Our heavy bombers," said Hull, "could get over Japanese home naval bases and the home fleet, as well as over the cities." The Secretary strongly urged:

the extreme importance right now and each day hereafter of obtaining these two bases for the purpose of permitting our aircraft to operate over all portions of Japan from the air. . .

---

prompted Marshall to suggest that a B-24 be sent into Siberia without advance diplomatic clearance. See memo, Kuter for Secretary, General Staff, November 21, 1941 (File: Russia, OCS, in WWIIRD/NA). The idea was probably rejected because of the explosive effects such a mission would have had upon American relations with Japan and Russia.

13. Msg., Michela to Milid, December 1, 1941 (File: 635, ID, ASF, in WWIIRD/NA).

14. Msg., from Griffiss, December 16, 1941, paraphrased in msg. Chaney to Agwar, December 18, 1941 (File: 400.3295, AG, in WWIIRD/NA). Before Pearl Harbor the Japanese charged that American aid to Russia was based upon a *quid pro quo*—namely, bases in the Maritimes. For example, the *Shanghai Times* in August, 1941, expressed concern that oil shipments to Vladivostok would be exploited by the United States to establish bases there. See msg., Lockhart to Secretary of State, August 23, 1941; msg., Grew to Secretary of State, August 2, 1941 (File: 861.24/546 and 526, in DS/NA).

15. Cordell Hull, *The Memoirs of Cordell Hull*, 2 vols. (New York: The Macmillan Co., 1948), II, 1111.

Alsib: Russo-American Link in the Pacific

we could scarcely do without them, and that, therefore, it is a matter of great importance to the present resistance to Japan by us—that, in fact, there is no substitute for effective attacks just now when compared with the injury that we could and would inflict from the air.

Hull linked the question of bases in the Far East with growing domestic criticism of Lend-Lease to the Russians because of their failure to cooperate in the Pacific.[16] Litvinov politely reaffirmed the Russian position: his country was too heavily committed against Germany to risk a war with Japan.[17]

Post-Pearl Harbor pressures for AAF operations from Siberia were convincing. A few days after the Japanese assault on Pearl Harbor, General Douglas MacArthur stressed that a "heavy air attack on Jap [*sic*] objectives would not only pull in much of present [Japanese] widely dispersed air strength but would destroy much of their exposed oil supply." He emphasized that a "Golden opportunity exists for a master stroke while the enemy is engaged in over-extended initial air efforts."[18] AAF planners shared the same opinion: the key to an offensive against Japan depended upon air power. They were certain that if the United States had the bases from which to attack enemy objectives, the situation in the Far East would be altered in favor of the Allies. But if denied these bases the AAF anticipated that the Allied position in the Far East would progressively deteriorate. In AWPD/4, a study prepared shortly after the attack on Pearl Harbor, the AAF emphasized the priority of the offensive against German-occupied Europe, but implied that air power for the European offensive might be seriously diminished if the United States operated from Siberia.

If Russia can be induced to make her bases available, then the opportunity to strike a telling and perhaps decisive blow in the Far East should be seized and acted upon, even though it may be necessary to reduce our air strength elsewhere.[19]

16. Memo of conversation by Hull, December 11, 1941, U. S. Department of State, *Foreign Relations of the United States, Diplomatic Papers, 1941*, Vol. IV: *The Far East* (Washington: United States Government Printing Office, 1956), pp. 743-44.
17. Hull, *The Memoirs of Cordell Hull*, II, 1112.
18. Quoted in U. S., Department of Defense, *The Entry of the Soviet Union into the War against Japan: Military Plans, 1941-45* (Washington: 1955), p. 1.
19. AWPD/4, p. 6 (File: 145.82-4, in USAF/HA).

100 EAGLES EAST

The plan was never tested. Soviet suspicions of America's Pacific strategy resulted in formal refusals to earlier requests for data about Siberia. On December 19, 1941, the Soviet government officially rejected the request of the American Embassy for the information.[20]

Official Washington had to reconcile itself to the fact that Russia would probably maintain its neutrality for some time in the Pacific war. But the AAF argument for future operations from Siberian bases could not be ignored in the light of increased Russo-Japanese tension in the Pacific. The President realized this. Early in March, he directed the Joint Chiefs of Staff to review the Far-Eastern situation and to advise him on military policy in the event of Soviet involvement.[21] Once again AAF planners differed from their colleagues in the Army. Air force officials optimistically believed that the Soviet Union would allow a survey party in Siberia to gather information about air routes and facilities provided the United States promised more than a token force of bombers for future operations there.[22]

Army planners raised sound strategic and logistic arguments against the project. One study pointed out:

> The most valuable assistance which can be rendered to Russia is to contain Japanese forces, mainly her air force, in the South Pacific and the sooner our action indicates to Russia that we shall do this the greater advantage she can gain from that assistance.[23]

Another study, discussing the difficulties involved in carrying out the AAF scheme, observed:

> The logistical difficulties, personnel and material losses that would be incurred, lack of adequate facilities in Siberia, inability of Russia to supply vital necessities upon arrival and during operation, and lack of sufficient U.S. shipping facilities available for this purpose preclude the possibility of sending

20. Msg., Chaney to Agwar, December 7, 1941 (File: 400.3295, AG, in WWIIRD/NA); msg., Michela to WD, December 27, 1941 (File: 635, ID, ASF, in WWIIRD/NA).
21. U. S., Department of Defense, *The Entry of the Soviet Union*, pp. 6-7.
22. Memo, Harmon for ACS, March 8, 1942 (File: H. H. Arnold Decimal File, in MD/LC).
23. Quoted in Maurice Matloff and Edwin M. Snell, *Strategic Planning for Coalition Warfare, 1941-1942* (Washington: Department of the Army, 1953), p. 143.

Alsib: Russo-American Link in the Pacific 101

supplies, reinforcements and airplanes to Siberia for combat purposes in the event of war between Japan and Russia.[24]

In other words, Army planners believed that the AAF desired to do far more than strategic and logistic realities allowed.

The War Department was not intrepid enough to suggest using the second front issue as a lever to exert pressure upon the Soviet Union to get the information about Siberia. American diplomacy, however, had gone so far as to link the second front with the question of Soviet participation in the Pacific war.[25] No doubt because of the serious political risks, this approach was not seriously pressed again.

In response to Roosevelt's inquiry regarding American policy in the event of Russo-Japanese hostilities, the Joint Chiefs informed the President that "The possibility of employing United States forces in and near Siberia depends on the ability of the Soviet forces to hold sea, land, and air bases to which the United States could proceed, and from which they could operate." They cautioned:

> It would be unwise for the United States to undertake active operations in Siberia until after its military officials were in possession of complete information as to Soviet strengths and plans, and unless the validity of this information had been confirmed by a careful and exhaustive examination, by United States officers, of Soviet forces and facilities in the Siberian theater.

The Joint Chiefs concluded that the only way to secure this indispensable information was by an agreement between Roosevelt and Stalin. If this agreement were achieved, the logical results would include a survey trip of Siberia and Russo-American staff conversations. The President returned the memo without comment, and the matter rested there.[26]

While military planners grappled with the problem of how to approach the Soviet Union regarding the use of the air route to and bases in Siberia, the AAF took preliminary steps to develop Alsib for ferrying Lend-Lease aircraft. As early as March, 1942, the

24. *Ibid.*, p. 144.
25. Memo of conversation by Welles, February 23, 1942, *Foreign Relations, 1942*, III, 694-95.
26. U. S., Department of Defense, *The Entry of the Soviet Union*, pp. 7-8.

102 EAGLES EAST

Director of Military Requirements suggested optimistically that all of the planes allocated to the Russians could soon be delivered by way of Alsib.[27] In fact, the AAF anticipated that by the end of 1942, 1,000 fighters would be ferried over the route.[28] Although the AAF planned to develop facilities to Nome, Fairbanks was scheduled as the tentative transfer point if the Soviet government refused to allow American pilots to fly the planes all the way to Russia.[29] The desirable goal was to have Americans fly the planes across the entire Alsib route because the vital experience gained by the pilots would obviously be useful if, in the future, they were to engage in combat operations from Siberian bases against Japan. However, Arnold was willing to compromise on this point if it jeopardized the opening of Alsib. He expressed this position to Admiral William Standley shortly before he assumed his position as the new Ambassador to the Kremlin.[30]

Shortly after he arrived in Moscow, Standley conveyed Arnold's proposal to Stalin. He also brought up a State Department suggestion of a shuttle service between Alaska and Siberia. Stalin, however, expressed his preference for a shuttle service from Canada to Archangel via Iceland. The Ambassador observed that the route via Iceland had probably been investigated by American authorities but rejected because of the weather conditions.[31]

After proposing the idea of a shuttle service, Standley went on to raise the question of ferrying planes to the Soviet Union via Alsib. Stalin showed no particular interest in the project. His preference was clearly for the North Atlantic route but he offered a glimmer of hope by promising to have the matter studied. Stalin made a special point of mentioning possible Japanese objections to the ferrying of planes over Alsib. But this, Stalin assured, "would not be an insurmountable obstacle."[32]

27. U. S., Army Air Forces, Air Transport Command, "Alaskan Division, Air Transport Command, Historical Record Report," II, 240 (File: 306.01, in USAF/HA).
28. *Ibid.*, pp. 240-41.
29. Memo, Brewer for CG, Ferrying Command, April 30, 1942 (File: H. H. Arnold Decimal File, 580 ATC, in MD/LC); msg., Arnold to George, May 10, 1942 (File: 145.95, Alaska, Bk.2, in USAF/HA).
30. Ltr., Arnold to Standley, March 10, 1942 (File: Arnold Special-Official File, in MD/LC).
31. Msg., Standley to Roosevelt and Hull, April 24, 1942, *Foreign Relations, 1942*, III, 546.
32. *Ibid.*

Alsib: Russo-American Link in the Pacific 103

Before the conclusion of the interview, Stalin referred to an American bomber which had landed in Siberia a few days earlier.[33] This was a B-25, which along with 15 others, took part in the famous Tokyo Raid under the command of Lieutenant Colonel James H. Doolittle. One of the bombers, piloted by Captain Edward J. York, was forced to land in Siberia because of insufficient gasoline.[34] Although Stalin showed "no annoyance at the incident" during his interview with Standley,[35] he could not have been pleased with an event which contributed greater strain to the tense relations between the two countries.[36] The Soviet government interned the five American airmen for several months as a sop to Russo-Japanese neutrality before a bogus escape was arranged to evacuate them from the country. As the aerial offensive against the Japanese developed intensity, there was a corresponding increase in the number of American flyers who were forced down in the Soviet Union. This required three more contrived "escapes" of American airmen before the Russians went to war with Japan in August, 1945. The men were well treated during their detention before they were clandestinely evacuated to the American base at Amirabad near Tehran.[37]

Japanese pressures in the Far East in 1942 highlighted the need to open Alsib and develop facilities in Siberia for AAF operations. Informed military sources expected Japan to attack Siberia during the summer.[38] Now Arnold was more determined than ever to keep the question of American air operations before the Russians. On May 5, he told Major General Dwight Eisenhower

33. *Ibid.*, p. 548.
34. Memo, Maj. O. J. Sands, for Chief, Intelligence Group, April 23, 1942 (File: 170.22781, in USAF/HA).
35. Msg., Standley to Hull, April 24, 1942, *Foreign Relations*, 1942, III, 548. In his memoirs, Standley reported that Stalin was apprehensive over the landing of the American plane. See Standley, *Admiral Ambassador*, pp. 157-58.
36. Memo, Sands, for Chief, Intelligence Group, April 28, 1942 (File: 170.22781, in USAF/HA).
37. "Deane Report," Part II, pp. 199-204, which is now accessible in Richard C. Lukas, "Escape . . . American Internees In the Soviet Union: From General Deane's Report," *Aerospace Historian*, XVI (Spring, 1969), 14-17. Soviet behavior was curious. While the Russians exerted considerable efforts and took great risks in helping the Americans escape in February, 1944, and in January and May, 1945, they doggedly blocked the repatriation of AAF personnel from eastern Europe when that area came under their control. Perhaps the friendly action on behalf of AAF pilots downed in the Pacific was done to ease America's persistent pressure on Moscow to enter the war against Japan.
38. Ltr., Stimson to Hull, April 14, 1942 (File: 381, AG, in WWIIRD/NA).

that "We must develop the facilities [in Siberia] as quickly as possible." He added firmly: "Furthermore, we must move into them so that when world conditions make it necessary there can be no argument about that matter."[39] In a message to Michela a few days later, the chief of the AAF emphasized the urgent need for the information in order to plan for later operations. The AAF wanted data which would provide for the movement of combat planes of all types over Alsib. Information was also needed to plan for the movement of long-range bombers over the Polar Cap to western Russia. A few days later, Marshall requested Michela to provide similar information for ferrying operations over Alsib and via Iran. In both cases, American equipment and pilots for ferrying operations were contemplated.[40] State Department machinery had also been enlisted to obtain results.[41]

For a brief time, at least, it appeared as though circumstances would force the Russians to open the route for both supply and strategic reasons. In addition to the possibility of a Japanese invasion of Siberia, German victories in Africa under Field Marshal Erwin Rommel grimly presaged the loss of the Middle East as a supply line to the Soviet Union. Lieutenant General H. A. Craig, former Assistant Chief of Air Staff, Plans, wisely observed:

> The loss of Egypt by the British would close the air ferry route across Africa to Russia, India and China. The Alsib route was a logical alternative for delivering aircraft (1) to the hard pressed Russians and (2) to China and India in the event Egypt was lost.[42]

As Craig pointed out, the deteriorating situation for the Allies in the Middle East dramatically added another dimension to Alsib as an alternative route of supply to the Chinese and Russians. Arnold directed Craig to discuss the matter with Major General Alexander I. Belyaev, Chairman of the Soviet Purchasing Commission in the United States. If Belyaev argued that Japan would object to the usage of the route to supply the Chinese, Arnold told Craig "to find ways and means of combating that line of argument."[43]

39. Memo, Arnold for Eisenhower, May 5, 1942 (File: 452.1, Russia, OPD, WDGS, in WWIIRD/NA).
40. Msg., Arnold to Military Attaché, May 7, 1942; msg., Marshall to Military Attaché, May 12, 1942 (File: Cables to Russia, ACS, G-2, in WWIIRD/NA).
41. Msg., Hull to Standley, May 11, 1942, *Foreign Relations*, 1942, III, 702-03.
42. Ltr., Craig to writer, February 20, 1963.
43. R & R, Arnold for Craig, May 9, 1942 (File: 145.96-182, IV-I-5, in USAF/ HA).

Alsib: Russo-American Link in the Pacific

During this interview with Belyaev, it is unclear whether Craig discussed the idea of developing Alsib as a supply line to China.[44] But Belyaev did indicate interest in the route for the delivery of Lend-Lease planes. However, if it were opened, Belyaev said Soviet pilots would ferry the aircraft.[45]

This sudden change in Soviet policy was confirmed by subsequent reports from American representatives in Moscow. Now that the door to Siberia was open, the United States hoped to have its pilots deliver the aircraft. If this failed, Marshall and Arnold were prepared to accept Russian pilots flying the planes.[46] President Roosevelt actively joined in jarring the door to Siberia by suggesting the establishment of civilian air and ferry services to Foreign Minister Molotov during the latter's visit to Washington during May and June, 1942.[47]

After Molotov's departure from the United States, the matter of opening Alsib began to crystallize, notwithstanding its confusion and contradiction. On June 8, Litvinov visited Hopkins and conveyed what was ostensibly a result of Molotov's recent visit. Hopkins' memorandum of his conversation with Litvinov is significant because a short time later a contradiction in, or a misunderstanding of, Soviet policy arose. Hopkins noted that "the Russian Government had agreed to *our* flying bombers to Russia via Alaska and Siberia." He added: "I imagine the real reason the Russians approved *our* flying planes through Siberia is that in the

44. Craig does not recall a discussion of China with Belyaev at that time. See ltr., Craig to writer, February 20, 1963. The Chinese were anxious to develop air and land routes between China and the Soviet Union for logistical reasons. In May, Hull asked Standley to secure information concerning air routes between China and Siberia. Standley advised against it because of political factors, but later took up the matter with Stalin. See msg., Hull to Standley, May 15, 1942; msg., Hull to Gauss, May 23, 1942; msg., Standley to Hull, May 29, 1942; msg., Standley to Hull, July 3, 1942, U. S., Department of State, *Foreign Relations of the United States: Diplomatic Papers, 1942*, Vol.: *China* (Washington: United States Government Printing Office, 1956), pp. 593-96, 600.
45. Ltr., Arnold to Belyaev, May 14, 1942 (File: H. H. Arnold Decimal File, 686 Russia, in MD/LC).
46. R & R, AFAEP for AAG, May 22, 1942, containing message, Marshall to London for transmittal to Standley (File: 145.95, Great Britain, Bk. 1, in USAF/HA).
47. Memo of conference at White House by Cross, May 30, 1942, *Foreign Relations*, 1942, III, 578; memo of conference at White House by Cross, June 1, 1942, *Foreign Relations*, 1942, III, 579. Prior to this meeting, Hull had sent a memo to Hopkins and suggested that these matters be discussed with Molotov. See Sherwood, *Roosevelt and Hopkins*, p. 560; memo of conversation by Hull, June 3, 1942, *Foreign Relations*, 1942, III, 586.

106 EAGLES EAST

event Japan attacks them we will already have organized a quick method of getting planes to Vladivostok."[48]

At the time of the Litvinov-Hopkins meeting, the Japanese were already in the Aleutian Islands. This appeared to be a prelude to full-scale operations against Siberia. On June 17, Roosevelt communicated the gravity of the situation to Stalin:

> Should such an attack materialize the United States is ready to assist the Soviet Union with American air power provided the Soviet Union makes available to it suitable landing fields in the Siberian area. The efforts of the Soviet Union and of the United States would of course have to be carefully coordinated in order promptly to carry out such an operation.

He urged that "detailed information be immediately initiated between our joint Army, Navy and Air representatives in order to meet this new danger in the Pacific." Roosevelt suggested that both of them appoint representatives to confer in Moscow and Washington and expressed pleasure with Stalin's approval of the movement of American planes via Alaska and Siberia.[49]

Subsequent events disclosed that Moscow was undecided about opening Alsib after all.[50] This vacillation in Soviet policy apparently was conveyed to Roosevelt because the nature of his remarks to Stalin sound as though he was selling Alsib again to a fickle buyer. On June 23, Roosevelt informed Stalin:

> I wish to emphasize that if the delivery of aircraft from the United States to the Soviet Union could be effected through Alaska and Siberia instead of across Africa, as is now the practice, a great deal of time would be saved. Furthermore, the establishment of a ferry service through Siberia would permit the delivery by air of short range aircraft to the Soviet Union instead of by sea, as is now the case.

He added:

> I am prepared to instruct the American ferry crews to deliver aircraft to you at Lake Baikal. This air route could be easily connected up with the landing fields leading into the Vladivostok area. In the event of a Japanese attack on the Soviet

48. Memo by Hopkins, June 9, 1942, *Foreign Relations*, 1942, III, 590-91.
49. Msg., Roosevelt to Stalin, June 17, 1942, *Foreign Relations*, 1942, III, 597.
50. Memo, George for Arnold, June 22, 1942 (File: 145.95, Alaska, Bk.2, in USAF/HA).

Alsib: Russo-American Link in the Pacific   107

Maritime Provinces, such a Siberian airway would permit the United States quickly to transfer American aircraft units to the latter area for the purpose of coming to the assistance of the Soviet Union.[51]

The President urged that an American survey party be authorized to fly over the area to determine the requirements of establishing airfields and navigational services. The survey, he said, would enable his representatives to discuss intelligently the problems of operating in the area at the proposed Soviet-American military conversations.[52]

Finally, on July 1, Stalin replied to Roosevelt's communications. At last, all doubt was removed: Stalin agreed to open Alsib. But the Soviet chief made it clear that his pilots would go to Alaska to accept the planes and fly them away. He showed no interest in an American survey of Siberia and wanted the joint military conversations held in Moscow, not Washington. He conspicuously ignored the President's suggestions regarding American air operations from Siberian bases.[53] He left little doubt that he accepted Washington's proposals with respect to ferrying Lend-Lease planes and nothing more.

Thus, early in July, 1942, the United States got Soviet consent to open Alsib—a route that later became the major passage for the delivery of Lend-Lease planes to the Russians during World War II. Although it was desirable to have AAF pilots fly the planes, the American government did not allow Russian refusal of this proposal to stand in the way of opening the route. As Standley related, Stalin accepted the plan "similar to the one proposed by General Arnold which was presented by me at my first interview."[54]

The Soviet position with respect to Alsib must be viewed within the larger framework of the war itself. It should be borne in mind that the Soviet Union, heavily committed to the war against Hitler, consistently pursued a policy of pressure upon Great Britain and after Pearl Harbor, upon the United States for large scale involvement against the Germans. To encourage America with the Alsib project—especially its strategic aspects against Japan—would

---

51. Msg., Roosevelt to Stalin, June 23, 1942, *Foreign Relations*, 1942, III, 599.
52. *Ibid.*, pp. 599-600.
53. Msg., Stalin to Roosevelt, July 1, 1942, *Stalin's Correspondence*, II, 28.
54. Msg., Standley to Roosevelt and Hull, July 4, 1942, *Foreign Relations*, 1942, III, 605. Standley's reference was to Arnold's letter of March 10, 1942.

108 EAGLES EAST

not have served Russian interests against Germany. In concentrating its efforts against Germany in 1941 and 1942, Russia was anxious to maintain peace with Japan, a policy which could have been jeopardized if Americans had flown planes from Alaska to an area adjacent to Japanese-occupied territory.

Although the much anticipated Japanese invasion of Siberia did not materialize, the possibility of such an attack must have convinced Stalin to open Alsib. It also appears very probable that the reduction of Lend-Lease deliveries to Russia's northern ports and the ominous threat by the Germans to the Middle East persuaded Stalin to develop Alsib as an alternate route of supplying his air force with American aircraft.

CHAPTER VIII

The Washington Protocol

MID-1942 WAS A TRANSITIONAL PERIOD in United States-Soviet relations. It still saw the West trying to prove its commitment against Hitler to Russia. Although not yet clearly apparent to American military planners, significant changes had occurred in the status of air power on the eastern front. The Soviet Air Force had recovered from its serious setback of the previous year and now outnumbered the Luftwaffe. Although still technically inferior to the Luftwaffe, it was making progress to correct this deficiency. As the balance of air power shifted in favor of the Soviet Union, the Moscow Protocol was nearing the end.

Therefore, Washington again had to decide the question of future aircraft commitments to the Soviet Union. In the process of reaching decisions on this question, the White House and the War Department were once again at opposite poles. As was to be expected, the White House wanted commitments to be continued at the same rate as before and if possible, to be increased. In view of projected operations against Germany, the War Department was most anxious to strengthen the air arm of American military power. In the end, aircraft commitments under the Second, or Washington, Protocol revealed a compromise between War Department and White House views.

Remarkable changes had occurred in the distribution of air strength on the eastern front since June, 1941. The disastrous losses suffered by the Soviet Air Force during the early months of the war had been a setback, not a lethal blow. Luftwaffe failures to exploit

109

110   EAGLES EAST

Russian losses by sustained attacks against industrial installations were, as German writers later bemoaned, catastrophic. By concentrating primarily upon close support of ground forces, the Luftwaffe did not really affect the ability of the Soviet Union to produce aircraft and, as a consequence, to re-equip its air force.[1] Russian aircraft production increased from a low point of 600 planes in November, 1941, to 850 in January, 1942, and 1,300 in March, 1942. By June, the figure was placed as high as 1,750 planes, 550 more than the number produced during the same month in 1941.[2]

The winter of 1941-42 saw the Luftwaffe facing a resurgent Soviet Air Force which recaptured numerical superiority on the eastern front while the strength of its opponent fell substantially below the figure it started the campaign with.[3] Several factors explain the depletion of the Luftwaffe. The Germans were unprepared for the severe Russian weather conditions, lacked adequate facilities, and suffered from insufficient replacements of planes and personnel. As a consequence, Berlin overused its units by committing and withdrawing them to meet the ever changing combat situations along a 2,000 mile front.[4] It was under these conditions that the Germans had to meet a Soviet counter-offensive.[5] As one

---

1. Richard Suchenwirth, *Historical Turning Points in the German Air Force War Effort* (USAF Historical Studies No. 189, USAF Historical Division, Research Studies Institute, Air University, 1959), pp. 72-83; Schwabedissen, "From Barbarossa to Stalingrad," *The Soviet Air and Rocket Forces*, p. 56; Air Ministry, "A Survey of German Air Operations, 1939-1944," p. 6.
2. U. S., War Department, "Preliminary Report," 8A-4.
3. The British Air Ministry placed German strength on the eastern front during the winter of 1941-42 at 1,700 aircraft. See Air Ministry, *The Rise and Fall of the German Air Force*, p. 172. German military authorities estimated that the Soviet Air Force had 2,600 aircraft on the eastern front in February, 1942 while the Luftwaffe had 1,900 planes there. See U. S. War Department, "Preliminary Report," TAB VIII-5A. The Karlsruhe Document Collection at the USAF Historical Division, Maxwell AFB, shows Luftwaffe strength at 1,550 during the period January through March, 1942. Even Stalin admitted to Eden in December, 1941, that the Soviets had more planes than the Germans.
4. Air Ministry, *The Rise and Fall of the German Air Force*, pp. 173-74; U. S. Department of the Army, *The German Campaign in Russia*, pp. 139-40. J. F. C. Fuller points out that the German offensive against Moscow "petered out, not so much because of Russian resistance but because of the frost." See Fuller, *A Military History of the Western World*, III, 443. Russian historians take strong exception to this interpretation. For example, see Telpukhovskii, *Velikaia Otechestvennaia Voina*, pp. 104-05.
5. For a brief survey of the condition of the German armed forces during the Russian counter-offensive which began in November, 1941, see U. S., Department of the Army, *The German Campaign in Russia*, pp. 97-108, 120.

The Washington Protocol

111

German dolefully wrote: "The winter of 1941-42 was the beginning of the end of the Luftwaffe."[6]

Losses of tactical aircraft continued to mount from approximately 281 in January, 1942, to 549 in July.[7] Germany was rapidly becoming short of fighters. And there was no immediate prospect for improvement because, unlike the Soviet Union, it had neglected production of fighters.[8]

By the middle of 1942, the Soviet Air Force had recovered from its setback of the previous year and, in contrast to the Luftwaffe, was growing stronger. By June, the Soviet Air Force outnumbered its adversary on the eastern front by several hundred planes. The strength of the Luftwaffe declined steadily to 1,650 planes by December while the Soviet Air Force grew to 4,000-5,000.[9] This growing quantitative superiority eventually decided the battle of airpower on the eastern front in Soviet favor—the decisive turning point was the Battle of Stalingrad.

Soviet needs for aircraft from its Allies were obviously less urgent than they had been during the early phase of the war, although this was not yet clearly evident to American planners. The Soviet Union gave no indication that the situation had changed in any way; in fact, the Kremlin maintained that its needs were as critical as they had been during the early days of "Barbarossa" and even requested a greater number of planes from its Allies. Even after it became apparent to Washington that Soviet

6. Plocher, "The German Air Force Versus Russia on the Eastern Front," Ch. 12-14, p. 873.

7. These were losses due to enemy action. Air Staff Post Hostilities Intelligence, "Chart: Tactical Aircraft of the Luftwaffe, Losses Due to Enemy Action, January-December, 1942."

8. Generalleutnant Adolf Galland, "Defeat of the Luftwaffe," *The Impact of Air Power*, pp. 250-54; Schwabedissen, "From Barbarossa to Stalingrad," *The Soviet Air and Rocket Forces*, p. 57; Plocher, "The German Air Force Versus Russia on the Eastern Front," Ch. 1-2, p. 24. The Germans produced 4,600 fighters in 1942 while the Russians more than doubled this figure.

9. U. S., War Department, "Preliminary Report," TAB VIII-5A; memo, Jacobs for Wedemeyer, May 7, 1943 with report: "U. S. S. R. Aircraft Strength and Production" (File: 452.1, Section 3, 1/22/42, OPD, WDGS, in WWIIRD/NA). Robert Kilmarx maintains that "Soviet fighters actually outnumbered Luftwaffe fighters between four and five to one as early as the summer of 1942. The total number of German aircraft in Russia remained close to 2,500, while the Soviet Air Force had more than three times that number." See Robert A. Kilmarx, *A History of Soviet Air Power* (New York: Frederick A. Praeger, 1962), p. 184. Karlsruhe Document Collection, USAF Historical Division, "Strength of the Luftwaffe in the Eastern Theater of Operations, 1942." Taken from Luftwaffe Situation Reports.

112 EAGLES EAST

needs were less critical than they once had been, no corresponding reductions of aircraft commitments were made.

The political overtones that characterized military aid to Russia were apparent when the Second Protocol was under study in Washington. By then, Russia had shown that it was unimpressed with the West's military effectiveness, critical of the delays and deficiencies of the Anglo-American supply program, suspicious of its Allies' motives, and dissatisfied with the absence of a second front in Europe. Could such negativism, if unchecked, seriously affect Russia's committal against the Axis? In view of alleged German peace offers to Russia,[10] Washington and London could not be optimistic. Within the larger framework of the war, matters of political expediency continued to loom large in Russo-American relations.

There was no doubt about the position of the White House with respect to allocations under the Second Protocol. On March 24, the President clearly stated his position to Stimson:

> I understand that, from a strategical point of view, the Army and Navy feel that aid to Russia should be continued and expanded to [the] maximum extent possible, consistent with shipping possibilities and the vital needs of the United States, the British Commonwealth of Nations and others of the United Nations. I share such a view.[11]

Although the War Department accepted the strategic importance of Russia, it favored supplying the Soviets "only insofar as it would not interfere with preparations to open a 'new front in Europe.' "[12] This was the crux of the problem. In order to carry out active operations in Europe, the AAF urged a reduction of commitments to America's allies. Arnold expressed this view during a meeting at the White House on April 1:

10. At the time the Second Protocol was under consideration, Standley conveyed to Washington rumors regarding German peace offers to Russia. These persisted throughout 1942. Memo, Capt. Hugh O. Davis for Chief, Intelligence Group, May 8, 1942; Memo, Davis for Chief, Intelligence Group, May 30, 1942; memo, Sands for Chief, Intelligence Group, August 1, 1942; memo, Lt. Col. C. E. Jackson, for Chief, Intelligence Group, November 5, 1942 (File: 170.22781, in USAF/HA). Krylov points out that in September, 1942, the Japanese offered to act as mediators in a separate Russo-German peace. See Krylov, *Soviet Staff Officer*, pp. 200-02.
11. Ltr., Roosevelt to Stimson, March 24, 1942 (File: 400.3295, AG, in WWIIRD/NA).
12. Matloff and Snell, *Strategic Planning for Coalition Warfare*, p. 206.

The Washington Protocol 113

I stated that as far as equipment was concerned, the Air Forces were treated like a sort of stepchild. After all other nations were given the airplanes they asked for, the United States Air Forces received what was left. I pointed out we could not fight a war along those lines. Both the President and Secretary Stimson said that such procedure must stop; that hereafter the United States Air Forces were to receive their share of airplanes, based upon the tasks we had to perform.[13]

Roosevelt's agreement, unlike Stimson's, excluded the Soviet Union from proposed aircraft reductions. The President's consent to decrease allocations to Great Britain resulted in the Arnold-Towers-Portal Agreement in June, 1942. By its terms, Britain would receive fewer planes in combat theaters where the AAF also conducted operations.[14] But all aid to Russia, the President reaffirmed, "must be at least as great as today and actually increased as much as possible."[15] Stimson disapproved of the political aspects of aircraft allocations to Russia:

All requests for planes for areas not essential to our own plans must be refused. The time is past for all gifts of planes —all gifts of planes based upon sentimental or goodwill purposes.

And he suggested that in the near future, it might be necessary to stop allocations:

The time may even come when we will have to determine whether more effective efforts to save Russia will be made through our own air forces rather than through the planes turned over to her air forces.[16]

Following Stimson's lead, Arnold's staff prepared an elaborate plan which substantially reduced future aircraft commitments to the Soviet Union. If the AAF's plan were adopted, allocations to the Soviet Union under the new protocol would have been slashed by 963 planes, including 36 medium bombers, 480 light bombers and 447 fighters. Similar reductions were proposed to Great Britain. In submitting his recommendations, Arnold emphasized

13. Arnold, *Global Mission*, pp. 305-06.
14. Craven and Cate, *The Army Air Forces in World War II*, I, 566-70.
15. Quoted in Matloff and Snell, *Strategic Planning for Coalition Warfare*, p. 206, footnote 36.
16. *Ibid.*, p. 207.

114   EAGLES EAST

that the proposed reductions were necessary in order to meet the requirements of the nation:

> To meet the deficiencies in aircraft discussed above, it will be mandatory that there be effected an appropriate reduction of American aircraft production now allocated to Defense Aid. . . . I appreciate the seriousness of this proposal particularly as to the effect upon our Allies. However, it is the only action possible if we are to meet our present plans and operational commitments.[17]

Marshall, too, supported a decrease—even a cessation—of aircraft allocations to the Soviet Union. During a meeting of the Joint Chiefs of Staff toward the end of April, he stated that "the number of planes to Russia would have to be drastically reduced, if not altogether stopped, by August or at the latest in September."[18] The urgency of Marshall's statement stemmed from the unpreparedness of the AAF to wage extensive operations on the continent. Only seventy groups, sixteen of which were transport and observation units, were in the AAF in January, 1942.[19] Additional groups were needed, but Arnold remarked dolefully that the United States would never get them "on the fighting fronts or on our training fields at home if we continued to allocate so many planes to foreign countries."[20]

The War Department decided not to reduce aircraft to the Russians immediately. Stimson recommended to the President that planes be made available to them at the same rate as "in the existing Protocol."[21] This did not mean that the War Department planned to continue these commitments throughout the period of the Second Protocol. Planes would be made available at the same rate as in the preceding protocol but only for the first few months. After that, the War Department contemplated a reduction because the scale of operations on the eastern front during the winter

17. Memo, Arnold for ACS, April 11, 1942 (File: 145.96-166, IV-C, in USAF/HA).
18. Matloff and Snell, *Strategic Planning for Coalition Warfare*, p. 207.
19. Craven and Cate, *The Army Air Forces in World War II*, I, 251.
20. Arnold, *Global Mission*, p. 308.
21. Ltr., Stimson to Roosevelt, May 1, 1942 (File: 031.1, ID, ASF, in WWIIRD/NA). In January, 1942, the rate of deliveries was established at 212 planes per month. This was not a new commitment but an effort to meet the monthly rate under the Moscow Protocol. See ltr., Stimson to Roosevelt, December, 30, 1941.

The Washington Protocol 115

months would ostensibly reduce Soviet requirements. Arnold, objecting to this approach, believed that the requirements of the AAF rather than the situation on the eastern front should determine American allocations.[22]

Marshall endorsed Arnold's position, noting that all considerations should be subordinated to AAF needs in Europe. He wanted the country to deliver to Russia 100 fighters, 100 light bombers and 12 medium bombers per month, if the attrition suffered in the Anglo-American air offensive over Europe permitted. But Marshall added that the United States should only guarantee 50 fighters, 50 light bombers and 12 medium bombers per month.[23] As was to be expected, the President did not accept these recommendations because they constituted, in effect, a reduction of previous aircraft commitments to the Soviet Union, which was intolerable to the White House.

As presented to Molotov on May 29 and eventually signed in Washington, the Second Protocol committed the United States to supply through October 1942 an average of 100 fighters, 100 light bombers and 12 medium bombers per month. The review clause in the protocol, stating that "Commitments will be made for the balance of the year on the basis of developments incident to the progress of the war," was especially important to the AAF which hoped and expected that later deliveries would be reduced.[24] This proved to be wishful thinking.

Of course, the Russians wanted more planes than those allowed in the new protocol. Molotov requested that the monthly pledge of B-25's be increased from 12 to 50 and that 150 Bostons, instead of the current 100 A-20's, be delivered each month to Iran. Although the White House refused these requests, the subject was open to later consideration.[25] The Russians expressed their qualified satisfaction with the Second Protocol, but urged that the delivery

22. R & R, Arnold for Maj. Gen. M. F. Harmon, May 16, 1942 (File: Russia — 1942, ACAS/MS, in WWIIRD/NA).
23. Memo, Maj. Gen. Harmon for ACAS, May 22, 1942 (File: Russia - 1942, ACAS/MS, in WWIIRD/NA).
24. U. S., Department of State, *Soviet Supply Protocols*, pp. 15-16, 19. The protocol contained a general reservation: "It is to be understood this programme is subject to variations to meet unforeseen developments in the progress of the war."
25. Memo, Burns for Hopkins, June 4, 1942, *Foreign Relations*, 1942, III, 707-08.

116 EAGLES EAST

of airplanes after October, 1942, be increased as much as possible.[26]

To what extent did commitments to the Soviet Union under the new protocol affect the AAF? War Department planners acknowledged that the monthly pledge of 212 planes would not seriously affect the ability of the AAF to engage effectively in the projected invasion of Europe in 1942. The commitment to Russia was roughly equivalent to a monthly production of one light bomber and one fighter group. If an invasion of Europe did occur during the fall of 1942, few of these planes could have been sent abroad in time to be formed into combat ready units. Although these planes were not critically significant in guaranteeing America's ability to invade Europe in 1942, they constituted production which could have been used as reserves against attrition. Moreover, these planes would have enabled the AAF to give more thorough training to its crews, thus hastening their combat readiness.[27] Although the AAF's position was not so critical in mid-1942 as it had been when the United States first began to supply the Russians, it still lacked sufficient aircraft and parts to execute the increasing demands of offensive war.

Soviet requests for scarce types of planes were often denied by the United States. This not only applied to heavies but also to transports, which were critically needed by all of the Allies throughout the earlier part of the war. While allocations of combat aircraft under the Second Protocol were under consideration, Soviet requests for transports were pending before the War Department. The discussions concerning these requests revealed the critical importance of the planes to the AAF and the inability of the United States to offer any of them to the Russians. It was also clear that military planners were keenly aware of the political effects which their decisions would have upon America's relations with Russia.

No transports had been included in the Moscow Protocol, but in a letter to Hopkins, Gromyko had requested immediate delivery of 600 DC-3's. Little wonder that the Soviet request was so urgent. The transport had so low a place in Soviet priorities that production had declined from 45 in September to 5 in

26. Ltr., Litvinov to Hull, July 7, 1942, *Foreign Relations,* 1942, III, 712. The Second Protocol was formally signed in Washington on October 6, 1942, but it became effective on July 1, 1942.

27. R & R, AFDAS for AFAEP, May 31, 1942; R & R, AFAEP for AFDAS, June 13, 1942; memo, for Col. O. A. Anderson, unsigned, June 20, 1942 (File: 145.95, Western Russia, Bk. 1, in USAF/HA).

The Washington Protocol

117

January, 1942. The AAF situation was as bad. Well might the Deputy Chief of Staff, Major General R. C. Moore, say that "No assurance can be given at this time as to the possibility of furnishing the Russians even a small part of their request in the near future."[28] American factories delivered only 16 in September, 10 in November and 16 in January, 1942. Output did not substantially improve until the summer when they averaged 124 per month.

Colonel H. S. Aurand, Defense Aid Director, told Major General J. H. Burns that the Joint Aircraft Committee decided that 1943 was the earliest date when transports could be available to Russia.[29] But the Soviet Union continued to ask for the scarce planes. Early in March, Hopkins, frequently acting as intermediary between the Russians and the War Department, conveyed the new Russian request. Lovett suggested that if transports to Britain were substantially reduced, it might be possible for the United States to provide the Soviet Union with approximately 100 of them by the end of 1942.[30] This suggestion was not pursued because of the serious effects on the British program.

A token delivery of 25 C-47's and 4 C-53's to Russia for May and June, 1942, was approved by the Munitions Assignments Board which had earlier received a little nudge from the White House.[31] Arnold reacted strongly to insure that his nest of birds had enough of carriers:

> To meet the training requirements for and to have in combat the 200 transport airplanes in August and 400 airplanes in November which have been allocated for airborne, parachute, and glider troops for the main effort, and to provide in addition the essential minimum requirements of the Ferrying Command, the Air Service Command, and all overseas areas

28. Ltr., Gromyko to Hopkins, November 21, 1941; memo, for Lt. Col. L. Jaynes, unsigned, December 14, 1941; ltr., Moore to Burns, December 24, 1941 (File: 400.3295, AG, in WWIIRD/NA); Translation, Luftwaffe Operations Staff, Intelligence, No. 35 449/43, October 29, 1943 (File: Karlsruhe Document Collection, USAF/HA); Army Air Forces, *AAF Statistical Digest: World War II*, p. 129.
29. Memo, Col. H. S. Aurand for Burns, January 7, 1942 (File: Russia Correspondence—Lend-Lease No. 1, ID, ASF, in WWIIRD/NA).
30. Ltr., Hopkins to Lovett, March 6, 1942; ltr., Brig. Gen. R. Olds to Lovett, March 23, 1942; ltr., Lovett to Hopkins, March 28, 1942 (File: 091 Russia, ASWA, in WWIIRD/NA).
31. Memo, Chairman, MAC (Air) for Meyers, April 10, 1942 (File: 145.96-206, in USAF/HA).

118   EAGLES EAST

where the Army Air Forces are operating, will require every transport airplane that is now available, or that can be provided by our entire production.[32]

Finally, during a meeting on April 21, the Combined Chiefs of Staff considered the matter. The discussion revealed that the chiefs were keenly aware of the political aspects of the question:

> Rear Admiral John H. Towers, Chief of the Bureau of Aeronautics, 'stressed the importance of making at least a small allocation to Russia in view of the political considerations.' Sir John Dill observed that in case no transport planes should be allotted to the Soviet Union, 'it would be necessary to give a very well reasoned explanation.' Marshall agreed that 'a very carefully phrased reply would have to be made.' He observed that 'the operational effect of such a small number of aircraft in Russia would be small although the political effect might be considerable.'[33]

In a rare move the Combined Chiefs of Staff overruled the order of the Munitions Assignments Board and refused the Soviet request.[34] Admiral King, impressed by the views of Admiral Towers, questioned the wisdom of the decision. Marshall completely disagreed with Towers who, he felt, was "not fully informed on the very large undertaking to which the Army is committed by order of the Commander-in-Chief." He stated the opening of a second front "at the earliest possible moment to relieve pressure on Russia," involved the use of parachute troops, airborne infantry, and gliders "in amounts considerably in excess of planes allocated to the Army at the present time." One of the objections of British officials to an invasion of Europe in 1942, he said, "was based on the lack of sufficient equipment for such a hazardous operation, especially landing boats and transport planes." He added:

> The small number of transport planes stated in the United States memorandum submitted to the British was wholly insufficient for the task and must be materially increased in the next few months, if we are to give Russia the vital assistance required. The necessity for this equipment is a

32. Memo, Arnold for Stimson, April 11, 1942 (File: RG 18, Box 949, AAF, in WWIRB/NA).
33. Matloff and Snell, *Strategic Planning for Coalition Warfare*, p. 208.
34. Memo, Chairman, MAC (Air) for Meyers, May 5, 1942 (File: 145.96-206, in USAF/HA).

The Washington Protocol 119

present one and cannot be satisfied by allocations in the future in view of the time schedule under which we are directed to operate and which I have confirmed on my recent visit to London. I therefore agree with General Arnold's statement in this connection to the Combined Chiefs of Staff.[35]

Marshall illustrated the seriousness of the situation by pointing out that the AAF would lack 379 transports of the projected minimum requirements for 1942. He concluded grimly: "Neither of us can be expected to fight a war and still give away our weapons beyond some reasonable point. As far as I am concerned, we have passed that point in aircraft."[36]

On the same day Marshall, communicating to the President the needs of the AAF for the planes, again advanced the War Department view that the invasion of Europe would be far more beneficial to the Russians than the provision of war materiel and opposed the allocation to Moscow of materiel which was vital for that operation.[37]

Roosevelt could not understand how the AAF was short of transports when planes in commercial airlines were available for the armed forces if needed. The expression "pigs is pigs," the President urged, should be translated into "planes is planes."[38] Marshall was hesitant to take carriers from commercial lines but made it clear that if this were done, he wanted them earmarked for the AAF. Faced with the strong opposition of the War Department, Roosevelt reluctantly went along with the decision against the allocation of the transports. Hopkins, acting in this matter for the White House, preferred to communicate the decision personally to Litvinov rather than use a letter prepared by the General Staff in order to soften its impact.[39]

The United States hoped that the rate of deliveries to the

35. Memo, Marshall for Adm. King, April 27, 1942 (File: 400.3295, AG, in WWIIRD/NA).
36. *Ibid.*
37. Memo, Marshall for Roosevelt, April 27, 1942 (File: 400.3295, AG, in WWIIRD/NA).
38. Memo, Roosevelt to Stimson and Marshall, May 5, 1942, quoted in Arnold, *Global Mission*, p. 331.
39. Matloff and Snell, *Strategic Planning for Coalition Warfare*, p. 210. However, Lovett expressed the opinion that 47 planes could be taken from commercial airlines for the Russians without hurting America's reserve pool of aircraft. See memo, Lovett for Stimson, April 26, 1942 (File: 452.1, in WWIIRD/NA).

Soviet Union under the new protocol would be substantially higher than under the preceding one. Considering the difficulties involved, the record of aircraft shipments under the Moscow Protocol had been respectable.

By the terms of the Moscow Protocol, the United States had agreed to provide 1,800 planes by the end of June, 1942. These were to be delivered at American factories. When the protocol terminated on June 30, 1942, the United States had virtually met this commitment:[40]

Moscow Protocol Commitment		Amount Available at American Factories	
Bombers	900	Bombers	875
(72 B-25's and		(77 B-25's and	
828 A-20's)		798 A-20's)	
Fighters	900	Fighters	875
(P-40's)		(P-40's)	
Total	1,800	Total	1,732

The record of exports to north Russia and Iran was not so impressive. The United States had voluntarily assumed the difficult task of transporting the planes to Soviet acceptance points because of Moscow's inability to do so. Exports were primarily hampered by the shortage of shipping and by the limitations of the air route to Iran. This is reflected in the following figures which indicate the number of planes exported through June 30, 1942, the number exported in July but credited to the Moscow Protocol, and the final status of aircraft exports under the agreement:[41]

	EXPORTS		
	October – June, 1942	July, 1942	Total Against Moscow Protocol
B-25's	76	0	76
A-20's	552	74	626
P-40's	657	93	750
Total	1,285	167	1,452

Exporting the planes from the United States and delivering them to Soviet acceptance points in northern Russia and Iran were entirely different matters. There were a host of difficulties which delayed the arrival of the planes at the acceptance points.

40. Ltr., Stimson to Roosevelt, August 18, 1942, with final report of military items on the Moscow Protocol (File: 031.1, Protocol, I, ID, ASF, in WWIIRD/NA).
41. *Ibid.*

The Washington Protocol   121

Some of these included the severe weather conditions, the spirited action of German naval and air forces, and the inadequate port conditions at Archangel and Murmansk. These difficulties particularly applied to the north Russian run. Deliveries of planes to Iran were delayed by the long distance involved, the lack of facilities at port and assembly areas, and the limitations of the air route. As a consequence, less than half of the planes exported from the United States had arrived in northern Russia and Iran at the end of the Moscow Protocol. Most of the B-25's and A-20's were sent to Iran, and the P-40's were shipped via the northern route.[42]

As the Second Protocol began, the prospects for an improvement in the rate of deliveries looked very bleak. The successful German assaults against the Allied convoys plying to northern Russia forced the United States and Great Britain to stop using this supply artery. This crucial decision was made after the Germans virtually annihilated PQ 17. On June 27, this heavily escorted convoy, composed of 34 merchantmen, departed Iceland. On July 1, the Germans spotted it and a series of air attacks followed. The British Admiralty, anticipating a major naval assault by the enemy's capital ships, the most famous of which was the *Tirpitz,* feared the loss of both merchant and escort vessels. Churchill wrote of the situation:

> Admiral Hamilton's cruisers would be of no avail against the force the Germans could employ, and it seemed that the only

42. Statistics relating to deliveries of American aircraft in north Russia and Iran during the Moscow Protocol reveal that somewhat less than half of those exported from the United States arrived at their destinations. The remainder were either in route, lost, or diverted. Approximately 286 aircraft arrived in north Russia, including 259 P-40's, 19 O-52's, 3 A-20's, and 5 B-25's. Approximately 348 aircraft arrived in Iran. Of these 248 were delivered to the Russians and consisted of 117 A-20's, 93 DB-7's, and 38 B-25's. The undelivered balance were mostly A-20's. See: Worksheets of plane arrivals in Russia, 1941-1942 (File: 913406, ACS, G-2, in WWIIRD/NA); Office of Lend-Lease Administration, Status of the Soviet Aid Program as of July 31, 1942 (File: 031.1, Protocol, I, ID, ASF, in WWIIRD/NA); Air Materiel Command, "Special One-Time Report;" Motter, *The Persian Corridor,* pp. 135-36. The arrivals of aircraft under the British commitment to Russia were considerably higher. By the end of June, 1942, approximately 1,284 planes arrived in Russia, including 1,161 Hurricanes, 30 P-40's, and 93 P-39's. See note from E. P. Taylor, British Supply Council in North America, July 13, 1942 and memo, Col. James F. Olive Jr. for Col. Betts, September 11, 1942 (File: 913401 and 913406, ACS, G-2, in WWIIRD/NA).

122   EAGLES EAST

hope of saving a proportion of the convoy lay in scattering as widely as possible before the enemy arrived.

The fateful order for the withdrawal of the cruisers and the dispersal of the convoy soon led to one of the most disastrous Allied losses of the war. German capital ships never attacked the convoy but instead returned to Norwegian waters. The helpless vessels were then ravaged by German airplanes and submarines. The Germans claimed that the convoy was totally annihilated, but the British only admitted the loss of twenty-three ships.[43] After this disaster, the commanding general of the Fifth Air Fleet enthusiastically informed Field Marshal Hermann Goering:

> Reich Marshal! I report the destruction of the large convoy PQ 17. Reconnaissance on 10 July 1942 in the White Sea, the navigable western waters, and along the coast of the Kola Peninsula and farther north found no trace of any merchant ship. The interpretation of reconnaissance photos of Jokanga, the last point for which units of Convoy PQ 17 were steering, show that not a single merchant ship from that convoy reached that port.[44]

The disaster convinced Churchill that firm action was necessary to prevent such prohibitive losses in the future. There seemed to be no alternative but to stop, at least temporarily, deliveries to northern Russia. On July 17, Churchill informed Stalin that the difficulties of the route required a suspension of the sailings until arrangements were devised which gave a reasonable chance of a fair proportion of the contents of the convoys getting to their destination. Meanwhile, merchantmen for the next scheduled convoy to northern Russia were to sail to Iran instead. To cushion the impact of his decision Churchill suggested the idea of sending British air forces to operate on the Russian front.[45]

Stalin was not pleased. In a stern note to Churchill on July 23, he told the Prime Minister that the reasons for the suspension were quite unconvincing. His advisers, said Stalin, believed that

43. This account is based upon Churchill, *The Hinge of Fate*, pp. 262-66. Morison's account is basically the same. See Morison, *History of United States Naval Operations in World War II*, I ,179-92.
44. Quoted in Plocher, "The German Air Force Versus Russia on the Eastern Front," Ch. 4-8, p. 678.
45. Msg., Churchill to Stalin, July 17, 1942, Churchill, *The Hinge of Fate*, pp. 267-70.

The Washington Protocol 123

with "good will and readiness to honour obligations" these convoys could be regularly undertaken and heavy losses could be inflicted on the Germans. The Soviet Marshal stated flatly that "It should be obvious that deliveries via Persian ports can in no way make up for the loss in the event of deliveries via the northern route being discontinued." Also disturbed by the contents of Churchill's message which implied that there would be no second front in Europe in 1942, Stalin stated his government could not tolerate that.[46]

Stalin's surly message revealed how serious the strain was in the Grand Alliance. The Russians had often complained about the delivery of supplies. Now the suspension of the convoys to north Russia and the continued absence of a second front in Europe threatened to disrupt seriously Anglo-American relations with the Soviet Union. As a consequence, the White House and No. 10 Downing Street concerted measures to restore Russia's confidence in the West. In this regard American aircraft again played a significant part.

The first step in improving relations was not to respond in kind to the bitter message to the Prime Minister. Roosevelt reminded Churchill of "the very difficult and dangerous situation" which confronted Stalin and explained that "no one can be expected to approach the war from a world point of view whose country has been invaded."[47] Churchill fully understood this and, as he said, "let Stalin's bitter message pass without any specific rejoinder."[48]

Both western statesmen felt that several practical steps had to be taken to improve relations with the Kremlin. The President advised Churchill that the Soviet Marshal be informed of proposed Anglo-American military operations in 1942—namely, the invasion of North Africa which had been decided a few days earlier. He also urged that another convoy be sent to north Russia. Roosevelt then promoted the idea, suggested earlier by Churchill, that the United States and Britain send a combined air force to operate on the Russian front. The President, emphasizing the salubrious

46. Msg., Stalin to Churchill, July 23, 1942, Ministry of Foreign Affairs of the U. S. S. R., *Stalin's Correspondence*, I, 56.
47. Msg., Roosevelt to Churchill, July 29, 1942, Churchill, *The Hinge of Fate*, p. 271.
48. Churchill, *The Hinge of Fate*, p. 272.

124 EAGLES EAST

political effects of placing an air force on the Russian front, said: "It would mean a great deal to the Russian Army and the Russian people if they knew some of our air force was fighting with them in a very direct manner."[49]

Roosevelt wanted to send fifteen planes, a "token gift," as an immediate measure to pacify Stalin. When Roosevelt conveyed his intention, Arnold was having difficulty finding twelve additional planes for service in Egypt. But aircraft for the Russians was a matter of priority, and in asking Major General G. E. Stratemeyer, Chief of the Air Staff, to find the planes for the Russians, Arnold revealed the serious political considerations involved:

> Can't we look around and get ten, or fifteen airplanes of some type and give them. If we do so, it may mean keeping the Russians in the fight. That should be prepared for the Joint Chiefs of Staff. We will just take them away from something.[50]

As the Second Protocol began, Britain and the United States initiated measures to restore Stalin's confidence in the West. One of the most significant of these involved placing an Anglo-American air force on the Soviet front. This project, code named *Velvet,* constituted a western effort to collaborate actively with the Soviet Union against Hitler. The strained relations with the Kremlin also emphasized the need to improve radically deliveries of aircraft —still the military item most prized by the Russians. The opening of the Alsib route appeared to be the answer.

49. Msg., Roosevelt to Churchill, July 29, 1942, Churchill, *The Hinge of Fate,* pp. 271-72.
50. Conference, Arnold and Stratemeyer, July 31, 1942 (File: 145.95, Western Russia, Bk. 1, in USAF/HA).

CHAPTER IX

The Bradley Mission to Moscow

WHEN STALIN CONSENTED to a survey of Siberia and military conversations in Moscow, he made it unmistakably clear that these matters were to further only one objective—namely, ferrying operations over Alsib.[1] Even so, American military planners still cherished the hope that the projected survey and the proposed military discussions might be broadened to lay the basis for collaboration in the Pacific war.

Thus the mission of Major General Follett Bradley, appointed to represent the United States in the proposed conversations in Moscow, had a twofold purpose—to arrange for deliveries of Lend-Lease planes via Alsib and to explore the question of collaboration against Japan. In directing Bradley to arrange for the delivery of war-aid airplanes, Stimson observed that although the Soviet Union desired its crews to accept the planes at Nome or Fairbanks, it was, nevertheless, desirable for Americans to ferry the planes into Siberia. Stimson also told Bradley to explore thoroughly "all possibilities" of mutual aid between the two countries, particularly collaboration in the Pacific. Bradley was authorized to swap detailed information regarding the Pacific and to propose a similar exchange of military missions to undertake detailed surveys of Alaska and Siberia.[2]

Bradley conferred with the President and found him most optimistic about the success of the mission. Believing that "the ice had been broken" with Stalin, the President was confident that

1. See Chapter VII.
2. Ltr., Stimson to Maj. Gen. Bradley, July 20, 1942 (File: 201-Bradley, OPD, WDGS, in WWIIRD/NA).

125

126 EAGLES EAST

the Russians would cooperate in opening Alsib and in providing information on facilities in Siberia. During his interview with Bradley, the President showed enthusiastic interest in the AAF project of using Alsib to send supplies to China and he asked the general to explore its possibilities. The President, affirming his abounding determination to aid the Russians, instructed Bradley to "tell Stalin to let us know what he wants and in what priorities and show us how to get it to him." The President beamed: "there was practically no limit to the aid we would furnish the Russians if they would do this."[3]

Before Bradley's departure no agreement had been reached with the Russians concerning the composition of the proposed survey party. It will be recalled that Stalin had informed the President on July 1, that the survey of Siberian facilities would be made by Soviet personnel. Only after Standley prevailed upon him did Stalin agree that American personnel could participate.[4] The President informed Stalin that the United States could send a plane to make the survey trip to Siberia with "three or four Russian officers to accompany it. On the other hand," the President stated, "we would be very glad to have American officers accompany a Soviet plane."[5] Stalin had no intention of allowing the survey party to be composed primarily of American personnel. "They could accompany a Soviet contingent in a Soviet-operated plane," he said.[6]

Shortly before Bradley's departure for Moscow, he conferred with General Belyaev and requested that the Soviet Union permit eight American members to participate in the combined survey group.[7] A few days later, the President informed Stalin that the American members of the survey party would be prepared to leave Nome by August 1 in their own bomber if it were needed. Stalin was obviously in no particular hurry to initiate the survey or to be pressured by the President. On August 2, he replied that a Soviet B-25 would be at Nome "between the 8th and 10th of August and on leaving for the projected survey flight will take on

3. Memo, Bradley for Marshall, July 22, 1942 (File: 201-Bradley, OPD, WDGS, in WWIIRD/NA).
4. See Chapter VII.
5. Msg., Roosevelt to Stalin, July 7, 1942, *Foreign Relations*, III, 1942, 607.
6. Msg., Stalin to Roosevelt, July 18, 1942, *Foreign Relations*, III, 1942, 610.
7. Ltr., Bradley to Belyaev, July 18, 1942 (File: H. H. Arnold, Official Files, in MD/LC).

The Bradley Mission to Moscow

board three American participants in the flight."[8] This number was hopelessly inadequate for the task of obtaining a realistic picture of the facilities which were to be surveyed. As a consequence this became Bradley's first item of business after arriving in Moscow.

During the first meeting with the Russians on August 6, Bradley sought to secure agreement to an increase in the number of Americans in the survey team, urging that the number be expanded from three to six or preferably to eight members. After much haggling, the Russians agreed. In view of the size of the survey group, Bradley then suggested that an American B-24 be used in lieu of a Soviet plane. But the Russians rejected the offer on the grounds that most Siberian airfields could not accommodate heavy bombers; instead they decided to send a DC-3 to join a Soviet B-25, then on its way to Alaska, in order to accommodate the party. By August 13, the planes arrived at Fairbanks. But the survey group did not depart for Siberia for almost two weeks due to Russian vacillations concerning the opening of Alsib and their reluctance to approve visas for all AAF members of the contingent. In the end, seven of the eight Americans under the command of Colonel Alva L. Harvey, departed Alaska for Siberia.[9]

Meanwhile other matters directly bearing on the opening of Alsib were under discussion in Moscow. During Bradley's first conference, the Russians appeared to be quite eager to develop the route to its full capacity and asked for American help. Bradley erroneously assumed they were asking for American ferrying services in Siberia. General Sterligov, Bradley's counterpart in the discussions, quickly dispelled that notion by claiming the SAF had sufficient pilots to conduct operations over Alsib from any point in the United States. In the face of continued Russian opposition to American pilots ferrying planes over the route, Bradley did not press further and told Sterligov that Fairbanks would be the transfer point of planes to Soviet pilots.[10]

---

8. Msg., Roosevelt to Stalin, July 23, 1942; msg., Stalin to Roosevelt, August 2, 1942, *Foreign Relations*, III, 1942, 614.
9. "Report of Bradley Mission to Russia, July 26-December 3, 1942," TAB I, pp. 3-5 (File: 201-Bradley, OPD, WDGS, in WWIIRD/NA). Army Air Forces, Air Transport Command, "Alaskan Division, Air Transport Command, Historical Record Report," II: "The Pre-Wing Period," p. 250 (File: 306.01, in USAF/HA).
10. "Report of Bradley Mission to Russia," TAB I, pp. 1-2.

128   EAGLES EAST

No sooner had the question of whose pilots would ferry the planes been explored than Russian negotiators curiously raised doubts whether Alsib could be used at all. Admitting that their segment of the route was not entirely prepared for operations, the Russians revealed that until one particular airfield had been constructed, no fighters could make the long flight from Alaska. The picture was equally unpromising with respect to emergency airfields which were either poor or non-existent on the entire segment of the route east of Krasnoyarsk. These revelations shocked Bradley who had assumed, because of earlier Soviet boasts, that the Russians could accommodate a large scale movement of aircraft.[11]

Soviet requests for transports proved to be the critical issue which seriously jeopardized the negotiations, revealing doubts and suspicions on both sides. Since the beginning of the American aid program, the Russians had repeatedly asked for transports. Critical shortages of these planes in the AAF prevented a favorable response to the requests.[12] After Bradley revealed the number of planes of all types to be sent via Alsib, the Soviets once again requested the carriers. Before he left for Moscow, Bradley had communicated a proposal to General Belyaev in Washington that within ten days of final approval of the route, the United States would have 50 A-20's and 12 B-25's at Fairbanks for the Russians to fly away. Within three weeks of approval, 43 P-40's and 50 P-39's would be at Fairbanks. Thereafter, deliveries would continue at the rate of 100 fighters, 100 light bombers, and 12 medium bombers per month. In other words, the entire American monthly commitment would be ferried to the Soviet Union via Alsib.[13] In conveying acceptance of this proposal, Belyaev made it appear that the Kremlin's consent was contingent upon the receipt of 43 transports in order to carry Russian crews to Alaska.[14]

Again the Soviet request for the 43 transports was repeated to Bradley in Moscow. Russia was "too hard-pressed on her fighting fronts," Sterligov bemoaned, "to divert transports from frontal supply service to use on this route." The Russian formula exag-

11. *Ibid.*, pp. 2-3.
12. See Chapter VIII.
13. Ltr., Bradley to Belyaev, July 18, 1942.
14. Ltr., Belyaev to Arnold, August 3, 1942 (File: Russia-1942, ACAS/MS, in WWIIRD/NA). However, Belyaev denied that Soviet consent to open Alsib was contingent upon provision of the 43 transports. See ltr., Belyaev to Arnold, August 5, 1942 (File: 306.01, 1939-1942, III, in USAF-HA).

The Bradley Mission to Moscow   129

gerated the number of personnel required to ferry the planes; Bradley observed that the number could be substantially reduced by using the same size ferry crews as used by the AAF. As a result he proposed that the Soviet requirement could be reduced from 43 to 20 planes. The Russian negotiators were unreceptive because, they explained, "Their system of individual training was such that no member of a crew could be dispensed with."[15] Failing to bring the Russians around, Bradley cabled their request for the carriers to Washington.

The War Department was frankly unimpressed with the alleged need for so many planes, believing 10 transports would be quite sufficient to handle the movement of the entire commitment of Lend-Lease planes.[16] In addition, the War Department suggested a *quid pro quo* arrangement which it had not seriously advocated earlier. In view of the fact that Russian pilots would ferry the planes across Alsib, it seemed eminently fair to the War Department to suggest that American crews operate the transport service.[17]

As Bradley was not anxious to get involved in another debate over the entry of American personnel into the Soviet Union, he objected strongly to the War Department's proposal. American operation of the transports would have been difficult to defend except on the basis of superior efficiency. And this, Bradly correctly observed, the Russians would be unlikely to accept. Moreover, he warned that the suspicious Russians would undoubtedly regard the idea as a subterfuge to establish foreign personnel within their frontiers, not to mention the jeopardy to their neutrality with Japan. And there were practical difficulties involved: How could an American transport service operate in Russia without interpreters, equipment and supplies? The Russians could obviously operate such a service more efficiently in their own country. Bradley was convinced that if the War Department proposal were pursued, it would merely complicate an already difficult situation and perhaps end entirely negotiations to open the route. As an alternative he suggested that after operations over Alsib had been

15. The Russians claimed that five men were needed to ferry a B-25 and four for an A-20. Bradley told the Russians they needed only three for a B-25 and two for an A-20. "Report of Bradley Mission," TAB I, pp. 6-8.
16. Msg., Street to Bradley, August 12, 1942 (File: Russian Flyaway Cables, AAF, ACAS/MS, in WWIIRD/NA).
17. *Ibid.*

130   EAGLES EAST

fully established, the United States could then try to ease into the picture.[18] Bradley won his point and the War Department abandoned its proposal.

Bradley was less successful in getting more transports for the Soviet Union. In defending the Russian request for a larger number, he remarked that although 10 transports were adequate to operate the route, this did not allow for weather and maintenance problems which could reduce the number of serviceable planes committed to the operation.[19] While he awaited a reply from Washington, he informed the Russsians that his country could only offer them 10 transports. The War Department, reaffirming that only 10 transports could be offered, was quite apprehensive that the Russians might refuse to open Alsib after delivery of the planes. It did not want deliveries made until Bradley was absolutely certain that Alsib would be activated by the Russians. To allay its suspicions, the War Department wanted Russian assurances that the planes would be used exclusively over Alsib.[20]

This brought a stalemate in the negotiations. The Russians believed that the number of transports was inadequate to insure delivery of sufficient aircraft to make operations on the route worthwhile. Bradley, who was as intelligent as he was tactful, quickly saw a way to force a change in the Russian position. He told the Russians that his country "would be glad to take over entire control of operations and supply of Alsib." Stunned by the proposal, the Russians immediately agreed to open Alsib on the basis of the transports which Washington had offered.[21]

After the transport question ceased to be a critical issue in the negotiations, the Russo-American survey party, which had lingered for so long in Alaska, was finally cleared to make the survey. Bradley wanted to join the group at Krasnoyarsk, a point along the proposed ferry route, and to accompany the flight back to Moscow. He made this request several times, but by the time the Russians consented, the survey had been completed.[22]

18. Msg., Bradley to Street, August 13, 1942 (File: Russian Flyaway Cables, AAF, ACAS/MS, in WWIIRD/NA); "Report of Bradley Mission," I, p. 8.
19. Msg., Bradley to Street, August 13, 1942.
20. "Report of Bradley Mission," TAB I, p. 8.
21. *Ibid.*; msg., Bradley to WD (No. 34), August 25, 1942; msg., Bradley to WD (No. 35), August 25, 1942 (File: Russian Flyaway Cables, AAF, ACAS/MS, in WWIIRD/NA).
22. "Report of Bradley Mission," TAB I, pp. 4-5, 13.

The Bradley Mission to Moscow   131

The American members of the group presented their observations to Bradley after they arrived in Moscow. In order to determine the technical feasibility of the route, the Americans had to rely more upon their own observations than upon discussions with their Russian colleagues. One member of the group, Major P. J. Prossen, commented that the Americans were treated politely, but Soviet cooperation with respect to the technical matters of the survey was very poor.[23] Colonel Alva Harvey, the commander of the American team, reported that most of the airfields east of Krasnoyarsk were primitive with neither hard-surfaced runways nor observable storage facilities. But if adequate supplies existed in this area, he believed that there would not be a great deal of difficulty in ferrying fighters across Siberia. Airfields west of Krasnoyarsk were modern. Harvey confirmed what the AAF had long suspected. When American combat units operated from Siberian bases, they would have "to start from scratch."[24]

On the basis of Harvey's report, Bradley informed the Russians on September 1 of his government's approval of Alsib.[25] By then, Russian ferry pilots were on their way to accept the first combat planes. Even the Department of State had facilitated matters by allowing the Russians to enter Alaska without visas.[26] Presumably no obstacles remained to initiate operations over Alsib.

But still another crisis had to be weathered. New difficulties began with the Soviet refusal to allow Harvey's group to make a more detailed survey on its return trip home. Another inspection by the Americans, the Russians declared, was "without purpose, since the route had already been approved on the basis of the survey made on the western flight." As a consequence, on September 19, Harvey and his men departed Moscow aboard a Soviet DC-3 for Alaska.[27]

23. "Report of Air Service Command Representative on the Flight of the Siberian Ferry Route—Maj. P. J. Prossen" (File: H. H. Arnold, Decimal File, 686 Russia, in MD/LC).
24. Intelligence Service, AAF, "Summary of an Interview with Col. Alva Harvey, Chief of Mission to survey ferry route, Alaska to Moscow," October 24, 1942 (File: 145.95, Western Russia, September 1941-December, 1942, Bk. 1, in USAF/HA).
25. "Report of Bradley Mission," TAB I, p. 5.
26. Msg., Standley to Hull, August 22, 1942, *Foreign Relations*, III, 720-21. Also see p. 721, footnote 22.
27. Bradley suggests that the Russians had consented earlier to allow Harvey's group to make a more detailed survey on its return flight. See "Report of Bradley Mission," TAB I, pp. 4-5. There is some indication that Bradley made

132   EAGLES EAST

On the same day, General Belyaev in Washington confronted Arnold with a staggering message. "According to instructions from my government," he dryly stated, "due to various reasons the ferry route Fairbanks-Nome-Eastern Siberia is not suitable for us and therefore cannot be utilized in the future." Planes already at Fairbanks would be accepted by Soviet pilots, but thereafter, Moscow wanted the planes delivered to Iran or northern Russia.[28] When the AAF learned of this sudden and unexplained change in policy, it immediately stopped all Lend-Lease planes in route to Alaska.[29]

Bradley promptly inquired about the matter in Moscow but the Russians curiously professed complete ignorance of Belyaev's remarks.[30] Admiral Standley sought out Molotov who did little to raise the cloak of mystery. Molotov, with his characteristic disregard of facts, implied that there were no planes in Alaska for the Russians to fly. The United States, he carped, "could not keep Russian pilots sitting there [in Alaska] with no planes to fly."[31] What Molotov meant by this is unclear because as early as September 17 there were forty-one planes ready for acceptance.[32]

The conflict between Belyaev's remarks in Washington and those of Soviet officials in Moscow never was unraveled. The Russians seem to have feared that the United States would not provide the transports which had been promised. There was some basis for their concern because as late as September 23, only six of the planes had arrived at Fairbanks.[33]

But there was a more important reason for this contradiction in Soviet policy: there was serious doubt concerning the success of

---

this request after Harvey's group completed the initial survey of Siberia. See Army Air Forces, "History, Eastern Command, USSTAF, 1941-1945," Ch. 4, p. 9 (File: 522-01-2, in USAF/HA).

28. Ltr., Belyaev to Arnold, September 19, 1942 (File: Russia-1942, ACAS/MS, in WWIIRD/NA).

29. R & R, Hanley for AFATC, September 19, 1942; R & R, Hanley for AFASC, September 19, 1942 (File: 306.01, 1939-1942, III, USAF/HA).

30. "Report of Bradley Mission," TAB I, p. 10.

31. Msg., Standley to Hull, September 23, 1942, *Foreign Relations*, 1942, III, 649-50.

32. Ltr., Maj. Kitchingham to Col. W. H. Tunner quoted in Army Air Forces, Air Transport Command, "Northwest Route Under the Ferrying Division, Air Transport Command: June 16, 1942—November 1, 1942," p. 131 (File: 301.04-5, in USAF/HA). Kitchingham commanded the 384th Base Headquarters, Ladd Field, Fairbanks, Alaska.

33. "Report of Bradley Mission," TAB I, p. 10.

The Bradley Mission to Moscow

large scale ferrying operations over Alsib. On September 24, a few days after Belyaev's statement in Washington, Sterligov told Bradley that Moscow's consent to open Alsib was contingent upon the success of the movement of the first group of planes from Fairbanks to Siberia. He even implied that after the first group of planes was successfully ferried across Siberia, the Russians might close Alsib anyway.[34]

Soviet apprehensions concerning their ability to handle extensive operations over their segment of the route were confirmed by the statements made by Russian officials in Alaska and Washington. Members of the Russian Military Mission in Alaska remarked to AAF officers that the route across Siberia was not completely operational. They pointed out that a segment of 1200 miles existed without a suitable airfield, thus precluding the movement of fighters.[35] In Washington, Belyaev himself expressed concern with respect to the operational capacity of the route. On August 31, he informed Arnold that his country could not handle the number of planes originally outlined in the American proposal. Accordingly, the AAF revised the schedule of planes to be flown from 212 to 142 planes per month.[36]

Since Soviet vacillations raised grave doubts about the use of the air corridor, officials in Washington questioned Russian motives in the negotiations in Moscow. Anxious to avoid the possibility that the Russians would either take the promised transports and close the route or continue negotiations in an effort to get more of them, Marshall cabled Bradley that none of the planes would be turned over in Alaska until Alsib was opened as planned.[37]

But Bradley's revelation that the Russians would probably close Alsib after accepting the first group of combat planes forced a complete reappraisal of War Department policy. The AAF urged an end to the negotiations, advising that subsequent deliveries of aircraft could be made in Iran and northern Russia.[38] On October

34. Msg., Bradley to WD, September 24, 1942 (File: Russian Flyaway Cables, AAF, ACAS/MS, in WWIIRD/NA). This was apparently repeated to Bradley on the following day. See "Report of Bradley Mission," TAB I, p. 14.
35. Army Air Forces, Air Transport Command, "Northwest Route," pp. 124-25.
36. Ltr., Belyaev to Arnold, August 31, 1942; memo, Hanley for CG, ATC, September 6, 1942 (File: Russia-1942, ACAS/MS, in WWIIRD/NA).
37. Msg., Marshall to Bradley, September 27, 1942 (File: 452.1 Russia, OPD, WDGS, in WWIIRD/NA).
38. Memo for record (initialed G.E.S.), October 3, 1942 (File: H. H. Arnold Decimal File, 686 Russia, in MD/LC).

134 EAGLES EAST

4, Bradley was told that the United States would not use Alsib to deliver planes to the Russians.[39] Yet, on the same day, Bradley cabled Washington that the Russians had decided to open Alsib and keep it open![40]

Before these policies were reconciled, Bradley, who heroically managed to maintain his professional poise through all this, had conveyed the War Department's decision to close Alsib. This produced so much furor in the Kremlin that a sudden interview was arranged on Soviet initiative between Bradley and Stalin. The Marshal protested that he was genuinely anxious to use the route but that the earlier decision to close it was made because of alleged failure of the AAF to get planes to Alaska. This had no factual basis and Bradley politely but firmly told Stalin so. The War Department's decision to close Alsib, Bradley patiently explained to Stalin, was an excellent example of what could be expected in the future as long as direct contact with responsible Soviet authorities was denied him.[41]

After the War Department had learned of the reversal of Soviet policy, it agreed to open the route and release the transports in Alaska to Soviet crews.[42] On October 9, Bradley formally communicated the War Department's decision to the Russians.[43] Ferrying operations had begun before the official change in the American position had been communicated to Moscow. On September 24, Soviet pilots had arrived in Alaska. After five days of transitional flying, conducted by members of the 7th Ferrying Group, the Russians flew the first group of planes, A-20's, from Fairbanks to Nome. On October 9, the P-40's followed.[44]

The long and difficult negotiations that preceded the opening of the air corridor between the two countries revealed a nagging doubt on the part of the Russians that they would be able to carry out the movement of so many aircraft across Siberia. Once the Russians decided to use Alsib, Bradley felt that they were

39. Msg., Marshall to Bradley, October 4, 1942 (File: 452.1 Russia, OPD, WDGS, in WWIIRD/NA).
40. Msg., Bradley to WD, October 4, 1942 (File: Russian Flyaway Cables, AAF, ACAS/MS, in WWIIRD/NA).
41. "Report of Bradley Mission," TAB V, p. 1.
42. Msg., Marshall to Bradley, October 7, 1942 (File: Russian Flyaway Cables, AAF, ACAS/MS, in WWIIRD/NA).
43. "Report of Bradley Mission," TAB I, p. 11.
44. Army Air Forces, Air Transport Command, "Alaskan Division, Air Transport Command, Historical Record Report," II, 269-72.

The Bradley Mission to Moscow 135

serious about the matter.[45] After his return to Washington he related: "Russian efforts to develop this route to its maximum capacity are continuing with initiative, vigor, and foresight. . . ."[46] His analysis was probably not far from the truth.

Some of Soviet vacillation in opening Alsib can also be attributed to the question of transports, an issue which raised mutual suspicions in the Kremlin and in Washington. When all of the transports had not arrived at Fairbanks, the Russians doubted Washington's commitment; on the other hand, the War Department equally mistrusted the Russians.

Before he flew home, Bradley attempted to pursue the other objective of his mission—extending his conversations to include joint military planning in the Pacific war. Anticipating tangible results of his efforts in this regard, the AAF planned to send a task force to Siberia in the event of Russo-Japanese hostilities. Some members of the General Staff even favored the idea of taking units away from *Bolero*, the code name for the build-up of armed forces in Britain, for this purpose.[47]

During his discussions concerning ferrying operations over Alsib, Bradley did not consider that the time was opportune to bring up the subject of the Pacific.[48] Bradley's meeting with Stalin, however, provided a unique opportunity to raise the question. He conveyed the President's feeling that Japan might attack Russia early in August and his desire that a detailed survey of bases and facilities in Manchuria be made in order to determine the needs of AAF units which could operate there.[49]

Stalin was keenly aware that Japan might attack at any moment but indicated no enthusiasm for American participation on Russian territory in hostilities against the Japanese in the event Russia and Japan went to war. Stalin was more concerned about

45. Minutes, Meeting of the General Council, December 7, 1942 (File: 170.31, in USAF/HA).
46. Ltr., Bradley to Marshall, December 14, 1942, transmitting "Report of Bradley Mission."
47. Memo, Arnold for Marshall, July 24, 1942; memo, Handy for Arnold, August 7, 1942 (File: 145.95, Alaska, May-December 1942, in USAF/HA); R & R, AFAEP for AFADS, September 13, 1942; memo with enclosures Brig. Gen. O. A. Anderson for Assistant Chief of Staff, OPD, Nov 6, 1942 (File: 145.95, Siberia, 1941-1944, in USAF/HA).
48. Msg., Marshall to Bradley, August 31, 1942; msg., Marshall to Bradley, September 9, 1942 (File: 201-Bradley, OPD, WDGS, in WWIIRD/NA).
49. "Report of Bradley Mission," TAB V, pp. 2-3.

136 EAGLES EAST

the Germans in the Caucasus and wanted the aid there. But if Bradley wanted to make the survey of Manchuria, Stalin said he had "no objections."[50]

Stalin assumed a pose of aggrieved resignation in respect to American delays in delivering supplies. With reference to future aid, Stalin hoped "but no longer" expected it. According to Bradley, the Marshal magnanimously displayed "a genuine willingness to afford us every facility for increasing our aid; whether to clear Russia of any blame in case of further failure, or to facilitate our efforts to make good."[51]

In view of Stalin's lack of confidence in American aid efforts, Bradley recommended that no survey of Manchuria be undertaken at that time. As he later explained: "Since we have led the Russians to believe that they will get a great deal more than they have actually obtained, no visits to Manchuria which will involve further commitments should be made until the commitments can be fulfilled."[52]

The War Department's request that he return to Washington for consultation came at an opportune time. The Russians were quite anxious to see Bradley leave and told him so![53]

Bradley still hoped to accomplish something in the way of obtaining information about Manchurian installations. Since he had advised Washington against an inspection of the area at that time, he hoped at least to get second-hand information before he left Russia. He asked Molotov to arrange a conference for him with a SAF officer, but the Commissar affirmed Soviet interest in the Caucasus, not the Far East. Bradley, explaining that a special mission led by Air Marshal R. M. Drummond and Brigadier General Elmer E. Adler was to deal with the question of Anglo-American aid in the Caucasus, pointed out that he was authorized to deal with the Far East with a view to the future. Molotov, not to be outdone by Stalin's frequent references to the deity, replied from the Bible: "Sufficient unto the day are [is] the evils [evil] thereof."[54]

50. *Ibid.*; ltr., Bradley to Marshall, December 14, 1942.
51. "Report of Bradley Mission," TAB V, p. 3.
52. Minutes, Meeting of the General Council, December 7, 1942.
53. Standley, *Admiral Ambassador*, pp. 255-56.
54. "Report of Bradley Mission," TAB VII, pp. 1-2. Also see memo, Thompson for Henderson, November 21, 1942, and Bradley's aide memoire, October 26, 1942, *Foreign Relations*, 1942, III, 660-62.

The Bradley Mission to Moscow   137

For days the Russians did nothing to facilitate Bradley's requests. This was too much for him and so, on November 4 in a letter to Stalin, he expressed his impatience: "In contrast with your expressed wishes regarding my contacts, my previous contact with General Sterligov has been severed and no other officers have been designated. Nine days after my request I have not even been informed when I might expect a reply."

His letter paid dividends. The next day General Korolenko, a stiff unimaginative officer, had been appointed to confer with him.[55] This was the first of several conferences between Soviet and American officers concerning collaboration in the Pacific that resulted in so few substantial results, revealing how chary the Russians were about sharing information with their ally. During the conference on November 11, Korolenko predictably repeated what Molotov had told Bradley earlier. Again Bradley explained that he was authorized only to deal with the question of collaboration in the Far East. Finally, Korolenko provided some general information, mostly known to the AAF, regarding facilities in the Far East. Before the end of the conference, Bradley asked that the Russians forward a study which would be useful in planning future AAF operations from Siberia.[56] Washington presumably is still waiting for it.

After his conference with Korolenko, Bradley boarded a B-24 and departed for home via Alsib. His plane was forced to land at Yakutsk because of mechanical difficulties, and another aircraft took him the rest of the way. The disabled B-24, subsequently transferred to the Soviet Union, was the first heavy bomber that the Russians received from the United States.[57]

Bradley's report brought a flurry of activity in Washington—sparking a Siberian project, code-named *Bazaar*—and led to an important exchange of correspondence between Roosevelt and Stalin. The President promised Stalin that the United States would send an American air force, composed of 100 four-engine bombers, in the event of Russo-Japanese hostilities.

He also asked the Soviet leader that Bradley continue his

55. "Report of Bradley Mission," TAB VII, pp. 1-2.
56. *Ibid.*, TAB VIII, pp. 1-2; ltr., Bradley to Marshall, December 14, 1942; minutes, meeting of the General Council December 7, 1942.
57. Memo, Bradley for Arnold, December 17, 1942 (File: 452.1 Russia, OPD, WDGS, in WWIIRD/NA); ltr., Belyaev to Arnold, February 22, 1943; ltr., Arnold to Belyaev, March 3, 1943 (File: 145.95, in USAF/HA).

138   EAGLES EAST

discussions with Soviet staff officers and that an American survey of Siberian installations be undertaken immediately.[58] Stalin, unimpressed and perhaps dismayed by American pressures, made it clear to the President that the Soviet Union was concerned with the war against Germany, not Japan.[59]

Furthermore, he wrote the President, "What we need is not air force units, but planes without pilots, because we have more than enough pilots of our own. . . ." And he added with a touch of pique, "It should be perfectly obvious that only Russians can inspect Russian military objectives, just as U. S. military objectives can be inspected by none but Americans. There should be no unclarity in this matter."[60] That doomed *Bazaar* to the file cabinet.

Although the United States was unsuccessful in laying the basis for collaboration with the Russians in the Pacific war, it did succeed in opening Alsib for the delivery of Lend-Lease planes. The number ferried over the route during the early months of operations was not impressive. But in time, after certain technical problems were resolved, Alsib became the most used artery for delivering aircraft to the Soviet Union.

58. Msg., Roosevelt to Stalin, December 30, 1942, *Foreign Relations*, 1942, III, 683.
59. Msg., Stalin to Roosevelt, January 13, 1943, Ministry of Foreign Affairs of the U.S.S.R., *Stalin's Correspondence*, II, 50.
60. *Ibid.*

CHAPTER X

The VELVET Project: Hope and Frustration

GIVEN THE WIDELY SEPARATED THEATERS of operation, it was apparent that the most feasible form of military collaboration between the United States and the Soviet Union involved air forces. From the American and British point of view, the employment of Anglo-American air units on the eastern front would not only bolster Soviet military strength but would also solidify the somewhat shaky allied alliance.

By the middle of 1942, London and Washington had endorsed a project, code named *Velvet*, for sending an air armada to the Caucasus. Although military considerations were partially responsible for its formulation, this project had strong political overtones. In July, Churchill and Roosevelt made two crucial decisions which, they felt, would significantly threaten good relations with the Kremlin—namely, the suspension of convoys to north Russia and the postponement of the second front in Europe. *Velvet* was supposed to counteract the effects of these decisions upon the Kremlin.

The idea of establishing direct military relations with the Russians dated back to the early days of the invasion.[1] Russia was so hard pressed that Stalin uncharacteristically accepted British Hurricane units at Archangel[2] and asked Churchill to send additional planes and crews to bomb the Rumanian oil fields from his homeland. Even the United States, not a belligerent yet, was

1. Msg., Churchill to Stalin, July 20, 1941, Churchill, *The Grand Alliance*, pp. 385-86.
2. Military Attaché Report, U.S.S.R., November 1, 1941 (File: 452.1, Deliveries of Planes to Russia, ID, ASF, in WWIIRD/NA); ltr., Zemke to writer, January 28, 1963; Richards and Saunders, *Royal Air Force*, II, 77-80.

139

140   EAGLES EAST

cordially invited to operate "on any part of the Russian front."[3]
After the disastrous loss of sixteen to twenty divisions near Uman
and the impending fall of Kiev, Stalin had very compelling reasons
indeed to ask Churchill on September 15, 1941, that he send twenty-
five or thirty divisions to Archangel or southern Russia, "for
military cooperation with the Soviet troops on Soviet soil in the
same way as was done during the last war in France."[4] But British
military commitments elsewhere prohibited the dispatch of the
sorely needed troops.[5] This, however, did not preclude continued
interest in the idea: Churchill pointed out to Stalin that as soon
as the British cleared the Germans from Libya, "considerable
forces, both air and army" would be available "to cooperate upon
the southern flank of the Russian front."[6] During the Moscow
Conference Stalin again suggested that Britain send troops to the
Ukraine; Lord Beaverbrook replied that forces from his country
were being sent to Iran and some of them might be spared for the
Caucasus. Stalin, not pleased with the suggestion, remarked:
"There is no war in the Caucasus but there is in the Ukraine."[7]

President Roosevelt also took considerable interest in sending
military forces to the eastern front. In May, 1942, he suggested that
American air units be sent to protect the Caucasian oil fields;[8]
General Arnold promptly directed his staff to prepare a study of
the matter.[9]

Before the completion of this study, the War Department
made its first serious attempt at direct air force collaboration with

3. Memo by Hopkins of conference, July 31, 1941, *Foreign Relations*, I, 811, 814.
4. Msg., Stalin to Churchill, September 13, 1941, Ministry of Foreign Affairs of
the U.S.S.R., *Stalin's Correspondence*, I, 24.
5. General Directive by the Prime Minister, September 22, 1941, Churchill,
The Grand Alliance, p. 852.
6. Ltr., Churchill to Stalin, September 21, 1941, Churchill, *The Grand Alliance*,
pp. 465-67.
7. Sherwood, *Roosevelt and Hopkins*, pp. 387-88. Churchill discussed the possibilities of Polish and British forces operating in the Caucasus with Gen.
Wladyslaw Sikorski, President of the Polish Government in Exile. See msg.,
Biddle to Roosevelt and Hull, October 14, 1941; msg., Biddle to Hull, October
24, 1941, *Foreign Relations*, 1941, I, 256. Also see Sikorski's remarks to Stalin
on December 6, 1941, in U. S. House of Representatives, *Polish Documents
Report of the Select Committee on Communist Aggression, 83rd Cong.*, 2nd
Sess., 1954, p. 20.
8. "History, Eastern Command, USSTAF, 1941-45," Ch. I, p. 29 (File: 522.01-1,
in USAF/HA).
9. R & R, AFDAS to AFABI, May 19, 1942 (File: RG 18, Box No. 950, AAF,
in WWIRB/NA).

The Velvet Project

the Soviets. Early in June, the War Department negotiated with Russian officials concerning the use of airfields by the Halverson Detachment, a task force of twenty-three B-24's intended to bolster American air strength in China. Before its departure for the Far East, the Halverson Detachment was to initiate a modest shuttle bombing operation from bases in the Middle East and Russia against the Ploesti oil fields. But approval for the task force to use Russian bases came too late to be of any use. On June 12, the unit conducted its air assault on Ploesti from Middle East bases, thus executing the first AAF mission against a strategic target in German-occupied Europe.[10]

Perhaps the initial blow of the Halverson Detachment against Ploesti would have been followed by the establishment of shuttle bases in the Soviet Union if the mission of this unit had not been suddenly changed. In June, 1942, the success of the *Afrika Korps* confronted the forces of the western allies with an extremely perilous situation. As a consequence, the Detachment was diverted from its original mission to bolster British strength there. American reinforcement of the British position also resulted in siphoning units from the already anemic 10th Air Force in India, and its able commander, Major General L. H. Brereton, was called to command the newly formed Middle East Air Force.[11]

The growth of AAF operations in a theater adjacent to the Soviet front had obvious implications for later operations from Russian bases. The Air Staff recommended that as soon as the conflict in the Middle East abated, the AAF should send two bombardment groups to Soviet bases. These combat groups, the Air Staff advised, could undertake strategic operations against enemy targets in southeastern Europe, principally the Rumanian oil fields. Serious damage to these targets would interrupt the flow of fuel to German armies on the eastern front.[12]

During the latter part of July, 1942, Washington and London

10. Ltr., Marshall to Litvinov, June 4, 1942; ltr., Marshall to Litvinov, June 5, 1942; memo, Eisenhower for Marshall, June 6, 1942 (File: OCS, Russia, in WWIIRD/NA); Wesley Frank Craven and James Lea Cate, *The Army Air Forces in World War II*, Vol. II: *Torch to Pointblank, August 1942-December 1943* (Chicago: The University of Chicago Press, 1949), p. 10.
11. Assistant Chief of Air Staff, "The AAF in the Middle East: A Study of the Origin of the Ninth Air Force" pp. 50-70 (Unpublished official study, in USAF/HA).
12. Memo with study, Col. O. A. Anderson for Arnold, July 3, 1942 (H. H. Arnold Decimal File, 381 War Plans, in MD/LC).

142   EAGLES EAST

decided to suspend convoys to north Russia and to postpone the second front in Europe. This raised the serious question: What could be done to offset the negative effects of these decisions on Anglo-American relations with the Kremlin? Churchill himself suggested the answer when he informed Stalin: "We are studying how to help on your southern flank." He added, "We might be able to send powerful air forces in the autumn to operate on the left of your line."[13] A few days later, he outlined the military values of the project to Anglo-American military representatives attending high-level talks in London.[14] But privately Churchill also elaborated other reasons for the project to Marshall, King, and Hopkins, the President's representatives at the London talks.

Upon their return to Washington, the "Three Musketeers," as they were genially dubbed, related the Prime Minister's views to the President who liked the idea so much that he made it his own.[15] The President believed that the project should not be conditional upon any other operation. Suggesting the salubrious effects of air force assistance on relations with the Russians, he explained: "Russia's need is urgent and immediate. I have a feeling it would mean a great deal to the Russian Army and the Russian people if they knew some of our air force was fighting with them in a very direct manner."[16]

Meanwhile Churchill had decided to go to Moscow and break the news concerning the second front to the sullen Soviet dictator. This was not an easy task and as Churchill himself said: "It was like carrying a large lump of ice to the North Pole."[17] Though there would not be a second front in Europe, the western allies would invade Africa. Churchill hoped this would pacify Stalin. Moreover, the convoys to northern Russia would not be suspended too long. Another convoy, PQ 18, would be sent in September.[18]

13. Msg., Churchill to Stalin, July 17, 1942, Churchill, *The Hinge of Fate*, pp. 267-69.
14. Prime Minister's Notes on Meeting, July 20, 1942, Churchill, *The Hinge of Fate*, p. 446. From London, Hopkins urged the President: "It is also my hope that you will consider putting some of our air squadrons into Russia." See Sherwood, *Roosevelt and Hopkins*. p. 611.
15. Msg., Roosevelt to Churchill, July 28, 1942, Churchill, *The Hinge of Fate*, p. 449.
16. Msg., Roosevelt to Churchill, July 29, 1942, Churchill, *The Hinge of Fate*, p. 272.
17. Churchill, *The Hinge of Fate*, p. 475.
18. Msg., Churchill to Stalin, July 30, 1942, Churchill, *The Hinge of Fate*, pp. 453-54.

The Velvet *Project* 143

And in order to take the edge off Russian disappointments concerning the lack of a second front in Europe and the temporary suspension of convoys to northern Russia, Churchill planned to suggest the idea of British and American air force assistance in the Caucasus.[19]

The unanswered question was: Would Stalin accept these half measures instead of a full resumption of convoys to Russia and an invasion of Europe in 1942? Churchill and Roosevelt hoped so. During Churchill's first meeting with Stalin, the Soviet Marshal was glum over the news that the second front was to be postponed. But his spirits noticeably improved when he learned about western plans to invade North Africa.[20] Then the Prime Minister suggested the idea of sending air force assistance to the Soviet front. Averell Harriman, who joined Churchill in the Middle East and accompanied him to Moscow, described this aspect of the meeting to the President:

> the Prime Minister brought the discussion back to the Russian front stating that you [Roosevelt] and he were exploring the possibility of sending an air force to the South Russia [*sic*] front but only after Rommel was defeated. He asked how such a suggestion would be received by Stalin. Stalin's answer was brief and simple, 'I would gratefully accept it.'[21]

On the following day, the Prime Minister's meeting was tense and difficult. Stalin, who said many disagreeable things, presented an aide-memoire in which the failure to open a second front in Europe in 1942 was described as a "moral blow" to Soviet public opinion.[22] He suggested that British fear dictated the decision and promptly criticized the failures of his allies to deliver Lend-Lease supplies.[23]

Before the conclusion of the talks, British, Soviet, and American military leaders explored the question of air force operations in Russia. Although most of the discussions centered on the second front, a matter constantly urged by Soviet military authorities,

---

19. Msg., Churchill to Roosevelt, December 3, 1942 (File: H. H. Arnold Special-Official File, 1941-45, E-W, in MD/LC).
20. Churchill, *The Hinge of Fate*, pp. 477-83.
21. Msg., Harriman to Roosevelt, August 13 and 14, 1942, *Foreign Relations*, 1942, III, 620.
22. Aide-Memoire, Stalin to Churchill and Harriman, August 13, 1942, *Foreign Relations*, 1942, III, 621-22.
23. Churchill, *The Hinge of Fate*, p. 486.

144   EAGLES EAST

Field Marshal Sir Alan Brooke, Chief of the Imperial General
Staff, introduced the question of direct air force assistance on the
eastern front. The Russian representatives, Marshal Kliment E.
Voroshilov and Marshal Boris M. Shaposhnikov, favorably received
the idea and repeatedly asked how many planes would be involved
in the operation. No definite reply could be made since a definite
offer had not been made yet to the Soviet government. All that
the military representatives could do was to agree that staff studies
be undertaken as soon as the question had been approved by their
governments.[24]

Churchill left Moscow with considerable anxiety about Stalin's
faith in the West. Although allegedly encouraged by his visit,
the Prime Minister found it necessary to suggest that the President
send a "consoling or heartening message" to the Soviet chief.[25]
Roosevelt obliged by informing Stalin that supplies were moving
forward and that "We are coming as quickly and as strongly to
your assistance as we possibly can. . . ." The President, too,
betrayed his anxiety when he added: "I hope that you will believe
me when I tell you this."[26]

The dubious success of his mission to Moscow convinced the
Prime Minister that it was necessary to "aid Russia to the very
limits of our power."[27] Direct air force assistance seemed the
quickest and best way to prove good faith. The Prime Minister
outlined the details of *Velvet* in a lengthy message to Roosevelt
on August 30. Sending an Anglo-American air force to southern
Russia, Churchill declared, "must be viewed as a long-term policy
in our co-operation with Russia and for the defense of the Persian
oil fields." Other military reasons included strengthening Russian
air power "generally," forming "the advance shield" of Anglo-
American interests in Iran, and wearing down the Luftwaffe. But
there were political reasons for sending the force. Churchill made
it clear that the benefits of "moral effect of comradeship with the
Russians" would be "out of all proportion to the forces

24. Maj. Gen. Follett Bradley and Maj. Gen. Russell L. Maxwell represented
the United States in the Anglo-American-Soviet military discussions. Msg.,
Maxwell to Marshall, August 31, 1942; notes on Moscow Conference by Maxwell, August 17, 1942 (File: 168.605, in USAF/HA. Hereinafter cited as Adler
File).
25. Msg., Churchill to Roosevelt, August 16, 1942, Churchill, *The Hinge of
Fate*, p. 502; *Foreign Relations*, 1942, III, 626, footnote 29.
26. Msg., Roosevelt to Stalin, August 19, 1942, *Foreign Relations*, 1942, III, 626.
27. Churchill, *The Hinge of Fate*, p. 563.

The Velvet *Project*   145

employed."[28] Thus he stamped *Velvet* with distinct political overtones which assumed increasing significance in Anglo-American
military relations with the Kremlin.

After outlining the composition, strength and employment
of the projected air force, he urged that American and British air
officers be dispatched "forthwith" to prepare the way for the air
force. "It is urgently important," Churchill declared, "that this be
put in hand without delay."[29]

The President's earlier enthusiasm for the project, however,
had cooled. Before the Prime Minister's return to London, the
President had asked the War Department to explore the merits
of sending air units to the Caucasus. He was not so sure Britain
should join in the operation. "If such an enterprise could be
accomplished," he asked Marshall, "would it be advisable to have
British air [*sic*] also represented?"[30] A few days later, Marshall
advised against sending an American air force to the Caucasus in
1942; the earliest that a balanced air force could be sent was
January, 1943. But this still would involve diverting air strength
from other operations which were more urgent. Moreover, weather
conditions in the Caucasus would leave only a few months of
continuous air operations. In addition, the air force would have
to be supplied by facilities in Iran, thus inevitably reducing the
flow of Lend-Lease through that region to Russia. Marshall recommended, therefore, that the question of sending the AAF to the
Caucasus be tabled. However, if the project materialized in the
future, he believed British participation was necessary.[31]

Thus by the time Churchill's urgent message concerning
Velvet arrived, the White House was not so anxious to push it.
Although the President was in full accord with the desirability
of the projected air operations,[32] he was reluctant to make a formal
proposal to Stalin yet. As a consequence, Churchill was unable
to follow up his earlier suggestion to Stalin by making a firm
offer of Anglo-American air force assistance. All he could do was

28. Msg., Churchill to Roosevelt, August 30, 1942, Churchill, *The Hinge of
Fate*, p. 564.
29. *Ibid.*, pp. 564-66.
30. Memo, Roosevelt for Marshall, August 21, 1942 (File: OCS, Russia, in
WWIIRD/NA).
31. Memo, Marshall for Roosevelt, August 29, 1942 (File: OCS, Russia, in
WWIIRD/NA).
32. Msg., Roosevelt to Churchill, August 31, 1942, Churchill, *The Hinge of
Fate*, p. 566.

146 EAGLES EAST

assure the Soviet chief that the matter was under study in Washington.[33]

The results of a subsequent War Department review of *Velvet* did not augur well for American participation in the project. Now Marshall was even more strongly opposed to American involvement in the operation and suggested it should be entirely a British affair. Conveying his doubts about the strategic value of sending American units so far afield, he said: "The use of available American Air Forces in the Caucasus is not likely to contribute more decisively to the success of our major strategic efforts than their use, or their retention for future use, in some other theater."[34] When the battle for Egypt permitted a diversion of air strength, Marshall wanted British units sent to the Caucasus while the AAF took their place in Egypt. In this way, American units in Egypt would be readily available to help *Torch* if they were needed. Moreover, said Marshall, concentration of the AAF in one theater would increase their combat efficiency and simplify supply and maintenance problems. After advancing these military reasons against involvement in the project, he questioned the political motives for sending the air force:

> Whereas the British, for political reasons, may feel obligated to send combat forces to fight beside the Russians for 'moral effect of comradeship,' our past and present policy of extending lend-lease [*sic*] aid to Russia to the fullest extent possible would seem to obviate the necessity for our sending combat troops for political or ideological reasons. So far as possible we should endeavor to deal with the military realities.[35]

Despite Marshall's eloquent exposition, the political aspects of the project could not be ignored, especially after the British decided to stop sending convoys to northern Russia for the remainder of the year. Suspension was necessary because of the critical need for warships for the forthcoming invasion of North Africa.[36] Hopkins thought the decision should be cushioned by a

33. Msg., Churchill to Stalin, September 6, 1942, Churchill, *The Hinge of Fate*, p. 568.
34. Memo, Marshall for Roosevelt, September 18, 1942 (File: OCS, Russia, in WWIIRD/NA). Also see memo, Col. F. N. Roberts and Col. Joseph Smith for Chief, Strategy and Policy Group, September 3, 1942, in Adler File.
35. *Ibid.*
36. Msg., Churchill to Roosevelt, September 22, 1942, Churchill, *The Hinge of Fate*, p. 572.

The Velvet *Project*   147

definite offer of air force aid. "If we must now tell Stalin that the convoys on the northern route are to be discontinued," he stated, "then it seems to me that it is almost imperative that we make a direct and firm offer to place our armed forces at his side in Russia against Germany."[37] Roosevelt agreed; he urged Churchill to defer making the announcement that the next convoy would not sail until they were in a position to offer Stalin the air force. But he was not ready to make a definite decision until he consulted again with the War Department.[38]

Meanwhile the ominous tremors emanating from Moscow spurred action on *Velvet*. While the Soviet press hammered away at the theme of a second front in Europe, Stalin criticized Anglo-American aid to his country. Churchill's mid-August visit did not end exhortations for another front in Europe.[39] When Wendell Willkie went on a goodwill mission to Moscow in September, he found that the theme of the second front was sung by Soviet official and muzhik alike. And Willkie joined in the chorus.[40] As one observer aptly put it: "Moscow was a buyers' market in the autumn of 1942. The Soviets were selling the second front 1942, preferred."[41]

Stalin's bitter remarks regarding western aid revealed the surly mood of the Kremlin. During a banquet held in Willkie's honor, Stalin proposed a toast—no doubt calculated to cause a great stir abroad. The toast began appropriately enough with a salute to the "airmen of the United Nations." Then he criticized Britain and the United States for not sending better planes. "The American Government," he stated, "has furnished the Soviets P-40 fighters not Aircobras [*sic*]; the British have supplied Hurricanes, not Spitfires. Both of these aircraft," he added caustically, "are inferior to German fighters they have to meet in combat." The

37. Msg., Hopkins to Roosevelt, September 22, 1942, Sherwood, *Roosevelt and Hopkins*, p. 638.
38. Msg., Roosevelt to Churchill, September 27, 1942, Churchill, *The Hinge of Fate*, p. 573.
39. Since Churchill's visit to Moscow, Ambassador Standley reported the persistent efforts of the Soviet press to keep the issue of the second front alive. See memo, Sands for Chief, Intelligence Group, August 27, 1942 (File: 170.22781, in USAF/HA).
40. Memo, by Standley, undated, unsigned, *Foreign Relations*, 1942, III, 637-39,647; interview with Maj. Richard T. Kight, November 12, 1942 (File: 300.601-5, in USAF/HA).
41. Henry C. Cassidy, *Moscow Dateline, 1941-1943* (Boston: Houghton Mifflin Co., 1943), p. 255.

148　　　　　　　　　　　　EAGLES EAST

Soviet Union, he bemoaned, did not understand "why some of these better planes aren't supplied to the Red Air Force."[42] After delivering this part of the toast, the Soviet chief attacked the British for their alleged failure to deliver 150 Airacobras, originally allocated to the Soviet Union. He neglected to mention, however, that the Russians had agreed earlier to the diversion of the planes to Britain.[43]

This episode was followed by another which confirmed Stalin's displeasure with western aid. On October 2, Henry Cassidy, Chief of the Moscow Bureau of the Associated Press, addressed a letter to Stalin, containing several questions about Lend-Lease. Stalin replied immediately, bluntly stating that assistance to the Russians was quite ineffective. But, he added, it could be improved if Britain and the United States fulfilled their obligations fully and promptly.[44]

Stalin's outbursts revealed the gloomy state of relations with Moscow. White House fears of Russo-German peace terms lay behind the urgency which the President now ascribed to *Velvet* and to the renewal of convoys. On October 5, the President informed Churchill: "We should make a firm commitment to put an air force in the Caucasus, and that operation should not be contingent on any other." He agreed with Churchill that everything be done to help:

> The Russian front is today our greatest reliance, and we simply must find a direct manner in which to help them other than our diminishing supplies. We shall on our part undertake to replace in the Middle East all of our own planes which are transferred, and assist you in every way possible with your air problems in the Middle East.

The President advised the Prime Minister to reverse his decision regarding convoys to northern Russia by sending the next one in successive groups with reduced escorts. "I think it better," he

42. Standley and Ageton, *Admiral Ambassador to Russia*, pp. 287-88; memo by Standley, undated, unsigned, *Foreign Relations*, 1942, III, 643.
43. Stalin was referring to the planes originally committed by Britain to Russia but diverted to the AAF in Britain in order to prepare units for the impending invasion of North Africa. The planes were to be repaid to the Russians as follows: 60 in October, 70 in November and 46 in December. See msg., Hopkins to Faymonville, October 5, 1942; memo, Edward Page for R. Atherton, November 12, 1942, *Foreign Relations*, 1942, III, 728, 745. Also see p. 745, footnote 63.
44. Quoted in Cassidy, *Moscow Dateline*, pp. 271-76.

The Velvet Project

149

stated, "that we take this risk than endanger our whole relations with Russia at this time." The President urged Churchill that both of them send similar messages to Stalin which "should be so phrased as to leave a good taste in his mouth."[45]

Churchill did not share the President's apprehensions. The Russians were angry, he observed, "but they were by no means in despair." *Velvet* had to be implemented but not before the battle in Egypt had been decided. The Germans, he warned, might "pull their Air Force off Russia and turn it on Egypt." Moreover, he added, "there is also the probability that they will be forced anyway to turn a large proportion on to *Torch*." For all the talk about immediate and unconditional employment of the combined air force, the President said nothing definite about the exact composition of the American contingent.

Opposing the President's proposal of floating the next convoy in successive groups, Churchill believed the best that could be done was to send a few individual ships. And Stalin, he said, should be told just that. If the United States and Britain offered *Velvet*, increased aircraft deliveries, and sent individual ships via north Russia, these measures, said Churchill, would "be sufficient to bridge the gap before *Torch* opens."[46]

Soviet criticisms merged curiously now with appeals for greater aircraft deliveries. The situation in the vicinity of Stalingrad had worsened. This was allegedly due to the large number of planes which the Luftwaffe deployed there. "We were short of fighters with which to cover our ground forces," Stalin complained. "Even the bravest troops are helpless without air cover. What we need particularly is Spitfires and Aircobras [*sic*]." In order to cope with the emergency, Stalin agreed to replace deliveries of tanks and guns for a time by increases in aircraft. He wanted Britain to send 300 and the United States to send 500 planes each month.[47]

Stalin's appeals were the catalyst which activated policy on *Velvet*. On October 9, Churchill and Roosevelt replied to the Kremlin. Churchill's message specifically dealt with three major

45. Msg., Roosevelt to Churchill, October 5, 1942, Churchill, *The Hinge of Fate*, pp. 576-77.
46. Msg., Churchill to Roosevelt, October 7, 1942, Churchill, *The Hinge of Fate*, p. 578.
47. Msg., Stalin to Churchill, October 3, 1942; ltr., Stalin to Roosevelt, October 7, 1942, Ministry of Foreign Affairs of the U.S.S.R., *Stalin's Correspondence*, I, 70; II, 35-36.

150 EAGLES EAST

questions—the *Velvet* project, the Soviet request for additional aircraft, and the question of convoys. The Prime Minister assured Stalin that orders had been issued to assemble the Anglo-American air force in southern Russia "so that they would be available for combat early in the New Year." Britain also planned to send 150 Spitfires above protocol commitments. Regarding the convoy situation, the Prime Minister informed Stalin that the shortage of warships prevented the dispatch of large scale convoys to northern Russia until January, 1943. Until then, most of these ships would be used for *Torch*.[48]

The President cautiously awaited the advice of the War Department before making a specific commitment of aircraft resources. Unlike the Prime Minister, the President merely told Stalin, "We are going to move as rapidly as possible to place an air force under your strategic command in the Caucasus." He also assured the Soviet chief of his efforts in searching for additional planes.[49]

Roosevelt was most anxious to follow up his message with a definite response to the requests for additional aircraft.[50] But he would not act until Marshall and others in the War Department told him what could be spared. Predictably Marshall objected strongly to the idea of increasing deliveries to the Russians. He warned that if these planes were taken from AAF units, it could negatively affect preparations for *Torch*. Again he returned to the position of the War Department—direct American military operations in the West would be the most effective kind of aid to Russia. Taking planes, as the President suggested, from coastal defense units was not an answer because they were unsuitable for operations in active combat theaters. Even if they were sent the United States would be inadequately protected against a possible surprise attack by enemy carriers. In lieu of sending additional planes, Marshall departed from his earlier position and recommended that the United States commit one heavy bombardment group to *Velvet*.[51]

48. Msg., Churchill to Stalin, October 9, 1942, Churchill, *The Hinge of Fate*, pp. 579-80.
49. Msg., Roosevelt to Stalin, October 9, 1942, *Foreign Relations*, 1942, III, 731.
50. Ltr., Hopkins to Marshall, October 10, 1942 (File: OCS, Russia, in WWIIRD/NA).
51. Memo, Marshall for Roosevelt, October 10, 1942 (File: OCS, Russia, in WWIIRD/NA).

The Velvet Project 151

Unable to find additional planes for the Russians, the President now wanted to initiate *Velvet* without delay. On October 12, he cabled Stalin: "Our heavy bombardment group has been ordered mobilized immediately for the purpose of operating on your southern flank." In sharp contrast to Churchill's position regarding the execution of *Velvet,* Roosevelt announced that the operation would not be contingent on any other.[52] Stalin, unimpressed with the promises, replied to the Prime Minister with a curt: "Thank you." To the President, Stalin was almost as brief. "I am grateful for the information," he said.[53]

Meanwhile British and American air staffs worked out detailed plans for the projected air force. By October 7, the AAF had a plan for the activation of the 376th Bombardment Group. Equipped with B-24's, the group was to be formed out of General Brereton's command and augmented by personnel and equipment from the United States. It would operate in the Middle East while awaiting transfer to the Caucasus. In addition to this combat group, the AAF plan also called for the organization of a transport group. On October 12, Arnold conveyed his plan to Air Marshal D. C. S. Evill.[54]

A week later, Evill submitted the British conception of the project which had been outlined earlier by the Prime Minister to the President. British units of the combined air force would include 1 long-range and 8 short-range fighter squadrons, 3 light bomber squadrons, and 2 medium bomber squadrons—a contribution of 252 combat planes. Since Britain would provide most of the combat strength, the London plan called for an Air Marshal to command the air force. Operating under the strategic control of the Russian High Command, the air force would support ground forces, attack land and sea communications in the Black Sea area, maintain control of the Caspian Sea, and protect such vital areas as Batum and Baku.[55]

The British urged that as soon as Stalin accepted the offer,

52. Msg., Roosevelt to Stalin, October 12, 1942, *Foreign Relations,* 1942, III, 733-34.
53. Msg., Stalin to Churchill, October 13, 1942; msg., Stalin to Roosevelt, October 15, 1942, Ministry of Foreign Affairs of the U.S.S.R., *Stalin's Correspondence,* I, 72; II, 37.
54. Memo, Anderson for Arnold, October 7, 1942; ltr., Arnold to Air Marshal D. C. S. Evill, October 12, 1942 in Adler File.
55. Ltr., with enclosures, Evill to Arnold, October 19, 1942, in Adler File.

152 EAGLES EAST

a joint mission be sent to Moscow in order to work out detailed arrangements with Soviet military officials concerning the operations of the air force and the facilities that it would require. Evill expected British units to assemble at Tehran by mid-January, 1943.[56]

The War Department tentatively accepted the British proposals but raised some objections on the subject of command. Despite the impressive number of planes which Britain planned to send, Arnold believed that by the time *Velvet* went into operation the AAF would probably be forced to provide most of the combat strength. That would require the appointment of an American commander, but the matter was not pressed.[57] As Anglo-American leaders fully realized, *Velvet* had yet to pass the first and the most critical step on the ladder to success—official Soviet acceptance of the offer.[58]

Since the idea was first suggested, Stalin curiously avoided references to the project in his correspondence with Churchill and Roosevelt. Yet, on October 6, Stalin told Major General Follett Bradley, who was on a special mission in Russia, that he was interested in Anglo-American air operations in the Caucasus. He even authorized Bradley to conduct a survey of the area where the air force was to operate.[59] Three weeks later, Molotov conferred with Bradley and again expressed Soviet interest in *Velvet*. Bradley replied that the survey of the Caucasus, promised earlier by Stalin, was necessary before actual air force operations began. Molotov, instead of facilitating the survey, expressed disappointment with western delays.[60]

But Stalin continued to remain non-committal about the projected air force in his correspondence with Churchill and Roosevelt. The Prime Minister decided to take the initiative and get a definite statement from him; on November 5, he cabled a desire to base twenty British and American squadrons in southern Russia as soon as possible. Before this could be done, the Prime Minister

56. *Ibid.*
57. Matloff and Snell, *Strategic Planning for Coalition Warfare*, p. 333.
58. Ltr., Arnold to Evill, November 2, 1942, in Adler File.
59. Since August, 1942, Bradley had been negotiating with the Russians to open Alsib for the delivery of Lend-Lease planes to the Soviet Union. Report of Bradley's Mission to Russia, July 26-December 3, 1942, TAB 5 (File: 201-Bradley, OPD, WDGS, in WWIIRD/NA).
60. Memo, Llewellyn Thompson for Henderson, November 21, 1942, *Foreign Relations*, 1942, III, 660-61; report of Bradley Mission, TAB 7, pp. 1-2.

The Velvet Project   153

pointed out that arrangements should be made between the military representatives of their countries.[61] Three days later, Stalin finally accepted, noting that the squadrons would be a very valuable help. He also permitted western representatives to come to Russia in order to work out the necessary arrangements concerning facilities, logistics, and operations.[62]

By early November the contingencies delaying implementation of *Velvet* had been removed. Stalin had accepted the air force. And the battle of Egypt, which had turned in favor of the Allies, now allowed the release of units for service in the Caucasus. In order to decide final plans with the Russians concerning operations, a British officer, Air Marshal Sir R. M. Drummond, was appointed to head a mission to Moscow. Brigadier General Elmer E. Adler, Commanding General of the 9th Air Service Command, was his American counterpart.

The Drummond-Adler mission departed Cairo by air on November 16 but was delayed en route due to bad weather. From Kuibyshev, the last leg of the journey was made by train. The thirty-eight hour trip from Kuibyshev to Moscow was grueling. Travelling in sub-zero cold in an unlit and unheated train which moved at a snail's pace, the members of the mission took to vodka and song to keep them warm. Finally, on November 21, they arrived in Moscow.[63]

In no particular hurry to begin meetings, the Russians convened the first session in the late afternoon on November 22, twenty-seven hours after the mission arrived.[64] During this session, Lieutenant General Fedor Falalaev, Chief of Staff of the Soviet Air Force, gave the impression that he had never heard of the Anglo-American offer to send the air force. Air Marshal Drummond, who conducted most of the discussions with Falalaev, had to outline the nature and scope of the whole project. To the surprise of Drummond and Adler, Falalaev acted like a man who searched for

61. Msg., Churchill to Stalin, November 5, 1942, Ministry of Foreign Affairs of the U.S.S.R., *Stalin's Correspondence*, I, 73.
62. Msg., Stalin to Churchill, November 8, 1942, Ministry of Foreign Affairs of the U.S.S.R., *Stalin's Correspondence*, I, 74.
63. Notes on Moscow Conferences, November 27, 1942; ltr., Adler to Mrs. Adler, November 27, 1942, in Adler File. The notes which Adler prepared while he was in Moscow have been edited by Maurer Maurer, "Notes on Velvet: General Adler's mission to Moscow, 1942," *The Airpower Historian*, IX (July, 1962), pp. 141-50. The unedited version has been used here.
64. Notes on Moscow Conferences, November 27, 1942, in Adler File.

154   EAGLES EAST

reasons to delay or scuttle the operation. The matter could not be delayed too long, Drummond warned, because it was necessary to supply the bases with 30,000 tons of materiel before combat units could be moved to them. Since supplies had to come via the route used to send Lend-Lease, Drummond advanced a formula which would substantially reduce the interference with the flow of this aid. If 500 tons of supplies each day were sent to the bases, the requisite total would have been reached at the end of two months. When this supply operation had been completed, then the combat units could be moved. Russian reservations about the effects of these supply operations upon the flow of Lend-Lease prompted Adler to suggest a modification of the plan—the American bombardment group might operate from North Africa instead of the Caucasus. In this way, Adler explained, supply and maintenance problems would be considerably reduced.[65]

Russian negotiators could not believe that the Allies were simply going to send an air force to help them. There had to be other motives. The air force would be a substitute for Lend-Lease, they suggested. No, they were assured. The meeting ended on a note of Russian suspicion.[66]

The inconclusive results of the first meeting were matched by those of the second which convened two days later. The Russians again expressed no particular interest in the air force and instead, offered a few of their own proposals. In view of the fact that the required tonnage to sustain the force would interfere to some extent with Lend-Lease deliveries, Falalaev proposed that Britain and the United States simplify matters by sending planes without the crews. Drummond and Adler could not discuss the Soviet proposal because they were authorized only to complete arrangements on the original Anglo-American offer—presumably accepted by Stalin. Drummond informed the Russians that their proposal had to be taken up at the highest level—by Stalin with Churchill and Roosevelt.[67]

65. Notes of Anglo-American Conversation with Russian High Command, November, 1942, First Meeting, in Adler File. During this meeting, Adler asked himself if *Velvet* was "symbolic—a gesture only." Handwritten notes by Adler in Adler File.
66. Notes of Anglo-American Conversation with Russian High Command, November, 1942, First Meeting.
67. Anglo-American Conversations with Soviet High Command, Second Meeting, November 24, 1942, in Adler File.

The Velvet *Project*   155

The Soviet maneuver raised the question as to whether the Russians had already decided to reject the proffered air force. Drummond pointedly asked Falalaev if this were so, but the Russian said nothing because he probably did not know himself. And so the negotiations dragged on the basis of the original Anglo-American offer.[68] Drummond and Adler mistakenly assumed that the Russians would convey their proposal through diplomatic channels to Churchill and Roosevelt, while they reported the new developments to military authorities in London and Washington.[69]

The results of the meetings of the technical committee, which explored various problems on a lower level, were also unproductive. Russian officers were reluctant to divulge pertinent information to their western colleagues until the Kremlin granted definite authorization to allow the foreigners to operate in the Caucasus.[70]

Drummond and Adler got the impression that Russian military men appreciated the values of Anglo-American air force operations but could not make a commitment until the political factors were solved. On his part, Adler was particularly impressed by the military advantages of strategic operations from Caucasian bases against targets in eastern Europe.[71] It will be recalled that during the first meeting Adler had suggested that the American group operate from bases in North Africa in order to simplify supply matters. But after a map of the Caucasus had been exhibited during the second meeting he became quite enthusiastic over the possibilities of AAF operations from the Soviet Union. He advised Marshall that the Soviet plan—if accepted by Washington and London—be modified to the extent of granting the AAF and RAF the right to use air bases in southern Russia for assaults against targets in southeastern Europe.[72] "In many ways," Adler remarked, "the territory [Caucasus] is to Central Europe as Vladivostok is to Tokyo."[73]

But the failure to complete arrangements on the basis of the Anglo-American offer irked the westerners. As Adler observed:

68. *Ibid.*
69. Notes on Moscow Conferences, November 27, 1942; msg., Adler to Marshall, November 25, 1942, in Adler File.
70. Notes on Moscow Conferences, November 27, 1942.
71. *Ibid.*, ltr., Drummond to Air Chief Marshal Sir Charles Portal, December 17, 1942, in Adler File.
72. Msg., Adler to Marshall, November 27, 1942, in Adler File.
73. Notes on Moscow Conferences, November 28, 1942.

156 EAGLES EAST

> The Mission feels that it is being treated in something of a cavalier manner. Our respective governments are not asking for any concrete items but instead are attempting to deliver a potent force to the area to assist in winning the war. The force offered is practically the same size as the force which won the battle of Egypt. It is composed of veterans.[74]

To Mrs. Adler the General was more candid. "You would think," he said, "that we were asking for something instead of trying to give."[75]

The Russians continued negotiations but not with the purpose of completing arrangements on the Anglo-American offer. During the next meeting on November 28, the Russians repeated their proposal that Britain and the United States send the planes assigned to the air force but without the crews. Then they made a staggering announcement: they had not conveyed this proposal through diplomatic channels, as had been assumed, and expected the mission to handle the matter. When Drummond pointed out that time would be required to get a definite reply from Washington and London, Falalaev complained about western delays in implementing the project. This was too much for even the phlegmatic Drummond who quickly retorted that the proposed air force was to begin operations in 1943, not 1942. Any delays in the matter, Drummond fired back, were due to Moscow's failures to respond to the original offer.[76]

After this exchange Falalaev advanced another proposal which revealed that the Russians were well aware of the political aspects of the project. The West could demonstrate its solidarity with the Soviet Union, he stated, by providing planes and air crews for integration into the Soviet Air Force. This proposal, although closer in agreement with the Anglo-American offer, still would have destroyed the unity of the air force. Until the mission received definite instructions from London and Washington, Drummond asked clearance to survey the Caucasus, but the Russians refused until the entire matter of Anglo-American air operations had been definitely decided. And so the third meeting ended without results.[77]

74. *Ibid.*
75. Ltr., Adler to Mrs. Adler, November 27, 1942.
76. Anglo-American Conversations with Soviet High Command, Third Meeting, November 28, 1942, in Adler File.
77. *Ibid.*

The Velvet *Project* 157

Drummond and Adler found themselves in an awkward situation. They had been authorized to settle technical details on a project which, everyone assumed, Stalin had accepted. After three meetings it was apparent that Moscow had no intention of accepting the air force, preferring instead the planes without the crews. As a concession, however, the Kremlin appeared to be willing to accept Anglo-American air units which would be integrated within the Soviet Air Force. The mission conveyed the Soviet proposals to London and Washington, still naively predicting that the Russians would probably accept the Anglo-American offer if their governments remained firm.[78]

There was one more meeting with the Russians. Drummond hoped it might be one in which the discussions would be informal. "Instead," Adler wrote, "again [it] was formal and nothing happened." This time the Russians offered a military reason for their reluctance to accept the western offer. Committing the entire air force to the Caucasus, the Russians argued, prevented effective utilization of some of its strength to cope with immediate situations elsewhere on the front. From a military point of view the argument had some merit because the Russians could attach their combat units to ground forces while *Velvet* groups would have to make a complete move.[79] Adler wrote: "I grow more and more convinced that for sound military reasons the Russians are right in their views."[80] But the principal point behind the project was not military anyway.

London and Washington reviewed the Soviet offers and finally rejected them. The British believed that acceptance of the proposals compromised the "overriding political benefits which were the object of the original plan [*Velvet*]." In the best statement of the political benefits which had been originally envisaged, London advised Drummond:

> It was hoped that by sending [the] 'Velvet' force to [the] Caucasus an example would be given of Allied forces working hand in hand with the Russians for the same military objectives and under unity of strategic control on a bigger scale

78. Msg., Drummond to Air Ministry, November 28, 1942; msg., Adler to Marshall, December 2, 1942, in Adler File.
79. Notes on Moscow Conferences, December 5, 1942 and December 9, 1942, in Adler File.
80. Notes on Moscow Conferences, December 9, 1942, in Adler File.

158   EAGLES EAST

than anything yet attempted. Not only would there have
been practical cooperation on a considerable scale but there
might also have developed a genuine spirit of comradeship in
arms which would have opened up considerable possibilities
in the political and military fields.[81]

To accept the Soviet proposals, then, "would destroy the
whole *raison d'etre* of the plan." This was Churchill's sentiment.
He informed the President that in view of successes in North
Africa and the improved military situation for the Russians in the
Caucasus, it was unnecessary "to force upon them what it costs us
so much to give."[82] The urgency behind *Velvet* had ceased to exist.

Sound military reasons existed for not accepting the Soviet
proposals. To send planes without crews meant in effect an increase
in American aircraft allocations to the Russians. As one member
of the War Department put it: aircraft commitments to the Soviet
Union were "already strangling us."[83] Moreover, as the Combined
Chiefs of Staff informed the mission, giving the Russians planes
without crews would break up the existing strength of combat
units.[84] Regarding the proposal to merge American units within
the SAF, the Combined Chiefs anticipated too many practical
difficulties: "Mixing air crews of different nationalities in one unit
was an unworkable arrangement."[85] The Combined Chiefs forwarded their objections to Adler and Drummond with a statement
that the original western offer still stood.[86]

The Drummond-Adler mission conveyed the rejection of the
Soviet proposals and repeated the original western offer. The Russians, in turn, rejected the Anglo-American offer and adhered to
their own proposals. This reply was so indecisive that the mission
was forced again to ask for a conference in order to determine

81. Msg., Churchill to Roosevelt, December 3, 1942, with enclosed messages
from London to Drummond (File: H. H. Arnold Special-Official File, 1941-45,
E.W., in MD/LC).
82. *Ibid.*
83. Memo, Brig. Gen. St. Clair Street for Arnold, November 30, 1942 (File: H.
H. Arnold Special-Official File, 1941-45, E.W, in MD/LC).
84. Memo, Arnold for Brig. Gen. John R. Deane, November 30, 1942 (File:
H. H. Arnold Special-Official File, 1941-45, E-W, in MD/LC); msg., Air
Ministry to Drummond, December 10, 1942 (Similar message to Adler), in Adler
File.
85. Memo, Arnold for Deane, December 1, 1942 (File: RG 18, Box 950, AAF,
in WWIRB/NA).
86. Msg., Air Ministry to Drummond, December 10, 1942.

The Velvet *Project*   159

positively whether the Russians wanted the air force.[87] Late in the evening of December 13, Molotov summoned Drummond to the Kremlin, where he personally confirmed Soviet rejection of the Anglo-American air force. Molotov advanced two reasons for the decision—namely, that too much time had elapsed since the original offer was made, and that supplies for the contingent would interfere with the flow of Lend-Lease to Russia via Iran. The first reason was unconvincing since the Russians had delayed the implementation of *Velvet* by offering counter-proposals after they accepted the western offer. When Drummond pressed him on the second one, Molotov was evasive at the outset but finally made a startling admission. Even if there were little interference with the flow of Lend-Lease, he said, the Soviet Union could not accept the air force. Drummond wrote glumly to London: "They never intended to proceed with the project."[88] Soon the Russians made it clear that negotiations concerning the project had been completed: Adler and Drummond were asked to leave the country! Understandably embarrassed, they wanted instructions to depart from Moscow. Adler, however, was ordered to remain until the Soviet proposals were reconsidered in Washington.[89] Unable to understand what the mission could accomplish further, Adler was concerned about injury to western prestige. "The Russians have said they don't want us any more," he wrote. "We give the impression of hanging around in a begging mood and no matter what happens now the aces are held by the Russians." He remarked a little later that "A continuation of our stay here will only lose prestige for the two governments."[90]

The President was reluctant to drop the project until he received final word from Stalin himself. In a message to the Marshal on December 16, the President departed from the decision

87. Msg., Adler to Marshall, December 14, 1942; ltr., Maj. Gen. A. V. Nikitin to Drummond, December 13, 1942; Notes on Moscow Conferences, December 17, 1942, in Adler File.
88. Msg., Drummond to Air Ministry, December 13, 1942, in Adler File. Soviet rejection of *Velvet* sparked several alternatives, one of which called for sending a bomb group to Aleppo. It was expected the group could operate against Rumanian oil targets and bolster America's position in the Levant. Memo, Col. C. P. Cabell for Arnold, December 16, 1942 (File: H. H. Arnold File, in MD/LC).
89. Msg., Drummond to Air Ministry, December 16, 1942; msg., Adler to Marshall, December 19, 1942; notes on Moscow Conferences, December 17 and 19, 1942, in Adler File.
90. Notes on Moscow Conferences, December 17 and 19, 1942.

160 EAGLES EAST

of the Combined Chiefs of Staff by not insisting that the air force operate as a separate entity under one commander. Instead he told Stalin that he was "fully willing to send units with American pilots and crews." He added: "I think they should operate by units under their American commanders, but each group would, of course, be under overall Russian command as to tactical objectives."[91] In other words, the President's proposal met the argument that individual units could be more easily detached to deal with situations on the front than those operating as a separate air force.

In his reply to the President's offer, Stalin proved that he had no intention of having foreign personnel in Russia even if they operated in separate units. He stated that the need for them had passed. But he repeated the Soviet request for the planes: "I should be most grateful if you would expedite the despatch of aircraft, especially fighters, but without crews, whom you now need badly for use in the areas mentioned." He added: "A feature of the Soviet Air Force is that we have more than enough pilots, but suffer from a shortage of machines."[92] The United States could not meet the request for planes without crews, Roosevelt explained, because the AAF also suffered from a shortage of planes for available crews.[93]

Meanwhile, in Moscow, Drummond had received a letter in which the Soviet government courteously refused the Anglo-American air force.[94] Adler described the reply as "a friendly closing to the mission's affairs and . . . [it] leaves the question open at a later date for rediscussion. . . ."[95] The end of the mission came in a terse order: "Proceed to Cairo. Terminate mission." On Christmas day, Adler and Drummond departed for Cairo.[96]

The fiasco of *Velvet* raises a pertinent question: Why did

91. Msg., Roosevelt to Stalin, December 16, 1942, *Foreign Relations*, 1942, III, 677.
92. Msg., Stalin to Roosevelt, December 18, 1942, Ministry of Foreign Affairs of the U.S.S.R., *Stalin's Correspondence*, II, 45.
93. Memo, Leahy for Roosevelt, December 21, 1942, with suggested message for Stalin (File: H. H. Arnold Special-Official File, 1941-45, E-W, in MD/LC). The President's message to Stalin on January 8, 1943, indicates that the suggested message of December 21 may have been sent. See msg., Roosevelt to Stalin, January 8, 1943 (File: H. H. Arnold Special-Official File, 1941-45, E-W, in MD/LC).
94. Ltr., Nikitin to Drummond, December 22, 1942, in Adler File.
95. Msg., Adler to Marshall, December 23, 1942, in Adler File.
96. Msg., unsigned, undated; notes on Moscow Conferences, December 19, 1942, in Adler File.

The Velvet Project   161

Stalin accept the proffered air force and then reject it? The entire project was pursued by Britain and the United States but was never enthusiastically received by the Kremlin. The diplomacy concerning *Velvet* reveals only a few fleeting indications of Stalin's interest—namely, during the Churchill-Stalin conference in August and during General Bradley's conversations with Stalin and Molotov in October. On the other hand, Stalin curiously ignored the air force in his correspondence with Churchill and Roosevelt until November when he reluctantly approved it and consented to allow the mission to come to Moscow. If Stalin wanted the air force, it is reasonable to assume that he would have pressed the matter early in October when he spoke of the need for air power on his front. Instead he asked for additional planes, not the air force.

Failing to get the additional planes which he requested, Stalin appears to have been willing to accept the air force if the military situation on the eastern front required reinforcement. Until the Russians launched their offensive at Stalingrad on November 19, Stalin may have thought it premature to reject categorically the additional air strength. After that offensive, however, it became increasingly apparent that there was no critical need either for planes or for an air force from the West. From October to December, 1942, the strength of the Luftwaffe on the eastern front had sharply declined. Prior to the offensive, part of this depletion was due to the withdrawal of units to meet the Allied offensive at El Alamein and the invasion of North Africa. During October-December, approximately 400 aircraft had been withdrawn from the Soviet and Arctic fronts for service in the Mediterranean. Moreover, the Luftwaffe was also forced to meet the increasing challenge of British and American air assaults in western Europe. The drain on German fighter strength was such that by February, 1943, almost 70 percent of the Luftwaffe's single engine fighters were in the European and Mediterranean theaters.[97]

The nature of the enemy's air operations on the eastern front hastened the process of decline. After the Russians launched the offensive which resulted in the encirclement of the German 6th

97. Great Britain, Air Ministry, *The Rise and Fall of the German Air Force*, pp. 145, 179, 182, 220-21, 224; Dispositions of the German Air Force and Italian Air Force; October 24, 1942 to June 19, 1943 (File: 142.041 K-2, in USAF/HA); "Strength of the Luftwaffe in the Eastern Theater of Operations, 1942," taken from Luftwaffe Situation Reports (File: Karlsruhe Document Collection, in USAF/HA).

162   EAGLES EAST

Army, the Luftwaffe was forced to withdraw from forward bases and was committed to the hopeless task of supplying the beleagured troops. Transports with fighter escorts and even bombers were assigned to supply operations. The continuing problems of over-using units which affected the serviceability of the aircraft and the efficiency of the pilots seriously limited the effectiveness of the Luftwaffe.[98] Little wonder that Soviet military officials expressed amazement over the lack of German air activity after the Russians launched their assault at Stalingrad.[99]

In sharp contrast to the Luftwaffe, the Soviet Air Force appears to have maintained its strength at 4,000-5,000 planes during the fall and winter of 1942. After that, its strength increased substantially.[100] In addition to its own resources, the Soviet Air Force could also rely on the deliveries of Lend-Lease aircraft from the United States and Great Britain. AAF deliveries to the Russians in Iran in the period July-November, 1942, came to 400 aircraft,[101] thus matching the number of known withdrawals by the Luftwaffe from the eastern front during the fall of 1942.

As the scale of operations unfolded during the battle of Stalingrad, it became increasingly apparent that the Luftwaffe was unable to match the strength of the Soviet Air Force. From that point until the end of the war, the Muscovites had virtually unchallenged air superiority on the eastern front.

These dramatic changes in the war on the eastern front had obvious implications for the failure of *Velvet*. While the Drummond-Adler mission lingered on in Moscow, it was increasingly apparent to Stalin that there was no military need for direct

---

98. Great Britain, Air Ministry, *The Rise and Fall of the German Air Force*, pp. 182-83, 217-18, 220.

99. Msg., Maj. Gen. Patrick J. Hurley to Roosevelt, December 8, 1942, *Foreign Relations*, 1942, III, 673. Hurley, who was in Moscow on a special mission for the President, was one of the few Americans to visit the Russian front during the early years of the war. He left Moscow for Stalingrad on November 27 and remained there until December 7. Later, he visited the Caucasus. Drummond and Adler had been denied access to both areas. For an account of Hurley's activities in Russia, see Don Lohbeck, *Patrick J. Hurley* (Chicago: Henry Regnery Co., 1956), pp. 173-79, 181.

100. Great Britain, Air Ministry, *The Rise and Fall of the German Air Force*, p. 223; U. S. War Department, "Preliminary Report," VIII-5A; memo, with report, Jacobs for Wedemeyer, May 7, 1943 (File: ABC, 452.1, WPD, WDGS, in WWIIRD/NA).

101. Air Materiel Command, "Special One-Time Report of Deliveries of AAF Aircraft to USSR."

The Velvet *Project*   163

western help. Even if there was no necessity for air reinforcement, this still does not adequately explain the rejection of an air force which would have been a valuable increment to the Soviet air arsenal. Stalin's reasons were probably more political than military. The shrewd Georgian who evaluated war not by casualties but by political consequences was probably apprehensive over the advantages which Britain and the United States would derive by placing an air fleet on Soviet soil during a critical time in the war on the eastern front. Western air operations there would dramatize their assistance to the Soviet Union, thus detracting from Russian prestige. Moreover, there was the danger that the contacts between Russian personnel on the one hand and westerners on the other would result in pressure for greater military and political collaboration—a situation which the Soviet Union wanted to avoid.[102] Stalin might have also feared that his partners planned to use the air force to further their interests in the Middle East—an apprehension that was probably confirmed in his mind by the large number of troops which arrived in Iran at the time *Velvet* was under negotiation.[103] Whatever Stalin's reasons were for refusing air force units of the United States and Britain to collaborate with the Soviet Air Force, they were real enough to wreck the project.

102. Adler stated that the Soviets did "not enjoy the thought of foreign soldiers mixing with their own troops and possibly contaminating them with better food, equipment, pay, and other items that would naturally appear with a foreign force. If forced to accept the [air] force they would prefer to place it in an area and draw a fence around it so that its operations would be independent but its control in their hands." Notes on Moscow Conferences, November 27, 1942. Churchill suggests that the failure of *Velvet* was due to the Soviet "feeling that if they could survive the winter they could reject any direct military aid from the West, which they regarded as an infecting contact and as a blow to their prestige." See Churchill, *The Hinge of Fate*, p. 582. Drummond believed that the primary reason for the failure of *Velvet* was due to the "almost fanatical urge to keep foreigners out of Caucasia." See ltr., Drummond to Portal, December 17, 1942.
103. The arrival of American troops in Iran represented the first contingent of forces of the Persian Gulf Service Command which was to improve the port and rail facilities in the region in order to expedite Lend-Lease deliveries to the Soviet Union. The Russians were apprehensive over the influx of so many troops. See Motter, *The Persian Corridor*, pp. 338, 437-38; memo, Col. R. S. Bratton for Chief, Intelligence Group, January 16, 1943 (File: 170.22781, in USAF/HA). Soviet historians now tell us that because of Russian opposition to *Velvet*, "The U. S. ruling circles retaliated by sabotaging deliveries of supplies to the Soviet Union at the height of the Volga Battle." G. A. Deborin, *The Second World War: A Politico-Military Survey* (Moscow: Progress Publishers, n.d.), p. 262.

CHAPTER XI

The Passing of the Crisis: The Status of Aircraft Aid (July 1942 — June 1944)

THE SECOND (WASHINGTON) PROTOCOL had established aircraft commitments for only three months. In October, 1942, these were to be fixed for the remainder of the year. Predictably, the War Department hoped that deliveries could be reduced while the White House, anxious to take the edge off Soviet disappointments regarding the suspension of convoys to northern Russia and the postponement of the second front, urged sending as much aid as possible without seriously crippling the strength of the AAF. Although a compromise solution eventually materialized—namely, continuing the existing rate of aircraft commitments—it became increasingly evident that air power was the most effective tangible way for the White House to demonstrate to the Soviets that the United States intended to continue the fight at their side.

The negotiations involving the Third Protocol, begun early in 1943, demonstrated the extent to which Lend-Lease, and especially aircraft aid, continued to play a crucial role in America's arsenal of diplomacy. Lend-Lease had never been exclusively a response to Soviet military need; it was more of a demonstration to the Russians of the western commitment to the anti-Axis alliance. That is why arguments in official circles for and against aid to Russia based on military considerations had the ring of a coin dropping in a well. Soviet officials who urged increasing aircraft commitments under the Third Protocol and American proponents of the Russian cause were the proverbial whistlers in the dark; the delivery routes could scarcely handle existing aircraft allocations, not to mention more of them.

164

The Passing of the Crisis 165

Dissatisfied with what they were getting, the Soviets declared that the gravity of the situation on the eastern front in August 1942, required a shipment of 250 bombers and 150 fighters each month from the United States. In other words, the Russians now asked for approximately twice the number of planes which had been committed during the first quarter of the Second Protocol. The Russians also persisted in trying to secure heavy bombers which had been consistently refused them.[1]

Arnold could not see how the requests could be met without delaying the activation of AAF units scheduled for operations in Europe and the Far East.[2] The White House toyed with the idea of meeting the requests but was reluctant to direct such a move if it meant a decline in the strength of the AAF in combat theaters.[3] It will be recalled that the President even urged the War Department to send at least 300 additional planes during the last three months of 1942 by taking them away from units patrolling the coast of the United States.[4] Marshall's opposition was endorsed by the Joint Chiefs of Staff who recommended that the current rate of 212 planes each month be continued until the end of the protocol period—i.e., June, 1943. The Joint Chiefs advised that it would be preferable to offer direct air force assistance than to decrease the strength of AAF units by sending additional aircraft.[5] But, as has been seen, Stalin did not consider this an acceptable substitute for additional aircraft.

Soviet pressure was eased to some extent when Arnold, again urged by the White House, revealed that the AAF was studying the possibility of sending 150 two-engine transports in 1943. And if production permitted, he said that an additional 150 of them would be scheduled for delivery.[6] A definite decision was not long

1. Ltr., Belyaev to Arnold, August 20, 1942; memo, MAC for MAB, TAB A, September 5, 1942 (File: ACAS/MS, in WWIIRD/NA).
2. Memo, Lt. Col. H. R. Paige for MAC, September 1, 1942; memo, Maj. J. A. Saalfield for Maj. Gen. G. E. Stratemeyer, September 8, 1942 (File: Case 121, ACAS/MS, in WWIIRD/NA); ltr., Arnold to Belyaev, September 11, 1942 (File: RG 18, Box 950, AAF, in WWIRB/NA).
3. Matloff and Snell, *Strategic Planning for Coalition Warfare*, p. 347.
4. See Chapter X of this study.
5. Memo, Leahy for Roosevelt, October 24, 1942 (File: H. H. Arnold Special-Official File, 1941-45, E-W, in MD/LC).
6. Ltr., Arnold to Belyaev, December 10, 1942. Also see R & R, Stratemeyer for ACS, A-3, December 1, 1942 (File: 145.96-166, in USAF/HA). The Soviets especially wanted the C-87. See Belyaev's request for 6 of these. Ltr., Belyaev to Arnold, November 26, 1942 (File: 145.95, Western Russia, Bk. 1, in USAF/HA);

166   EAGLES EAST

in coming. On January 9, 1943, the President personally related to Stalin that 200 transports would be sent in 1943 with deliveries to begin immediately.[7]

Increases in aircraft allocations were unrealistic. Experience clearly showed the extraordinary difficulty in delivering existing amounts to acceptance points. Arnold was correct when he told the President that "Hastening actual delivery of the airplanes to her, rather than the commitment to her of additional airplanes is the most practicable means whereby we may assist Russia in meeting her present emergency."[8] The following tabulation reveals that the problem was not one of production but of backlog:[9]

STATUS OF AIRCRAFT ON SECOND RUSSIAN PROTOCOL
July-December 1942

	DUE ON PROTOCOL	DELIVERED FROM FACTORY	EXPORTS
Medium bombers	72	83	45
Light bombers	600	590	408
Fighters	600	649	556

When the unexported planes furnished by the United States on the British account are considered, the backlog exceeded 400 planes.[10] Anxious to see a reduction, the President directed the

---

ltr., Arnold to Belyaev, December 10, 1942 (File: 145.96-162, IV-A, Procurement of Supplies and Equipment, July 1941-January 1943, in USAF/HA). The Soviets also wanted 30 AT-6 trainers: although MAC doubted the suitability of the plane for the operations which the Russians had in mind, the request was approved. Ltr., Belyaev to Burns, October 8, 1942; memo, Burns for MAC, October 9, 1942; ltr., MAC to Executive Officer, MAB, October 20, 1942; memo for OLLA, October 22, 1942 (File: Case 153, ACAS/MS, in WWIIRD/NA).

7. Msg., Roosevelt to Stalin, January 9, 1943, Ministry of Foreign Affairs of the U.S.S.R., *Stalin's Correspondence*, II, 50.

8. Memo, Arnold for Roosevelt, August 3, 1942 (File: 145.95, Western Russia, Bk. 1, in USAF/HA).

9. Ltr., with report, Stimson to Roosevelt, January 9, 1943; Office of Lend-Lease Administration, "Status of the Soviet Aid Program as of December 31, 1942" (File: 031.1, protocol, Vol. II, ID, ASF, in WWIIRD/NA).

10. During the Second Protocol the United States was sending 429 planes on the British account to Russia. 179 of these were to compensate the Russians for those which had been originally scheduled for British delivery to the Soviet Union but had been diverted to the AAF. The remainder of the planes was to apply against the British account to Russia in return for the equipment of some AAF units with British Spitfires. Ltr., with report, Stimson to Roosevelt, January 9, 1943. The number of planes in backlog status reveals that some of them constituted the unexported balance which the United States was to

The Passing of the Crisis 167

War Department to make deliveries according to protocol schedules by the most expeditious means, whether by ship or flight.[11] But in the event the schedules could not be met to a reasonable degree, the President wanted the War Department to consider the substitution of larger type planes for smaller ones on an estimated equivalent basis if this would improve the possibilities of delivery.[12]

The White House proposal was not a new one. The War Department had earlier considered the possibility of supplying 1 B-25 for 2 A-20's. Since the deficiency of medium bombers was as severe as that of light bombers the War Department rejected the idea.[13] When he conveyed the War Department's disapproval of the White House proposal, Arnold emphasized that the disappointing record of deliveries to the Russians was due to earlier Soviet indecision concerning the method of delivering the planes, citing Kremlin delays in opening Alsib.[14]

Arnold's explanation for the disappointing tally was not entirely correct. One of the basic reasons for the backlog of planes in the United States was the failure of flight deliveries to Fairbanks to meet expectancies. Although original plans called for sending the entire commitment via Alsib, the Russians, doubting their capacity to ferry so many, asked that the schedule be revised.[15] Accordingly, the monthly schedule for delivery to Fairbanks was reduced to: 60 P-40's, 20 P-39's, 50 A-20's and 12 B-25's.[16] In other words the major share of the commitment was still to be flown to Fairbanks. But the early months of operations revealed that the AAF had been too optimistic about its own ability to honor even

---

furnish on the British account. For some indication of the number of planes in backlog status see memo, Col. Richard H. Ballard for Maj. Gen. L. D. Clay, March 4, 1943; memo, Hopkins for Arnold, February 2, 1943 (File: USSR Delivery File, A-4, ACAS/MS, in WWIIRD/NA).

11. Memo, Roosevelt for Stimson, October 2, 1942 (File: 031.1, protocol, Vol. I, ID, ASF, in WWIIRD/NA).

12. Memo, Hopkins for Arnold, October 2, 1942 (File: 031.1, protocol, Vol. I, ID, ASF, in WWIIRD/NA).

13. Memo, Marshall for Hopkins, August 24, 1942 (File: USSR Deliveries to October 1, 1942, ACAS/MS, in WWIIRD/NA).

14. Memo, Arnold for Hopkins, October 6, 1942 (File: 031.1, protocol, Vol. I, ID, ASF, in WWIIRD/NA). Stimson gave the same explanation to the President. See ltr., with report, Stimson to Roosevelt, October 8, 1942 (File: 031.1, protocol, Vol. I, ID, ASF, in WWIIRD/NA).

15. See Chapter IX of this study.

16. Memo, Hanley for CG, ATC, October 7, 1942 (File: Russia 1942, ACAS/MS, in WWIIRD/NA).

168 EAGLES EAST

the revised schedule of planes. In the period September-December, 1942, only 148 planes were delivered to the Russians at Fairbanks.[17]

Obviously AAF planners had not anticipated the difficulties involved in delivering so large a number of planes. Aircraft operations in an arctic climate were difficult at best for man and machines alike. Before planes could operate effectively, they had to be winterized against the severe weather. Unfortunately, many of them leaving factories and modification centers had not been properly winterized. The problem was further complicated by the extent of Soviet winterization criteria which went beyond that practiced by the AAF. As a consequence, depots at Great Falls and Fairbanks, which lacked personnel and equipment, had the tremendous task of effecting modifications to meet Soviet specifications.[18]

Even without these problems, it would have been impossible to send more planes than were sent to Fairbanks during these months. The shortage of trained inspectors seriously delayed the processing of aircraft while the lack of adequate forecasting and communication facilities, the scarcity of trained mechanics, and the shortages of parts and equipment further hampered efficient operations.[19]

Deliveries continued to northern Russia and Iran. Although the convoys to northern Russia had not maintained a regular schedule because of U-boat and Luftwaffe attacks, approximately 390 planes had been delivered there during the last six months of 1942.[20] There was some improvement in the situation in Iran during this period over the sluggish beginnings earlier in the year, averaging 75 planes per month.[21] But as the historian of the Persian Corridor has pointed out, it was an uneven struggle. Shortages in personnel and equipment, difficulties in clearing ships from

17. Carr, "Great Falls to Nome," p. 192.
18. "Meeting to Discuss Ferry Shipment of Planes to Russia via Northern Route, November 13, 1942;" memo, Meyers for Ballard, November 24, 1942 (File: Russia 1942, ACAS/MS, in WWIIRD/NA); memo, Arnold for George, December 24, 1942; memo, Ballard for CG, Materiel Command, December 26, 1942 (File: USSR Deliveries, October 1, 1942, ACAS/MS, in WWIIRD/NA); "Report of Bradley Mission," TAB 2, pp. 1-4; memo, Col. L. G. Fritz for Lt. Col. R. M. Love, January 23, 1943 (File: Russian file beginning March 1, 1943, ACAS/MS, in WWIIRD/NA).
19. Carr, "Great Falls to Nome," pp. 181-84, 190-91, 117-19.
20. "Plane Arrivals, North Russia" (File: 913406, ACS, G-2, in WWIIRD/NA).
21. Air Materiel Command, "Special One Time Report."

The Passing of the Crisis

poor port facilities, and the problems of assemblying planes which differed in type and model delayed efficient operations.[22]

As in the case of flight deliveries to Fairbanks, planes sent to Iran by air did not meet expectations. It will be recalled that in March, 1942, B-25's began the flight across the South Atlantic and Africa to Iran. By the end of the year, 103 bombers had been delivered.[23] There was hope that A-20's could also be sent by air in order to avoid the excessive delays of water shipment—120 days by way of the Cape of Good Hope; 90 if the Mediterranean was open. Due to the difficulties in the installation of fuel tanks, however, the first flight-delivered A-20's were not turned over to the Russians at Abadan until September, 1942.[24]

Drastic measures to expedite the movement of aircraft were ordered by the White House. The top priority granted earlier to Soviet aid was translated to various aspects of the aircraft program —production, service, and movement—by early 1943. The Materiel, Air Service, and Air Transport Commands were directed to take specific steps to speed the movement of Lend-Lease planes.[25] Some of these included the movement of parts to repair inoperative planes along the ferry routes, the establishment of depots and sub-depots to tend to maintenance needs and the dispatch of skilled personnel to various points along the ferry routes.[26] Instructions were also issued to insure that planes were modified before arrival at Fairbanks and Abadan in order to avoid delays in turning them over to the Russians.

Administrative coordination, which was sorely needed, came with the appointment of Colonel Richard H. Ballard as Assistant

---

22. Motter, *The Persian Corridor*, pp. 135-36.
23. Air Materiel Command, "Special One Time Report."
24. R & R, AFAEP for AFCAS, August 1, 1942; draft memo, Arnold to Roosevelt, August 3, 1942 (File: 145.95, Western Russia, Bk. 1, in USAF/HA); ltr., Burns to Hopkins, August 21, 1942 (File: Case 90, ACAS/MS, in WWIIRD/NA); ltr., Lt. Col. P. I. Doty to Chief, International Section, Materiel Command, March 10, 1943 (File: New Russian Misc. file, ACAS/MS, in WWIIRD/NA).
25. Memo, Ballard for CG, Materiel Command, January 1, 1943; memo, Ballard for CG, Air Service Command, January 1, 1943; memo, Ballard for CG, Air Transport Command, January 1, 1943; note for record, February, 1943 (File: USSR Delivery File, A-4, January-February, 1943, ACAS/MS, in WWIIRD/NA).
26. Memo, Ballard for CG, Air Service Command, February 17, 1943; R & R, ACAS, A-4 for ATC, February 17, 1943; memo, Hanley for CG, Air Service Command, February 23, 1943; memo, Ballard for Executive, MAB, January 14, 1943 (File: USSR Delivery File, A-4, January-February, 1943, ACAS/MS, in WWIIRD/NA).

170 EAGLES EAST

Chief of Staff, A-4. Ballard's task was to monitor the flow of aircraft from factories to Soviet acceptance points.[27] In order to facilitate Ballard's work, the major commands were to forward regular reports concerning the progress of each plane earmarked for the Soviet Union.[28] Not even planes destined for the AAF received this kind of scrupulous attention.

In order to remove the bottlenecks in the movement of planes from factories to acceptance points, the AAF also turned its attention to the improvement of facilities.[29] This was in accord with the policy outlined earlier by the White House regarding the improvement of port and rail facilities in Iran. One of the persistent problems in Iran had been the lack of facilities to unload and clear cargo. By joint agreement with the British, American military forces were to improve and operate port and rail facilities. This was the task of the newly-created Persian Gulf Service Command which, under the command of Brigadier General Donald H. Connolly, began operations in December, 1942.[30]

These measures showed some uneven results by the end of the Second Protocol in June, 1943, when the United States had succeeded in exporting 96 per cent of the planes made available from factories.[31] On the basis of a monthly delivery of 142 planes, and the additional allocation of 10 to 20 C-47's each month, deliveries to Alaska by the end of the protocol should have reached 1,500 planes. By June, 1943, American personnel had actually flown 1,107 from Great Falls to Fairbanks.[32]

27. R & R, Stratemeyer for Hanley, December 16, 1942; R & R AFDAS for AFADS, December 16, 1942; ltr., Hanley to Belyaev, December 29, 1942 (File: Russia 1942, ACAS/MS, in WWIIRD/NA).
28. Memo, Ballard for CG, Materiel Command, January 1, 1943; memo, Ballard for CG, Air Service Command, January 1, 1943; memo, Ballard for CG, Air Transport Command, January 1, 1943.
29. Memo, Arnold for Hopkins, February, 1943, in Alaskan Division, Air Transport Command, "Historical Record Report," Vol. III: "November 1942-December 1943," Appendix II.
30. Msg., Hopkins to Faymonville, October 5, 1942, Foreign Relations, 1942, III, 728; Motter, The Persian Corridor, pp. 331, 338.
31. Ltr., Patterson to President, July 9, 1943, with enclosure, TAB C (File: 400.3295, AG, in WWIIRD/NA). 141 planes constituted the unexported backlog from the United States; the largest number of these were A-20's, some of which had been used for training purposes by the AAF. R & R, Director of Individual Training for ACAS, A-3, February 23, 1943 (File: USSR Aircraft Delivery File, A-4, ACAS/MS, in WWIIRD/NA).
32. Carr, "Great Falls to Nome," pp. 178-79. See appendix for deliveries at Fairbanks.

The Passing of the Crisis 171

If Alsib lagged a little behind expectancies, its record of deliveries was better than that of the Persian Gulf. Personnel of the Douglas Aircraft Company assembled planes there until the end of March, 1943, when the AAF assumed operations. But poor planning failed to make an easy and efficient transition. The 17th Depot Repair Squadron, on detached service with the 82nd Air Depot Group since January, 1943, learned the job of assembly operations from the Douglas civilians. But these skills were not used very long before the squadron followed the Douglas people from the area, leaving Abadan assembly operations without adequate personnel.[33] The situation was further aggravated by shipping almost 300 planes, originally scheduled for delivery to northern Russia, to Abadan.[34] By the end of the Second Protocol 415 planes were on hand, most of which needed to be assembled and delivered to the Russians, while expected arrivals from Britain and the United States pushed the figure up to 1,000 by July, 1943.[35] Personnel were sent to deal with the problem, but it was a classic case of "too little, too late" to prevent the backlog from assuming monumental proportions. This crisis influenced the decision to reduce the number of planes sent to the Middle East in favor of Alsib which carried more air traffic under the Third Protocol until it finally absorbed all but a few aircraft deliveries under the Fourth.

Early in March, 1943, a few months before the end of the Second Protocol, Ambassador Standley dropped a bombshell in Moscow. The honest but unpredictable ambassador was deeply disturbed by the lack of publicity in the Russian press concerning American aid. Convinced of the ingratitude of the Kremlin which gave the impression that it alone was fighting the war, the ambassador called a news conference and freely vented his opinions. Nothing quite like this had occurred in Russo-American relations since the war began. Admitting that his comments might "cause displeasure," he nevertheless did "not feel that we should sit back and continue to accept the ingratitude of the leaders of this

33. Motter, *The Persian Corridor*, pp. 266-67.
34. These were P-39's and P-40's which had to be shipped rather than ferried to Abadan because of a shortage of pilots. Msg., Hopkins to Harriman, April 7, 1943; msg., Harriman to Hopkins, April 11, 1943; excerpt of msg., Spalding to Harriman, April 13, 1943 (File: 421.1 Russia, OPD, WDGS, in WWIIRD/NA).
35. Memo, Paige for Meyers, July 6, 1943 (File: USSR Deliveries via Abadan, ACAS/MS, in WWIIRD/NA).

172   EAGLES EAST

country." Standley hoped his remarks would "clear the air by emphasizing to the Russian Government that we are not satisfied with their policy in this respect."[36] Of course, it went deeper: Standley may not have been diplomatic but he was perceptive. The lack of official comment about western aid was one of several indicators of a Soviet desire to go it alone.

Molotov quickly objected to the ambassador's comments, contending that both he and Stalin had on numerous occasions expressed their thanks for the aid. And one important reason it was not constantly emphasized, said Molotov, was that it would attract attention and result in greater pressure by the Germans on the northern convoys. Molotov even claimed "that the man in the street knew by heart the number of tanks and planes received from America."[37]

To what extent Standley's frank observations affected United States-Soviet relations is difficult to say. Relations, never really warm, had not been distinguished by mutual candor. Standley's defenders claim too much for the episode when they assert that the story of aid to Russia was now told by the Soviet press "for the first time."[38] When American aid was far less than it was in 1942, the Soviet press had given reasonably good coverage. On the other hand Standley's detractors, including Senator Thomas T. Connally who condemned his "ineptness" and the John Brown Club which wanted him recalled, exaggerated the impact of the incident.[39] Surely it caused some strain but not an irreparable breach. The real significance of the episode was that the Russians now had evidence of something they probably had long suspected —the growing dissatisfaction of numerous people, including those in official circles, with a relationship that was too one-sided and unrealistic. But they also had the satisfaction that no major reassessment in White House policy toward the Kremlin resulted because of the increased American commitments under the Third Protocol.

36. Msg., Standley to Secretary of State, March 9, 1943 (File: 861.24/1310, in DS/NA).
37. Msg., Standley to Secretary of State, March 11, 1943 (File: 861.24/1325, in DS/NA).
38. Walter Kerr, *The Russian Army: Its Men, Its Leaders, and Its battles* (New York: Alfred A. Knopf, 1944), p. 236.
39. Msg., John Brown Club to Hull, March 30, 1943 (File: 861.24/1366, in DS/NA); U. S., *Congressional Record*, 78th Cong., 1st Sess., 1943, LXXXIX, Part 2, 1701.

The Passing of the Crisis   173

It was customary during the first days of January to ask the Soviet Purchasing Commission for its requirements during the coming fiscal year. Equally customary was a memorandum from the President to government agencies involved in the Soviet aid program that emphasized Russia's crucial role in the defeat of Germany and the need to support her. In contrast to earlier protocols, the American and British drafts differed greatly in approach and tone. The British were inclined to be tougher, somewhat less generous, and oriented toward a *quid pro quo* as seen by their desire to have the protocol take the form of a treaty, to stipulate reciprocal aid from the Russians, and to avoid precise shipping commitments. The American draft followed the same generous approach that had marked the two earlier protocols. One particular demand of the British caused serious concern in American official circles. Troubled by the gruesome losses on the northern convoy run and the ineffectiveness of Russian measures to help in the protection of ships, the British insisted that an article be included in the protocol granting air bases to the RAF in Russia.[40] The high casualties of men—1,500 killed and hundreds more wounded—and the destruction of ships—about 100—were convincing justifications.[41]

The issue was so heated that at one point in the negotiations with the Kremlin, London threatened to stop all convoys to the northern ports unless it got the bases.[42] But this matter was not included in the protocol, and other disparate points in the two drafts were harmonized in accordance with the American position which maintained that no article should be included in the new supply agreement which would provoke Russian suspicion or antagonism. General S. P. Spalding, the highly placed and influential coordinator of the protocol before he went to Moscow to head the United States Supply Mission in the U.S.S.R., mirrored administration views when he urged the necessity to avoid provoking Soviet ill will because "the U.S.S.R. is so important to us not only in the present war against Germany, but after Germany is defeated in the all out effort against Japan and again in bringing

40. Memo, Spalding for Hopkins, May 3, 1943; memo, Spalding for Hopkins, May 3, 1943 (File: Soviet Protocol Committee Records, Box 2, in FDR/L).
41. Msg., Matthews to Secretary of State, March 2, 1943 (File: 740.0011, E.W. 1939/28300, in DS/NA).
42. *Ibid.*, memo from Spalding, May 17, 1943 (File: Soviet Protocol Committee Records, Box 2, in FDR/L).

174   EAGLES EAST

about an enduring peace."[43] Even a War Department suggestion
to include a clause in the protocol urging a reciprocal exchange of
information between the military attachés of both countries was
turned down by the administration. It was argued that such a
clause was not really needed in view of the alleged improvement
in Soviet cooperation in providing useful military information
to the United States. Moreover, these pundits argued that the
Soviets would respond cooperatively to offers of generosity, not to
those rooted in *quid pro quo*.[44]

Despite a decline in munitions requests under the Third
Protocol compared with the Second, the request for aircraft—still
the top priority item in Russia's arsenal—was staggering: 8,160,
consisting of a monthly delivery of 500 P-39's, 100 A-20's, 50 B-25's,
and 30 C-46/C-47's,[45] more than had been asked for in June, 1941,
during the darkest days of the debacle on the eastern front.
Although the Soviets never offered precise justifications for their
requests, a few American voices now questioned the alleged need
for so many planes when the Germans were now on the defensive
and Soviet industry had recovered from its worse shocks of earlier
years and was probably producing enough to meet its needs. There
was even the suggestion that the Russians were building up reserve
stocks of planes.[46] Significantly, there was a direct relationship
between the improvement in Soviet military fortunes since the
Battle of Stalingrad and the exacting standards which the Russians
imposed on American aircraft before the planes were accepted.
Moreover, as the extent of Anglo-American air operations unfolded
in the Mediterranean and Europe, by far the greater portion of the
Luftwaffe was deployed against the West.[47]

43. Memos, Spalding for Hopkins, May 3, 1943.
44. Memo, Marshall and King for President's Soviet Lend-Lease Committee,
n.d.; memo, from Spalding, May 11, 1943; memo, Spalding for Hopkins, May
24, 1943 (File: Soviet Protocol Committee Records, Box 2, FDR/L).
45. Memo, Arnold for Somervell, April 19, 1943 (File: Misc., in USAF/HA).
46. Minutes, meeting of the General Council, October 26, 1942, pp. 8-9;
Arnold, *Global Mission*, p. 387; memo, Wedemeyer for Handy, December 10,
1942 (File: H. H. Arnold Special-Official File, 1941-1945, E-W, in MD/LC).
Official statistics of Soviet aircraft production are not available. See estimates of
Russian aircraft production during the war in Institute for Research in Social
Science, *The Soviet Aircraft Industry*, pp. 90-91; U.S., War Department, "Preliminary Report," 8 A-4.
47. See British estimates of the distribution of German air strength early in
1943 in ltr., Churchill to Stalin, March 11, 1943, Ministry of Foreign Affairs of
the U.S.S.R., *Stalin's Correspondence*, I, 102.

The Passing of the Crisis 175

The AAF did not support an increase in current levels of aircraft commitments—100 P-39's, 100 A-20's, 12 B-25's and 20 C-47's per month (150 fighters on Britain's account). Several factors made it impractical to increase allocations. The most important one was that the existing rate was about all the combined capacities of shipping and ferrying facilities available to the United States and the Soviet Union could effectively bear. The suggestion was frequently made to provide the Russians with the material to build the planes themselves. But initial Soviet requests for aluminum were larger than available supply and threatened serious decreases in finished aircraft production in the United States. Steel production was much larger, but the shortages of shipping left large unshipped stocks on the seaboard. Thus the limitations of shipping during the early years of the war worked as a control factor in forcing the Russians to determine more essential needs by the allocation of shipping space.[48]

Wherever possible flight delivery of critical materiel for the Soviet munitions industry was made. For example, the AAF was used to fly tin and mercury from China to India where it was unloaded and sent to Russia. From August, 1942 to August, 1943, almost nine million pounds of such cargo was carried by the AAF: more than 25 percent of the strategic raw materials shipped by the United States all over the globe was for the Soviet Union.[49]

Of the types requested by the Russians under the Third Protocol, the P-39, B-25 and C-47 posed special problems. The model change from the P-39 to P-63 retarded the Bell Company's production which, added to delays in producing other types, meant a decline in AAF fighter expectancies. Shortages in B-25's were also expected because of the development of a low-level attack version, the B-25H, to compensate for deficiencies of light bombers. But the situation with respect to the C-47 was the gloomiest. Despite the President's promise to Stalin, Douglas Aircraft could not produce enough transports to meet demands. "Our transport position con-

48. Memo, Burns for Hopkins, October 13, 1942 (File: Soviet Protocol Committee Records, Box 18, in FDR/L); meeting of Protocol Sub-Committee on Supplies, December 26, 1942 (File: Lend-Lease Records, Box 93, in FRC); ltr. Nelson to Burns, February 16, 1943 (File: Soviet Protocol Committee Records, Box 18, in FDR/L); report, "The Lend-Lease and Other Export Programs," June 30, 1943 (File: RG 179, Box 785, WPB, in NA).
49. Ltr., L. P. Marcin to F. Linville, September 13, 1943 (File: 861.24/1680, in DS/NA).

176   EAGLES EAST

tinues to deteriorate," Arnold solemnly told General Brehon Somervell, Commanding General of the Services of Supply.[50] The White House accepted the AAF estimate but before a draft of the proposed Third Protocol was submitted to the Soviet Chargé d'Affaires on June 9, 1943, it insisted that an important qualifying statement be inserted:

> The offer will be re-examined at the earliest practicable opportunity for the purpose of determining whether in the light of operational requirements and production it is possible to increase the number of airplanes.[51]

Apparently to stem a large anticipated Nazi offensive in the summer, the Russians wanted far more fighters than the United States offered.[52] "Airplanes is (sic) the quickest and best way" to help them, the President told Arnold. A week later, Burns paraphrased the same observation to Arnold: "The delivery of airworthy planes to the Russians is the real measure of our aid to that country."[53] Arnold could not find more Airacobras, but he came up with an additional 600 P-40's and 78 B-25's for delivery in 1943. The President was gratified. He had reason to be. Considerable juggling of production and allocation estimates raised American pledges from 2,292 to 2,970, including deliveries on Britain's account, for the period July-December, 1943. Roosevelt personally informed Stalin of the increase over the new protocol and assured him that commitments would again be reviewed later in 1943.[54] The episode did not pass without the Russians urging a displacement of P-40's by P-39's which had shown somewhat better results on the eastern front. From the Russian point of view, one American fighter type would simplify training and maintenance programs. Arnold held out the hope that later reviews of the aircraft situation might result in the elimination of the P-40 from the schedule as soon as commitments could be met with the Bell P-63.[55]

50. Memo, Arnold for Somervell, April 19, 1943 (File: 145.95, Bk. 2, in USAF/HA).
51. Memo, Spalding for Hopkins, May 28, 1943 (File: Soviet Protocol Committee Records, Box 2, in FDR/L).
52. Msg., Davis to President, May 24, 1943 (File: 861.24/1473 PS/SF, in DS/NA).
53. Memo, Roosevelt for Arnold, June 10, 1943; memo, Burns for Arnold, June 18, 1943 (File: 145.95, Bk. 2, in USAF/HA).
54. Memo, Arnold for Roosevelt, June 14, 1943; msg., Roosevelt to Stalin, June 16, 1943 (File: 145.95, Bk. 2, in USAF/HA).
55. Ltr., Belyaev to Arnold, July 19, 1943; ltr., Arnold to Belyaev, August 1, 1943 (File: 145.95, Bk. 2, in USAF/HA). The Russians were prompt to ask

The Passing of the Crisis

A subsequent review of the situation under the Third Protocol during the fall revealed White House plans to maintain if not increase commitments during the last six months of the supply period. The AAF, convinced that the transition from P-39's to P-63's would result in less fighter production than required in combat theaters, sought a way out of the dilemma by suggesting an end to American fighter deliveries on Britain's account to Russia. The United States had delivered 150 fighters for the British in order to keep Spitfires on the western front. But the rationale for this arrangement disappeared when the P-38, P-47, and P-51 showed their superior combat performance against the Luftwaffe. The AAF therefore hoped to continue monthly fighter commitments on the basis of either all P-39/63's or 100 P-39/63's and 100 P-47's. Arnold anticipated no particular problem in meeting allocations in light, medium, and transport types.[56] Although the British opposed the proposal, the AAF approved offerings which retained allocations at the increased levels of 1943. Total allocations for the last half of the Third Protocol, January-June, 1944, included: 750 P-39/63's, 250 P-40's, 200 P-47's, 600 A-20's, 150 B-25's, and 120 C-47's, for a total of 2,070. When the 900 fighters on the British account are included, the figure for the period reached 2,970.[57] This meant that all allocations approved and accepted under the Third Protocol amounted to: 300 B-25's, 1,200 A-20's, 1,350 P-39/63's, 850 P-40's, 200 P-47's, and 200 C-47's, for a total of 4,140. The 1,800 fighters on the British account brought the tally to 5,940.[58]

---

for new fighters and bombers that were either not yet in full production or on the planning table. No sooner did Belyaev receive Arnold's letter concerning the substitution of P-39's for P-40's than he asked for several P-38's, P-47's, B-24's, and B-29's. Three P-47's were approved from September's production for Soviet test purposes. Ltr., Arnold to Belyaev, August 11, 1943 (File: H. H. Arnold, Box 129, in MD/LC).

56. Ltr., Hopkins to Arnold, September 30, 1943; ltr., Arnold to Hopkins, October 11, 1943 (File: 145.95, Bk. 2, in USAF/HA); memo, AC/AS for Arnold, October, 1943.

57. Memo, AC/AS, Plans, for Arnold, October 7, 1943; memo, Brig. Gen. Jamison for Gen. Giles, December 7, 1943; ltr., Portal to Arnold, November 9, 1943 (File: 145.95, Bk. 2, in USAF/HA); memo, Arnold for Burns, January 27, 1944 (File: H. H. Arnold, Box 129, in MD/LC). A request for three P-63's to familiarize Russian pilots with the fighter that was to replace the P-39 was approved. Ltr., Piskounov to Meyers, December 8, 1943; R & R, Deputy Chief of Air Staff to AC/AS, Plans, December 15, 1943 (File: 145.95, Bk. 2, in USAF/HA).

58. Memo, Meyers for CAS, May 4, 1944 (File: RG 18, Box 206, ACAS, in

178 EAGLES EAST

In the review of aircraft allocations for the last half of the Third Protocol, the White House wanted Arnold to allocate some heavy bombers to the Russians.[59] Heavies had a particular significance because of the persistent attempts of the Russians to acquire them and the forthcoming meeting of the Big Three at Tehran. Once again the different objectives of Lend-Lease shared by the War Department and the White House came to the fore. From a military point of view the War Department's arguments against such allocations were unassailable. Heavy bombers, vital to the air offensive against Germany, were not produced fast enough to keep up with consumption. One study predicted a net shortage of 212 B-17's, for example, by the end of 1944.[60]

To military leaders, giving a much sought after weapon to the Russians without some promise of tangible military gain was foolish. That is what made the War Department's arguments against the White House suggestion so telling. Soviet conceptions of air power meant that the planes would not be used strategically against the Reich. The Soviets would disperse the big birds which were not intended for that kind of warfare. Obviously this was not making the best and quickest use of this kind of military hardware. Even if the Russians intended to use the planes as the AAF did, it was doubtful if actual operational use could be made of the planes because it took approximately eighteen months to train and equip B-17 groups for combat. Furthermore, it required an allocation of 1,000 heavies to be assured that the Russians could muster 600 planes at any given time, exclusive of planes for trainers and replacements, for a strategic assault.[61] Arnold did not give a categorical negative to the White House; instead he pointed out that the AAF, largely because of the buildup of bomb groups to 48 airplanes, would be in no position to allocate any heavies to

---

WWIIRD/NA). Not included in these figures were the 48 PBY's that MAB assigned to the Russians in March, 1944. The Soviets originally requested 100-200 of this type but Deane's office believed that they did not need that many. Soviet pilots flew the planes from Elizabeth City, North Carolina, via Iceland to northern Russia, completing the movement early in June, 1944. But 90 more navy aircraft, PBN's, were subsequently allocated to the Russians who flew them home via Iceland as well as via the Aleutians. At the end of the war, the U. S. Navy was delivering the planes at 5 per month. "Deane Report," II, Ch. 13, 451-54.
59. Ltr., Hopkins to Arnold, September 30, 1943 (File: 145.95, in USAF/HA).
60. R & R, AC/AS, plans to AC/AS, MM & D, February 4, 1944 (File: 145.95, in USAF/HA). 61. *Ibid.*

The Passing of the Crisis 179

the Russians until after June, 1944.[62] The White House accepted his position, and the heavy bomber matter was not renewed seriously again except in discussions with the Russians concerning the role of the AAF in Siberia.

It was inevitable that sooner or later Alsib would assume a greater share of, and eventually absorb, all aircraft deliveries to the Russians. The perfection of facilities and procedures along the route made it the most efficient way to deliver the machines. It took an average of forty days to deliver a combat plane to Fairbanks. The closest competitive route was flight delivery to Abadan which consumed approximately sixty days.[63]

Delivery schedules under the Third Protocol called for 355 planes per month via Alsib and only 140 via the Atlantic to Abadan.[64] Although these figures were too ambitious, ferrying operations over Alsib proceeded much better than the previous year. Especially significant was the increase in air traffic during the winter months. The original schedule was altered to some extent in the fall when, upon Russian request, 200 fighters were sent by the southern route during the winter months. Most of the problems that plagued the early phase of operations over Alsib were either removed or mitigated substantially enough to assure more efficient operations. Now there was a larger number of mechanics, more facilities—particularly hangars to allow personnel to work inside and warehouses to store supplies—and fewer winterization problems. One index of the efficiency level achieved was the ease with which the planes were processed—less than five hours compared to two weeks for the first plane delivered to the Russians at Fairbanks.[65]

While Alsib eclipsed the route to Iran as the principal delivery route, much of the Third Protocol period was spent fighting the backlog of unassembled planes at Abadan. By the end of September approximately 1,000 planes still awaited assembly. Although the assembly rate improved to 250 per month, more machines had to be put together to make a dent in the mountain of metal that threatened to overwhelm the personnel there. The days of Iran as

62. Ltr., Arnold to Hopkins, October 11, 1943 (File: 145.95, in USAF/HA).
63. Memo, Brig. Gen. Saunders for Burns, June 25, 1943 (File: H. H. Arnold, Box 129, in MD/LC).
64. *Ibid.* Except in July when 100 P-39's were scheduled for water shipment to Abadan.
65. Carr, "Great Falls to Nome," pp. 193-98.

180   EAGLES EAST

a delivery corridor to Russia were numbered: phasing out aircraft activities began in August, 1944, and were completed on January 31, 1945.[66]

Considering the jump in monthly allocations from 212 to 495 planes per month between the Second and Third Protocols, the AAF record was impressive. All of the 5,940 planes committed under the protocol, including the satisfaction of the British account, were delivered at the factory and approximately 5,632 of these had left the country.[67] Either Russia did not need the planes so badly or she was generally satisfied with the effort that was made to deliver them, because there were fewer complaints from Moscow toward the end of 1943. As the ring closed around the Reich and the imperatives of the war in the Pacific assumed greater urgency, Russo-American relations focused closely on direct collaboration on the eastern front and in the Pacific, areas of special significance to the AAF.

66. Minutes, President's Protocol Committee, September 30, 1943 (File: Lend-Lease Records, Box 93, in FRC). Division for Soviet Supply, Lend-Lease Administration, August 12, 1944, and December 9, 1944, "Weekly Reports" (File: Lend-Lease Records, Box 74, in FRC). A comparison of Alsib's delivery record with that of Abadan dramatizes the gravity of the problem. At the end of September, 1943, 48 planes awaited delivery at Fairbanks in contrast to 1,000 at Abadan. See Motter's scholarly and comprehensive study of the difficulties encountered in American aid shipments to the Russians through Iran.
67. Carr, "Great Falls to Nome," p. 200, footnote 44.

CHAPTER XII

The Elusive Bomb Line

URING MOST OF THE WAR the United States and the Soviet Union could afford to wage their respective military operations against the Nazis without recourse to daily liaison. But this situation disappeared by 1944 when Russian forces plunged into eastern Europe, an area rich in strategic targets for the AAF. The proximity of American and Soviet forces obviously posed dangers of accidental conflicts. For that reason alone some kind of liaison was important. Moreover, the possibilities of sharing military information on a regular basis between adjacent commands suggested unique opportunities of mutual benefit in waging combined Allied warfare.

In February, 1944, Sir Henry Maitland Wilson, the Supreme Allied Commander, Mediterranean, raised the question of establishing contacts between Anglo-American air forces and the Russians in order to coordinate strategic air efforts against the Nazis in eastern Europe. Wilson, having in mind American and British procedures of attaching air force officers to ground units, suggested that a liaison officer from his theater be detailed for duty with the southern group of Soviet armies. The idea received the endorsement of the Combined Chiefs of Staff who authorized Major General John R. Deane to approach the Russians.[1]

The Russians were not interested in liaison between military commands because control of the Soviet war effort centered in

1. Msg., Wilson to British Chiefs of Staff, February 26, 1944; msg., Agwar to Deane and Burrows, April 16, 1944 (File: MAAF, 0603/10/335, in WWIIRD/ NA); msg., Deane to Spaatz, June 12, 1944 (File: 522.1621-1, in USAF/HA). Wilson also implied some political advantages for western representatives to be present when Rumania and Bulgaria left the war.

181

182   EAGLES EAST

Moscow—any liaison would have to be there, they said. Pending the establishment of liaison in Moscow, Deane proposed and the Soviets approved in April, 1944, the first temporary bomb line between Soviet and Allied forces operating in the Balkans— Constanta, Bucharest, Ploesti, Budapest.[2]

No sooner had the bomb line been adopted than the AAF submitted targets—Mielec, Riga and Galati—for the first *Frantic* mission. The AAF made the mistake of asking for Soviet approval when it was only necessary to do so in the case of Galati, which lay beyond the line. The Russians disapproved of the targets but later reconsidered their decision after some shrewd admonitions by Deane.[3] But the AAF learned something from the experience—in the future, it submitted the names of targets to be bombed but did not ask for Soviet approval.

The bomb line proved too restrictive both to the Mediterranean Allied Air Forces (MAAF) and to the Russians. It prevented MAAF units from hitting prime targets east of the line when the Soviets were not in the area. The Soviet General Staff was so displeased that upon its suggestion the bomb line was abolished on June 11, 1944. Meanwhile, the Russians accepted Colonel Samuel Gormly, Jr., as the AAF's liaison officer in Moscow and promised him regular contact with a representative of the Red Army General Staff. In lieu of liaison in the field, Gormly's mission was the next best thing, although Soviet reluctance to divulge information to him and the delay in communications between Moscow and MAAF's headquarters in Italy seriously compromised the value of his assignment.[4]

This disappointing beginning in liaison was offset to some extent by the results of contacts between American and Soviet officers in the Balkans during the fall of 1944. Anxious to exploit German retreats from southeastern Europe by coordinating opera-

2. Msg., Deane to Wilson (Part I), April 19, 1944; msg., Deane to Wilson (Part II), April 19, 1944; msg., Deane to Wilson, April 20, 1944 (File: MAAF, 0603/10/335, in WWIIRD/NA). The temporary bomb line followed the course: Constanta, Bucharest, Ploesti, Braov, Debrecen, Miskolc, Budapest.
3. Msg., Deane to Spaatz, May 31, 1944; msg., Deane to Marshall and Arnold, June 1, 1944 (File: 522.1621-1, in USAF/HA). Galati is also spelled Galatz.
4. *Ibid.*; msg., Deane to Eaker, June 11, 1944 (File: 522.161-2 in USAF/HA): "Deane Report," Part I, p. 41. The need for flexibility in bomb lines with efficient procedures to make changes was dramatized late in August when Eaker proposed a line from Cracow via Ploesti to Varna. Three days after Eaker made his proposal, the Russians were already in Ploesti (File: 522.01-1, in USAF/HA).

The Elusive Bomb Line 183

tions with the Russians, Lieutenant General Ira C. Eaker, the brilliant Chief of MAAF, sent a few of his officers to negotiate the entry of a liaison unit to Rumania. General Vorobiev, who completed arrangements for General Rodion Malinovsky, the Commander of the Second Ukrainian Army, exclaimed to General C. P. Cabell and Colonel P. M. Barr, the AAF representatives: "Now the matter is in the hands of the soldiers. Let us go ahead!"[5] As a consequence, a fifteen man detachment, commanded by Colonel John F. Batjer, went to Rumania in October and established regular contacts with officers of the Second Ukrainian Army. Batjer's team furnished MAAF with briefing material on missions, photo reconnaisance on targets, information on friendly and enemy troop dispositions, and in general, facilitated allied air force operations in southeastern Europe. Unfortunately, the experiment did not fulfill its potential because of the perennial difficulty of acquiring up-to-date operational information about Soviet military movements. Confined to Bucharest, Batjer's team found to its despair that "No Russian instrumentality [in Bucharest] has front line information or contact with the front other than through Moscow."[6]

On November 7, 1944, the Russians paid the price for their intransigence. Planes of the 82nd Fighter Group strafed a column of troops along a road in Yugoslavia where German traffic usually plied. This time Russians were there. The American unit killed Lieutenant General Kotov and five other soldiers. The air battle that followed between Lightnings and Yaks took two more Soviet lives. The incident was regrettable.[7] But considering the heavy AAF activity in areas near Soviet lines and the lack of effective liaison, it was remarkable that the first major American-Russian incident in eastern Europe did not come sooner and that similar ones were not more numerous. Between August 18 and November 11, 1944, the 15th Air Force flew approximately thirty-seven missions near Soviet lines in Yugoslavia and Hungary, claiming

5. Memo, Col. Barr for Anderson, November 28, 1944 (File: Portfolio entitled "Proposed Russian Bombline," in USAF/HA).
6. Msg., Eaker to Spaatz, November 5, 1944 (File: MAAF, 0403/11/413, in WWIIRD/NA); see the account in "History, Mediterranean Allied Air Forces," II, 381-82 (File: 620.354, in USAF/HA). The RAF had a liaison team in Sofia while Batjer's group was in Bucharest.
7. Msg., McNarney to AG, November 17, 1944; msg., Deane to Eaker, November 10, 1944 (File: MAAF, 0403/11/413, in WWIIRD/NA); "History, 82d Fighter Group," November, 1944 (File: GP-82-Hi, in USAF/HA).

184   EAGLES EAST

more than 600 planes destroyed and 300 damaged, not to mention
the destruction and damage to enemy vehicles, rolling stock, and
rail lines.[8] Arnold urged Eaker to press strongly for effective liaison
with Soviet field headquarters because "similar incidents can and
will happen in the future due to the lack of knowledge of the front
line situation both in our field headquarters and in the Soviet's
[sic]." Eaker expected the Russians now to demonstrate greater
interest in liaison without which more accidents were likely to
occur. "But what is more important," he commented dolefully,
"we are going to fail to attack valuable targets which would help
Russian ground forces for fear of having those incidents recur."[9]

Moscow was furious over the incident and acted as though the
AAF intentionally attacked the column. General Alexei Antonov,
the First Deputy Chief of the General Staff, demanded an immediate investigation by American authorities with full information
to the Combined Chiefs of Staff of the "deplorable facts." Antonov
denied the possibility of a genuine mistake by AAF pilots because
the Soviet planes allegedly had "clearly visible markings." He
added ironically that there was "no justification for these operations of American Air Forces not having been coordinated with the
General Staff of the Red Army."[10]

General Deane shrewdly used the incident to impress upon
Moscow the necessity of improving military coordination. He proposed that a liaison officer—either Russian or American— be
attached to the field headquarters of the other. The Russians
balked again at the proposal and returned to their oft-repeated
position that the only place for liaison was Moscow. But when
Deane cited the liaison team in Bucharest as a precedent to expand
contacts with other Russian units, Antonov disclaimed knowledge
of it.[11]

Soviet reluctance to accept the American liaison concept
forced Deane to search for some reasonable alternative: he went
further than most air force officers approved by suggesting that
the Russians establish a bomb line between their forces and the
air forces of the western Allies. A few days after the incident in

8. "History, Mediterranean Allied Air Forces," II, 385.
9. Ltr., Arnold to Eaker, November 16, 1944; ltr., Eaker to Arnold, November
21, 1944. These letters were shown to me by Dr. Alfred Sears who was editing
Arnold's letters to his commanders while I was at the USAF/HA.
10. Msg., Deane to Eaker, November 10, 1944.
11. Ibid.

The Elusive Bomb Line 185

Yugoslavia, Allied air forces operating near the Soviet front followed a self-imposed safety line procedure in order to avoid further incidents—bombers operated no closer than forty miles from Russian forward positions while fighters had a margin of eighty.[12]

No sooner had the safety line been adopted than Moscow proposed on November 23 that Anglo-American operations be confined to the west of a bomb line passing from Stettin through Sarajevo to the Yugoslavian-Bulgarian frontier. If the line were accepted in its entirety, Allied air force operations would have been compromised substantially, eliminating pressure on twenty top priority Nazi targets, including Blechhammer and Vienna. This line, naively ignoring topographical features, excluded AAF strategic operations in eastern Germany, Czechoslovakia, and Austria. All targets in Hungary were denied. The serious impact on strategic bombing in central and eastern Europe was obvious. After taking note of the objections of major field commanders—all of whom opposed it—the Combined Chiefs of Staff rejected the portion of the Soviet line extending from Stettin to Sarajevo and directed a continuance of the earlier safety-line policy for strategic operations. But the Combined Chiefs did accept the smaller portion of the line from Sarajevo to the southern border of Yugoslavia for tactical operations.[13]

The West reluctantly accepted the smaller section of the line. As Eaker complained, it was a "guide only," not a substitute for the long sought-after liaison with Soviet army units.[14] There were some commanders, however, who had deeper misgivings about the Combined Chiefs' decision. Wilson, angered for a long time by American approaches to the Russians about bomb lines without first consulting him, proposed a more practical one from Sarajevo to the south that would give greater freedom to his units to strike Nazi escape routes in particular from southern Yugoslavia. Deane approved the Wilson line, as it was called, and submitted it to the Soviets, emphasizing the western concept of flexibility in bomb lines and raising again the question of liaison in the field. To no

12. *Ibid.*; msg., Twining to CG, AAF, MTO (File: MAAF, 0403/11/413, in WWIIRD/NA).
13. Msg., Adm. Archer and Deane to CCS, November 23, 1944; msg., Wilson to CCS, November 24, 1944; msg., CCS to Wilson, Eisenhower, and Spaatz, November 24, 1944; msg., JCS to Deane, November 24, 1944 (File: MAAF, 0403/11/413, in WWIIRD/NA).
14. Minutes of meeting, November 29, 1944 (File: 519.1612, in USAF/HA).

186   EAGLES EAST

avail: the Soviets rejected the line as well as operational liaison.[15]

Deeply disturbed by the failures to work out effective methods of coordinating western air force operations in eastern Europe with the Russians, the Combined Chiefs early in December, 1944, approved the implementation of the Wilson Line without Moscow's agreement. The Combined Chiefs believed that the circumstances were sufficiently grave to warrant the drastic action—namely, the "urgent necessity to seize the opportunity to attack the heavy German concentrations between the present bomb line and that proposed to the Red Staff on 28 November [Wilson line]." The western *fait accompli* proved an effective method of dealing with the Russians: Moscow accepted the Wilson Line and in time even asked that the AAF fly missions east of it. Revised periodically by Wilson, who communicated the changes to the Russians through Deane's mission, it was a flexible demarcation between Soviet and Allied forces that functioned until the end of military operations in the Balkans.[16]

Early in December the Soviets returned to their idea of a strategic bomb line from the Baltic to the Balkans. Military considerations were not the only ones behind their pressures. General Slavin unabashedly admitted to Deane that the Soviet government was deeply concerned about the continuance of Allied supply missions to Polish partisans operating under the authority of the Polish Government-in-Exile in London. If accepted, the Soviet proposed line would have denied Allied missions to the pro-west Poles. From a military point of view, the line granted a larger zone of operations to western air forces than the Soviet proposal of November but still denied western attacks against top priority oil targets, including Blechhammer, Odertal, and Moravska Ostrava.[17]

The new Soviet proposal was no more satisfactory than the earlier one. Bomb lines established by governments, consistently

15. Msg., Wilson to CCS, November 27, 1944; msg., Deane to Wilson, November 28, 1944; msg., CCS to Military Mission, November 28, 1944 (File: MAAF, 0403/11/413, in WWIIRD/NA).
16. Msg., Deane to CCS, December 1, 1944; msg., CCS to Archer and Wilson, December 2, 1944; msg., Military Mission to CCS, December 2, 1944 (File: MAAF, 0403/11/413, in WWIIRD/NA); Ministry of Foreign Affairs of the U.S.S.R., *Stalin's Correspondence*, I, 283; "History, Mediterranean Allied Air Forces," II, 389; msg., Spaatz to Arnold, December 21, 1944 (File: MAAF, 0403/11/414, in WWIIRD/NA).
17. Msg., Archer and Deane to CCS, December 3, 1944; msg., Spaatz to Arnold, December 10, 1944 (File: MAAF, 0403/11/414, in WWIIRD/NA).

The Elusive Bomb Line

advocated by Moscow, were objectionable to the AAF which continued to urge western-style practices of military liaison on the army group level which could revise the lines on a day to day basis if necessary. Deane suggested a way out of the impasse: if the Soviets agreed to establish air liaison between field headquarters, then the United States would accept the Soviet strategic line.[18] In making this suggestion Deane clearly hoped liaison teams would exert an impact substantial enough to make the bomb line the flexible kind of instrument that Washington envisaged all along. But Soviet intransigence on the question of liaison did not augur well for the future of air force collaboration. The Strategy and Policy Group of the War Department General Staff observed gloomily:

> We have never had sufficient information regarding Soviet operations to bring about the best coordination of operations on the eastern and western fronts. Our experience to date indicates that it is unlikely that we will be able to improve this situation.
> . . . it is doubtful whether the Soviets will disclose their military plans or improve the procedures for the coordination of operations on the eastern and western fronts.[19]
> . . . the present indication is that the Russians do not intend to permit such Liaison Officers and this, when considered with their decisions regarding the Maritime Provinces, appears to be a part of firm Russian policy to keep the Allies out [of] Soviet operations.[20]

Yet, on a lower level, there were strong indications that Soviet military commanders wanted to improve contacts with their western colleagues. In September, it was General Yakoviev, the senior Russian officer in Bucharest, who proposed the general plan that later resulted in Colonel Batjer's group going to Rumania. On another occasion, General S. T. Biryusov confessed that he could

18. Meeting, Headquarters, MAAF, November 27, 1944 (File: 519.1612, in USAF/HA); msg., Archer and Deane to CCS, December 3, 1944.
19. OPD, WDGS, "Compilation of Existing Agreements, References and Trends relating to subjects of possible discussion at Argonaut," TAB E (File: Argonaut, in USAF/HA).
20. *Ibid.*, TAB E, 2. This refers to Soviet opposition to the entry of an American survey party which was to investigate the Vladivostok-Amur River region for the purpose of assessing AAF needs in later operations against Japan.

188   EAGLES EAST

achieve far more "on the spot" with Anglo-American officers than by referring matters to Moscow for action.[21]

No doubt Soviet officers recognized the fact that lack of coordination with the United States and Britain was a costly luxury. There were several instances of American offers to execute missions directly on behalf of the Russians that were unanswered or refused. For example, the AAF offered to bomb German forces, numbering perhaps *ten* divisions, on their way to Budapest if the Russians were unable to do so. The queries were ignored, and as a consequence, the Germans entered the city and set back the Russian offensive there for months. Collaboration with the United States would have eliminated one of the strongest pockets of Nazi resistance in 1945. The stubborn refusal of the Kremlin to help the AAF get Russian bases as a harbor for crippled and disabled planes, many hit by Russian flak and fighters, was another example of the abysmal level of military collaboration.[22] One would have thought after Air Chief Marshal Sir Arthur Tedder's meeting with Stalin in mid-January, 1945, when he explained western air strategy which was of such obvious benefit to the Russians, that Russia would have sought closer military contacts. No doubt this would have been the case if Stalin's objectives were closer to those of his Allies. But his tradition and training, dictating limited and cautious collaboration with the United States and Britain, conspired to prolong a war that probably could have ended sooner than it did.

A hopeful and yet frustrating point of the East-West dialogue respecting collaboration in eastern Europe came at the Yalta Conference. American, British and Russian representatives tentatively agreed that a limited zone of operations be established between the Russian front and a line passing from Stettin via Berlin and Vienna to Zagreb. Air force operations within the limited zone were not denied the West. The United States and Britain agreed to give the Soviets twenty-four hours' notice of a scheduled mission into .the zone. If the Russians raised no specific objection, the mission would proceed. But the Soviets sought to alter the arrange-

21. "History, Mediterranean Allied Air Forces," II, 390. Patrick K. Truesdell, who was in charge of the evacuation of one group of American pilots from the Soviet Union, sharply contrasted his dealings with Russian military and civilian officials. See memo, Truesdell to writer, February 2, 1969.

22. Ltr., Eaker to Arnold, January 19, 1945, with enclosures. The author saw this letter along with several others during the editing of Arnold's letters to his commanders by Dr. Alfred Sears at the USAF/HA.

The Elusive Bomb Line

ment a few days later by requiring their clearance of all contemplated missions within the limited zone before they began. The Combined Chiefs disapproved the rider; the agreement, like so many others, failed to be implemented at Yalta.[23] Unable to work out an accord with the Russians, the United States and Britain adopted arrangements similar to those stipulated in the defunct Yalta agreement—namely, adopting a zone of limited operations one hundred miles from known Soviet positions. Bombing missions within this zone were signalled to Moscow, usually twelve to twenty-four hours before time over target. Although Soviet approval of these missions was not required, Moscow had an opportunity to voice its objections. Even lists of priority targets within the area were forwarded for Moscow's benefit.[24] The Allied action left the Soviets with no alternative but eventually to accept the arrangements drawn up at Yalta. By the terms of an Anglo-American-Soviet agreement, effective March 10, 1945, Anglo-American air forces would not execute missions without twenty-four hours notice within a limited zone between the Soviet front and a line running through Posevalk, Berlin, Dresden, Vienna to Zagreb. Points on the line were considered within the unlimited zone. Soviet objections to a specific Allied mission within the zone would be respected. On the Soviet side, the Kremlin obligated itself to inform Allied military missions in Moscow forty-eight hours before any change was made in the zone of limitation.[25]

Agreement on strategic air force operations with the Russians came just one month before the end of Allied strategic bombing in Europe and the conversion of all groups to tactical units. No

23. See documents in U. S. Department of State, *Foreign Relations of the United States: Diplomatic Papers, 1945, The Conferences at Malta and Yalta* (Washington: United States Government Printing Office, 1955), 640-45; 800-01; 838-39; msg., Eaker to Twining, February 9, 1945 (File: MAAF, 0403/11/415, in WWIIRD/NA). The limited zone of operations extended only to Zagreb; previous arrangements concerning the tactical bomb line in the Balkans were in operation there.
24. Msg., Spaatz to Eaker, February 9, 1945; msg., Spaatz to Eaker, February 10, 1945; msg., Eaker to Twining, February 11, 1945; msg., Spaatz to Eaker, February 19, 1945 (File: MAAF, 0403/11/415, in WWIIRD/NA). The 8th Air Force had followed the procedure of bombing 100 miles west of known Russian positions prior to the Yalta meeting. The procedures of the 15th Air Force differed only slightly from the 8th; now both had common operational directives concerning missions near the Soviet front.
25. Msg., Hill to Arnold, February 27, 1945; msg., Spaatz to Arnold, February 28, 1945; msg., Eaker to Arnold, March 1, 1945; msg., Hill to Spaatz, March 7, 1945 (File: 0403/11/415 and 416, in WWIIRD/NA).

190 EAGLES EAST

sooner was the zone of limitation in official operation than several incidents involving the AAF and the Soviets marred the brief tryst of cooperation. Perhaps the most serious one involved the attempt of Lieutenant Myron King, who, after a forced landing in Warsaw, tried to smuggle a stowaway under the name of "Jack Smith" back to Britain. Moscow responded by grounding all AAF planes, except those of the Air Transport Command, in Soviet-held territory.[26] The increase of clashes involving the Soviet and American air forces—these were extraordinarily few considering the closeness and size of the forces—prompted the Joint Chiefs of Staff in April, 1945, to stop all tactical operations in support of the Soviets unless they explicitly asked for western air support.[27] This was wise policy. So long as the Soviets refused to accept the risk of a few incidents for the benefits of Allied bombing near their lines, it was ridiculous to help them against their will.

The United States and Britain never did persuade the Russians to approve the attachment of air force liaison groups with Soviet armies. The Batjer team, an exception that proves the rule, complained from the outset of its difficulty in acquiring military information from the Russians in Bucharest. The Kremlin held out during most of the war for bomb lines agreed to by governments rather than by regional military commanders. Soviet behavior can be explained not by the lack of understanding or appreciation for the flexible bomb line concept, but rather by the nature of the Soviet system itself. The Kremlin's rigid concept of zones of operation divided by a bomb line was the military counterpart to the political sphere of influence. For the Kremlin to have permitted liaison groups on lower military levels would have suggested a decentralization of monolithic operational control that Moscow scarcely wanted to convey to subordinate commands. Moreover, liaison by definition meant a sharing of information which the

26. Msg., MAAF to 15th AF, March 31, 1945 (File: 670.01-3E, Annex 65, in USAF/HA); see Eastern Command cables for period March-May, 1945. covering the incident and subsequent grounding of American planes in Russia (File: 522.1621, in USAF/HA).There was another incident in March, involving an American Liberator, commanded by Lt. Donald Bridge, which took off without Soviet clearance after being refueled in Mielec, Poland. The neurotic Soviet commander of the base was so shaken by this breach of protocol that he shot himself!
27. Msg., Deane to Marshall, April 6, 1945; msg., Marshall to Arnold, April 6, 1945; msg., Marshall to Olson, Eisenhower, Spaatz and McNarney, April 19, 1945 (File: 519.1612, in USAF/HA).

Russians were consistently reluctant to do with their allies during the war. One of the greatest ironies of World War II is that the Soviet westward advance made it progressively more difficult for the AAF to bring the full weight of its strategic air power to bear upon the Nazis in eastern Europe. In the final analysis much of the difficulty might have stemmed from Russian unwillingness to share credit with the United States in the subjugation of the enemy in central and eastern Europe.

Thus the western Allies were forced to adopt unilaterally a tactical bomb line in the Balkans and later the safety line and limited zone procedures for strategic air force operations before the Soviets finally acquiesced to an agreement. Though they lacked effective liaison on the operational level with the Russians, it is striking that so much damage in eastern Europe was done by Anglo-American air forces with so little cooperation from the Russians.

CHAPTER XIII

Eastern Command
United States Strategic Air Forces, 1944-45

THE ESTABLISHMENT and operation of American air force bases in Russia was the product of military and political objectives which thrust the connection with the Kremlin from the plane of Lend-Lease to the broader level of strengthening the relationship for wartime and postwar goals. The military objectives proved too ambitious and were reduced in significance as the war progressed. The political benefits which were supposed to accrue from the AAF being on Soviet soil failed because of a fundamental cleavage in American and Soviet views of the postwar world which became increasingly obvious by 1944.

Leaders in Washington and London had toyed for a long time with the idea of strengthening the wartime connection with the Kremlin by sending air force units to serve on the Soviet front. This was regarded as especially crucial during the difficult years before the Anglo-American invasion of France, the heralded "second-front" which had been postponed too often to the liking of the Russians. Western leaders hoped the decision to launch the invasion of North Africa instead of northwestern France in 1942, taken with full cognizance of the repercussions from the Kremlin, could be offset by the offer of a combined Anglo-American air force operating on the Russian front. But Stalin made it quite clear that he preferred greater deliveries of planes, not an air force, from the West.

The idea of basing the AAF on Soviet soil was not abandoned, only deferred to the halcyon days of the Tehran Conference. What followed was one of the most dramatic episodes in American military diplomacy. American objectives in establishing bases in Russia

192

started out modestly enough: the Joint Chiefs of Staff viewed them in relation to shuttle bombing operations between England and Italy on the one hand and the Soviet Union on the other. These missions were not to be isolated ones but related to the strategy contained in the Combined Bomber Offensive Plan which called for strategic bombardment of Nazi industrial—especially oil—targets in eastern Germany and Poland, not accessible from bases in Italy and England. Special importance was attached to the disruption of Germany's already weakened air defense system by forcing the Luftwaffe to spread its fighters over a wider area—obviously of crucial significance to the later invasion of France.[1]

The United States Military Mission to the U.S.S.R., created in October, 1943, in order to improve military coordination with the Russians, had the primary responsibility of procuring the bases for the AAF. The mission's perceptive commander, Major General John R. Deane, was quick to see that "if we play our cards right" the shuttle bombing project would establish a precedent to achieve another much cherished hope of the military planners—American bombing operations against Japan from Soviet bases in the Pacific.[2]

The matter of acquiring AAF bases in western Russia and planning Russo-American operations from the Pacific was taken up by President Roosevelt with Stalin at the Tehran Conference in November, 1943.[3] A month later, Ambassador Averell Harriman reported that the Russians approved "in principle" but needed more time to consider the question of collaboration in the Pacific war.[4]

In the days immediately following the Tehran meeting, Deane seemed to give more attention to the future operation of the AAF from the Maritimes by urging the Russians to build depots and centers at Irkutsk or Chita in Siberia to accommodate heavy bombardment units.[5] When Brigadier General Alfred Kessler, who was later to command American bases in Russia, visited Deane and Harriman in Moscow early in 1944, he found that both men viewed the shuttle bombing project primarily within the context of estab-

1. "History of Eastern Command," I, Ch. 1, para. 15; Ch. 2, para. 4-7 (File: 522.01-1 in USAF/HA).
2. *Ibid.*, Ch. 2, para. 3.
3. Msgs., Roosevelt to Stalin, November 29, 1943, Ministry of Foreign Affairs of the U.S.S.R., *Stalin's Correspondence*, II, 109-11.
4. "History of Eastern Command," I, Ch. 2, para. 2-3.
5. *Ibid.*

194 EAGLES EAST

lishing a precedent which allegedly would encourage Russian collaboration with the United States in the Pacific war.[6]

The months following the Tehran meeting saw a feverish pace of meetings among USSTAF officers and Soviet and American officials in Moscow to complete arrangements on Eastern Command, the name of the AAF headquarters in southern Russia, and the shuttle bombing missions, code named *Frantic*. At first no one had a clearly delineated plan of the scope of the operation. To the Russians their agreement "in principle" meant that details would have to be hammered out with the American representatives. The Americans avoided asking too much for fear of arousing Muscovite suspicions which might jeopardize the entire project. The mixture of occidental pragmatism and oriental caution produced in time a workable basis for the historic operations of the AAF from Soviet soil—a unique experiment in fighting and living together between the Russian and the American people.[7]

The Russians believed that the shuttle missions would be limited to hitting enemy targets en route to the Soviet Union, refueling there, and returning to AAF bases in Italy and England. This too had been the original assumption of the AAF. But as time went on military leaders became more keenly aware of the benefits of using Soviet bases in east-target-east missions in addition to west-target-east and east-target-west missions in siphoning off

---

6. *Ibid.*, See Kessler's memo for Commanding General, USSTAF in "Extracts from Major Lepawsky's Diary" (File: 522.117, in USAF/HA). While negotiations proceeded concerning the establishment of American bases in Russia, the Soviets approached Gen. Mason MacFarlane, head of the Allied Control Commission in Italy, and asked for bases there for supply missions to Tito and his partisans. The request was a modest one compared to the AAF project in Russia. Though some military figures, like Gen. Maitland Wilson, were critical of Russian diplomatic methods, there was no question of denying the request because of the fear of torpedoing the AAF project. After a carefully worded agreement was worked out which allowed a 24 plane detachment to operate out of Bari, the Soviets arrived with 4 additional aircraft for Marshal Tito. This was not exactly a breach of the agreement since the planes would be used by the Yugoslavs. But even slight departures by the AAF from Russo-American arrangements respecting Eastern Command without consultation with Russian officials usually brought swift and stern representations. Well might Gen. Wilson wonder whether a purely political present to Tito was a legitimate use of American Lend-Lease planes. Msg., Winant to Secretary of State, June 8, 1944; Ltr., Murphy to Secretary of State, July 29, 1944; msg., Murphy to Secretary of State, July 26, 1944 (File: 861.24565/6-844; /7-2944; /7-2644, in DS/NA).
7. "History of Eastern Command," I, Forward.

Eastern Command 1944-45 195

already weakened German fighter strength from the western front.[8]

If bombardment forces would make greater use of Russian bases, AAF proposals to bolster the task forces with escort fighters required even greater facilities and manpower to operate them. Particularly striking was Soviet agreement to American control of ground-air communications with AAF aircraft over Russian soil, probably the first time that a foreign military force enjoyed operational autonomy in the Soviet Union.[9]

The AAF initially limited the estimated number of permanent personnel required for service with Eastern Command in order not to prejudice the birth of the project. But as the scale of the operation unfolded, estimates increased to more than 2,000 which the Soviets reduced to 1,200. To accommodate special personnel, such as language experts and technicians, the figure was raised eventually to 1,270.[10]

While the Joint Chiefs of Staff estimated that ten bases would be needed, Stalin spoke in terms of six—three bases in the north and three in the south. After examining Soviet needs, geography, and climate, the AAF got three bases in the Ukraine—Poltava, the principal one, Mirgorod, and Piryatin.[11] Almost immediately these bases lost most of their value because of the rapid offensives which brought the Red Army well into eastern Europe. USSTAF observed late in July that strategic targets were becoming tactical ones and that many of them had to be preserved instead of bombed to help the Soviet advance.[12] By the end of August, half of Eastern Command's sixteen targets were in Soviet hands; by the end of November, only four of the original group were not under Soviet control.[13] The Russians promised new bases but these never materialized, and the future of the command grew dimmer after the summer of 1944.

8. *Ibid.*, Ch. 2, para. 15-16.
9. Historical Section, "Project Frantic: Russian [*sic*] Shuttle Bombing" (File: 622.430-6, in USAF/HA). This autonomy was compromised on one vital point— namely, notification to Soviet authorities of flights 24 to 48 hours in advance. Given the fluctuations in weather, this was impractical. The AAF preferred air corridors through the front for the passage of American planes but the Soviets rejected the idea in favor of reducing their notification requirements to 10 hours.
10. "History of Eastern Command," I, Ch. 7, para. 1-5. By the end of August, 1944, 1,323 people were associated with Eastern Command, although 130 had departed from Russia by that date.
11. "Deane Report," Part I, pp. 62-65; Part II, pp. 181-82.
12. "History of Eastern Command," I, Ch. 2, para. 23.
13. *Ibid.*, Ch. 2, para. 40-44.

196 EAGLES EAST

One aspect of AAF operations of special importance was photographic reconnaissance of enemy targets which were not readily accessible from bases in western and central Europe. During the early negotiations with the Russians, shuttle bombing and photo reconnaissance were treated separately, ostensibly because the latter might be implemented sooner. After he received Stalin's confirmation to his Tehran pledge respecting reconnaissance flights from Soviet bases, Harriman betrayed the delicacy of this aspect of the mission in the eyes of the security-conscious Russians by urging the appointment of Colonel Elliott Roosevelt, Chief of the Photographic Reconnaissance and Intelligence Section of USSTAF, to negotiate the matter. "It is our first step into Russia," Harriman declared. "It will set a pattern for future collaboration, especially with regard to the Japanese war . . . Because of his relationship, I feel that an atmosphere will be created by Elliott's presence in these negotiations." Elliot could not be spared, Arnold replied,[14] but Harriman's request pointed up the undeniable diplomatic and political overtones of Eastern Command. A USSTAF memorandum, describing the project under the code name *Baseball,* euphemistically observed:

> The main objective of Baseball itself is to prove to the other Ball Team how well we plan and play the game, so as to convince them to let us use their other Ball-fields. Whether they let us use their other Ball-fields or not, we are going to be playing somewhere in that League, and we must profit from both our lessons and our failures.
> The other Ball Team is a unique Ally with a state of mind and system of policies few of us understand. . . . Recommend therefore that 2nd Echelon of Baseball have 1 to 3 officers . . . possessing or ability to acquire a sympathetic understanding with the other Team's state of mind and society.[15]

One difficult aspect of establishing an AAF command in Russia was the problem of supply. The route to Archangel and Murmansk, a major artery for the delivery of Lend-Lease goods, had to be used along with the slower route from the Persian Gulf. The latter, though it had the capacity for year-round operation and excellent port facilities, lacked a complete rail connection with southern Russia. The heavy additional burdens upon existing

14. *Ibid.,* Ch. 8, para. 71.
15. *Ibid.,* para. 66.

Eastern Command 1944-45

supply routes—added to the long range plan of AAF operations from Siberia—prompted the Military Mission in Moscow to urge the opening of a new route through the Black Sea.[16] The proposal, however, was quite impractical in view of Turkey's firm neutrality and the operation of German units in the eastern Mediterranean.

What became clear during the planning conferences with the Russians was that Eastern Command would not be limited merely to servicing American task forces returning from missions in eastern Europe. Eastern Command opened up a wide arena of possibilities for military collaboration between the two countries. The very fact that Eastern Command existed and supervised American combat operations in eastern Europe from Soviet bases provided a point of contact from which to expand the scope of collaboration to include such high priority items as exchanging weather ciphers, establishing an air transport system between Moscow and Washington, sharing intelligence information, and improving military liaison. But combat operations, the principal *raison d'etre* of the AAF in Russia, was the immediate concern.

A. Operations

No mission can take place without a target. Despite the plethora of targets in eastern Europe, the first shuttle mission to Russia was complicated by a serious difference of opinion between American and Soviet officials. Curiously, the Russians were reticent at first in expressing their wishes about targets they wanted bombed. Yet, when General Spaatz decided on several possibilities, the Russians refused to approve them, urging instead that the AAF hit tactical ones in an area where Soviet ground forces were operating. The strategic-tactical target syndrome was characteristic of the difference in air force thinking between the American and Soviet military.[17] The AAF complied with Soviet wishes by launching its first shuttle mission on June 2, 1944, with a routine attack upon the marshalling yards at Debrecen, Hungary, which could have been bombed just as easily from bases in Italy. The historic mission made up in dignitaries what it lacked in success. The Commanding General of MAAF, Ira Eaker, accompanied the flight of the 127 Fortresses and 64 Mustangs. He was welcomed by a mixed Russian and American delegation in a drizzling rain, got a

16. *Ibid.*, II, Part 2.
17. "History of Eastern Command," I, Ch. 2, para. 14-21.

198   EAGLES EAST

bouquet of flowers from Major General A. R. Perminov, the Soviet Commander at Poltava, who in turn received the Legion of Merit. The impact of the mission on the Germans, however, was lost in the confusion accompanying the invasion of Normandy.

The two missions that followed were more effective, rated "good" by military evaluators, and were more economical from Soviet than Italian bases. However, neither of the missions, which hit airdromes in Rumania, were strategic operations.[18]

The first strategic attack did not come until 114 bombers and 70 fighters of the 8th Air Force struck synthetic oil facilities at Ruhland in lower Silesia on June 21, and followed it after an over-night stop at Russian bases by an attack on a hitherto immune target—oil refineries at Drohobycz, Poland.[19] "This event," relates Adolf Galland, "caused a considerable stir in the German High Command." The Germans grimly pondered whether this meant the opening of another air front that now placed key industries, moved at great cost to the east, at the mercy of American bombers. The German High Command clearly evinced its concern with this new dimension of strategic bombardment by emasculating the 4th Flying Corps by taking approximately 200 scarce JU 88's and HE 111's from bases in eastern Poland for an attack on Poltava in the early hours of June 22.[20] What followed was one of the most

18. *Ibid.*, Ch. 4, para. 2-4. Less than two weeks before the first shuttle mission, the United States approved the release of the M-9 Norden Bombsight and C-1 Automatic Pilot, both of which the Soviets had long hoped to get. The timing suggests that the American decision was tied to the negotiations with the Russians over *Frantic*. Ltr., Rudenko to Arnold, April 12, 1944; ltr., Giles to Rudenko, May 21, 1944; ltr., Rudenko to Giles, May 29, 1944 (File: H. H. Arnold, Box 129, in MD/LC).

19. "History of Eastern Command," I, Ch. 4, para. 5-8.

20. Adolph Galland, *The First and the Last: The Rise and Fall of the German Fighter Forces, 1938-1945* (New York: Henry Holt & Co., 1954), pp. 281-93. On the other hand, Craven and Cate tell us: "The much vaunted purpose of frightening and distracting the Germans did not materialize at all." Craven and Cate, *The Army Air Forces in World War II*, III; 318. This is not an accurate picture. If the Germans regarded Eastern Command and Frantic so casually, one wonders why they risked their scant fighters to raid Poltava in the first place? Statistics show an increase in GAF fighter strength on the eastern front—doubled—in the last year of the war, though the preponderance of fighter strength, it is true, remained in the West. But disposition of aircraft strength at a time when major offensives came from the West hardly proves the casual attitude toward the affair that some captured German generals such as Keitel, who was almost universally despised by his own cronies, would have us believe. Furthermore, there is evidence to show the deployment of scarce antiaircraft batteries to hydrogenation plants which were so vulnerable to *Frantic*. See "Transfer of Flak Artillery Because of the 'Shuttle Bombing' of the

Eastern Command 1944-45 199

destructive attacks in the history of the AAF, ranking with the Japanese assault on Hickam Field at Pearl Harbor. The Luftwaffe proved even at this late date in the war that it was still capable of launching a well-organized precision bombing spectacle, one of the most accurate ever witnessed by seasoned AAF task force commanders. The statistics bear out the assessment: 43 B-17's destroyed or damaged beyond repair, 26 B-17's damaged but repairable, and 6 transports destroyed or damaged. Since an overwhelming percentage of the bombs fell on the field, the damage and destruction to vehicles, supplies, and facilities was large. Surprisingly, however, only two Americans lost their lives, although fourteen were wounded. Soviet losses ran considerably higher—thirty dead and ninety-five wounded—figures that were increased by a later, not so successful Luftwaffe attack on the sister fields of Mirgorod and Piryatin. Toward the end of the attack, a general on inspection turned his flashlight into a slit trench. An enlisted man occupant blurted: "Put that damned light out," and then he recognized the general. Neither man apologized to the other.[21] The attack proved to be the first and the last effort of the Luftwaffe against the American operated bases in Russia.

The Luftwaffe attack, no doubt intended to demoralize the Allies, bared the gaping deficiencies in Soviet airdrome defense. Soviet anti-aircraft detachments, one observer commented wryly, did "a hell of a lot of shooting." But, he hastened to add, "Most of their efforts seemed to be just wild firing"[22]—testimony that was substantiated by the continuance of the anti-aircraft barrages long after the Germans returned to their bases without the loss of a single plane.[23]

The incident embarrassed the Russians and disturbed the Americans. Although a few doubts were raised by some American

---

American Air Force," excerpt from the Daily Situation Reports of the High Command of the Luftwaffe, Operations Staff, June, 1944 (File: Karlsruhe Document Collection, in USAF/HA).

21. "History of Eastern Command," Ch. 6, para. 11-14. The loss of 15 P-51's, though not mentioned in the "History of Eastern Command," was claimed by the Germans. See Walter Grabmann, "Analysis of Specialized Anglo-American Techniques," used for USAF Study 183 (File: Karlsruhe Document Collection, in USAF/HA). The two Americans who lost their lives were F. O. J. G. Lukacek and Lt. Raymond Estels.

22. Report, Col. Archie J. Old, Jr. to CG, 3d Bombardment Division, July 6, 1944, in "History of Eastern Command," II, Part I.

23. Craven and Cate, *The Army Air Forces in World War II*, III, 314.

officers about continuing the operation, the stakes were too high. Stalin initially approved an ambitious American proposal which called for a massive increment of more than 6,000 men to bolster the defenses of the bases.[24] But it was never implemented because Moscow soon grew chilly to the whole idea of continuing the shuttle operations.

The Americans recovered better from the incident than their hosts. Not only did the United States want to continue operations but also to expand the combat aspects into a permanently based air force from Soviet airdromes. The immediate objective, of course, was to resume the shuttle operations as soon as possible in order to demonstrate to the Nazis continuing Russo-American collaboration on the eastern front. Beginning on July 22 and continuing for the next several days, a series of strafing attacks by Lightnings of the 15th Air Force hit airdromes in Rumania and Poland with creditable results. This series of missions was followed by another task force of the 15th Air Force which hit Rumanian targets late in July and early August. But the losses and damage to fighters were so costly for the results produced, that General Kessler advised the discontinuance of the strafing missions.[25]

With the departure of the fighters, the 8th Air Force dispatched a huge force of seventy-six Fortresses and sixty-four Mustangs against a Focke-Wulf factory at Rahmel on August 6, followed by two more missions from Soviet bases against oil refineries in Poland and airdromes in Rumania. These were the most successful missions of the shuttle bombing series.[26]

A month passed before the AAF resumed the missions, delayed largely because of the tense political situation arising from the Warsaw uprising. Attacks against targets in Germany and Hungary and a supply mission to the beleaguered Poles concluded American operations from Russian bases.[27]

In summary, Eastern Command accommodated seven task forces—four from Great Britain and three from Italy. These forces executed a total of eighteen bombing and strafing missions and one supply-dropping mission. Seven of the eighteen combat missions were west-target-east shuttle missions to Russia, eight were east-

24. "History of Eastern Command," I, Ch. 6, para. 25.
25. *Ibid.*, Ch. 4, para. 5-11.
26. *Ibid.*, para. 12.
27. *Ibid.*, para. 13-15.

target-west missions from Russia to Italy, and three were east-target-east missions in which Soviet fields were used for take-off and return. More than 1,000 aircraft landed at Eastern Command bases, completing more than 2,200 sorties to or from Russian bases.[28]

Despite the impressive number of planes involved in these summer operations, the military significance of the missions was modest. Only six of the sixteen targets hit by American planes were strategic, and most of the targets could have been reached without the use of Soviet bases. As the Eastern Command historian put it, only three of the targets "would have been relatively out of economical range of USSTAF bombers had it not been for the availability of the Russian bases."[29] Moreover, there is no evidence that AAF bombing and strafing missions accomplished more than a brief disruption of operations in the target areas. Since more than half of the targets hit by the AAF were tactical, these missions contributed directly to the Soviet advance. But the strategic bombing missions, the Eastern Command historian stated frankly,

> accomplished less physical destruction of German life, production and military targets, than would have been accomplished by an equivalent expenditure of AAF manpower, machines and money continuing to operate from the U.K. and Italian bases.[30]

The real significance of the missions can not be found in sorties flown or bombs dropped but rather in the psychological impact of the entire operation. The United States and the Soviet Union had clearly demonstrated to the Nazis that the Allied alliance, despite growing political difficulties among the partners, was not the myth claimed by Dr. Goebbels. It was stable enough to give tangible evidence of its commitment to closing the ring around the Third Reich.

B. The AAF and the Warsaw Uprising

No event of the war demonstrated the real intentions of the Soviets toward Poland more than their attitude toward the uprising

28. *Ibid.*, para. 1. Battle losses incurred during Eastern Command operations included: 2 killed, 10 wounded and 41 missing in action. Losses from German attacks on AAF bases included 2 killed and 14 wounded.
29. *Ibid.*, para. 40-44.
30. *Ibid.*, Ch. 12, para. 5.

202   EAGLES EAST

of the Polish Home Army, known as the AK, under the leadership
of General T. Bor-Kormorowski. The Home Army had the authority from the Polish government in London to launch an uprising
in Warsaw in support of the approaching Russians.[31] The Soviet
advance and the Nazi retreat promised a swift liberation of the
Polish capital which had received several emotional messages from
Russian and Polish Communists to revolt against the Nazis.[32] The
Russians expected to be in Warsaw early in August.[33] The con-
catenation of favorable events, including the strong opposition
among leading German officers who tried to kill Hitler late in July,
led to General Bor-Komorowski's order to launch the ill-fated
uprising on August 1:

> In fifteen minutes an entire city of a million inhabitants was
> engulfed in the fight. Every kind of traffic ceased. As a big
> communication centre where roads from north, south, east,
> and west converged, in the immediate rear of the German
> front, Warsaw ceased to exist. The battle for the city was on.[34]

Almost immediately Prime Minister Churchill telegraphed Stalin,
telling him of British intentions to assist the Poles and relating the
appeals of Warsaw for Soviet assistance. Stalin doubted Polish
claims of controlling key installations in the city and offered no
help.[35] His grim reply confirmed earlier reports of the Soviet
attitude toward the Home Army which even before the uprising
assisted Russian forces in taking Vilna and areas in the Volhynia.
Polish officers were rewarded by arrest and, in some cases, execution. Stanislaw Mikolajczyk, the prime minister of the Polish government, urged Roosevelt to send American officers to the eastern
front to urge the Soviets to stop their violence. Nothing came of
the appeal.[36]

31. The London government unanimously empowered Bor "to proclaim the
insurrection at a moment which you will decide as most opportune. If possible,
let us know beforehand." Waclaw Jedrzejewicz (comp. and ed.), *Poland in the
British Parliament, 1939-1945*, Vol. III: *Summer 1944-Summer 1945* (New
York: Jozef Pilsudski Institute of America, 1962), p. 7.
32. *Ibid.*, p. 9.
33. Jan Ciechanowski, *Defeat in Victory* (New York: Doubleday & Co., Inc.,
1947), p. 322. Marvin W. McFarland, "Air Power and the Warsaw Uprising,
August-September, 1944," *The Airpower Historian* (October, 1956), p. 189.
34. Winston S. Churchill, *Triumph and Tragedy* (Boston: Houghton Mifflin
Co., 1953), p. 130.
35. *Ibid.*, pp. 130-31.
36. Ciechanowski, *Defeat in Victory*, p. 317.

Eastern Command 1944-45

The curious behavior of the Russians at the Vistula has been explained essentially in military terms. The Soviet offensive "had reached the end of its tether," declares Alan Clarke, the historian of the Russo-German war who believes that German counter-attacks and Soviet over-extension combined to dictate a halt at the Vistula.[37] The Russians may have needed some time to regroup and resupply, but an army with three times more tanks, four times more infantry, six times more artillery, and five times more aircraft than the Wehrmacht[38]—not to mention having a strong pro-Allied force in Poland itself—was in a position to take more decisive measures than it did to relieve the Poles. That it did so only when the Poles were defeated rings more like the Kremlin's political cynicism than the need to strengthen itself before a crumbling enemy.

Despite the failure to influence the Soviets to help the Poles, the RAF flew supply missions on August 4 and again on August 8 from bases in Italy. The attempts, declared Churchill, "were both forlorn and inadequate" since only five planes were involved. During the second week of August, ten to fifteen planes flew to Warsaw, but after the 14th of the month, these missions stopped almost entirely.[39] Crews had to fly over 700 miles and suffered high casualties from enemy flak and fighters while the Russians remained rooted less than ten miles away from the Polish capital. One observer told of seeing Germans and Russians bathing on different sides of the Vistula as if a truce existed while the Poles were being decimated.[40] From the middle of August until the end of the uprising, the RAF usually dropped supplies in the forest of Kampinos from where they were subsequently smuggled into the city.[41]

American military leaders were reluctant to air lift supplies to the Poles. Some, like Major General F. L. Anderson, who served as Spaatz's deputy for operations, vented an Anglophobia, unreasonably blaming the British for pressing a matter that stood to jeopardize Russo-American military collaboration.[42] To many of

---

37. Alan Clarke, *Barbarossa: The Russian-German Conflict, 1941-1945* (New York: The New American Library, 1965), p. 431.
38. *Ibid.*, p. 443; U. S., War Department, "Preliminary Report," TAB VIII-5A.
39. Churchill, *Triumph and Tragedy*, p. 131; T. Bor - Komorowski, *The Secret Army* (New York: The Macmillan Co., 1951), pp. 262, 266, 279.
40. Clarke, *Barbarossa*, p. 433.
41. Bor - Komorowski, *The Secret Army*, pp. 280-81.
42. McFarland, "Air Power and the Warsaw Uprising," pp. 190-91.

204 EAGLES EAST

these men, schooled in the bitter business of computing casualties and losses which had to be maintained at acceptable rates, the use of heavy bombers without fighter escort over long distances was militarily foolish. Then, too, there were the equally compelling reasons for them to use aircraft and crews for the invasion of southern France which developed at the same time as the Polish insurrection. Moreover, the Joint Chiefs of Staff had long written off eastern Europe as an area of its responsibility, leaving it to the British.

But the pleas of the Poles could not be ignored by the United States, which sought Soviet approval for an 8th Air Force supply drop using Russian bases. On August 14, the 8th Air Force filed alternate plans with Eastern Command for clearance with the Russians—one for a bombing operation against Konigsberg, the other a supply drop to Warsaw. On the following day, the Soviets refused both requests but had no objection to American or British planes dropping supplies "as long as Soviet bases were not used."[43] Stalin cynically described the Polish effort against the Germans as "a reckless and terrible adventure." Dismayed by this, Churchill reminded the President that "We are nations serving high causes and must give true counsels towards world peace even at the risk of Stalin resenting it. Quite possibly he wouldn't."[44] The experience shook the confidence of Ambassador Harriman who described Soviet policy as based upon "ruthless political considerations."[45]

The President had no intention of abandoning the Poles. Neither did he want to alienate the stubborn Russians. He tried through diplomacy to alter their attitude by having Harriman join the British ambassador in Moscow to exert pressure on the Russians. Then upon the insistence of Churchill, the President and Prime Minister sent a joint plea to Stalin on August 20, declaring there would be an outraged world opinion if the Poles were abandoned in their hour of desperate need. They pointedly asked Stalin to send aid or agree to let AAF-RAF planes do so and use Soviet

43. McFarland, "Air Power and the Warsaw Uprising," p. 190; msg., Harriman to Secretary of State, August 15, 1944, U. S. Department of State, *Foreign Relations of the United States: Diplomatic Papers, 1944*, Vol. III, *The British Commonwealth and Europe* (Washington: United States Government Printing Office, 1965), 1374-76; msg., Harriman to Secretary of State, August 17, 1944 (File: in DS/NA).
44. Churchill, *Triumph and Tragedy*, pp. 134-35.
45. Msg., Harriman to Secretary of State, August 15, 1944, *Foreign Relations, 1944*, III, 1376.

Eastern Command 1944-45

bases. Stalin was still unmoved. He bluntly labelled the leaders of the uprising "criminals" and explained Soviet problems in breaking German counter-attacks around Warsaw, all the while ignoring references to the western appeal to use Soviet bases for an Allied supply drop.[46]

The Polish question clearly revealed just how fragile the western alliance with Moscow was. Stalin demonstrated that he wanted the Polish affair resolved his way, even at the risk of a break with London and Washington. How else could the Soviet position of refusing to assist the Poles and to cooperate with England and the United States be explained but in terms of a blatant attempt to reduce the non-communist leadership of Poland? It was noteworthy that the Kremlin's refusal to bow to western pressures to use Russian bases for supply missions was linked with a counter-demand that the Eastern Command close out its operations and return the bases to Soviet use.

Failing to moderate the Soviet position, Churchill wanted the President to take a gamble, urging him to send American planes to drop supplies to the Poles and land in Russia without authorization if necessary. He seriously doubted that the planes and crews would be mistreated by the Russians. The President shied away from what he considered to be a too drastic solution[47]— one which risked rupture of an already fractured alliance that he was still so anxious to use against Japan and to continue into the postwar period. Even Churchill later commented in defense of his wartime colleague "that terrible and even humbling submissions must at times be made to the general aim."[48]

Despite Soviet opposition to assisting the Poles and cooperating with Britain and the United States by allowing their planes to use Russian bases, volunteer crews of the 205th RAF Group in Italy continued to fly missions to Warsaw during the critical months of August and September and suffered heavy casualties. In six weeks of operations these men chalked up 181 sorties and lost 31 aircraft.[49] Their efforts, however, contributed more to

46. Churchill, *Triumph and Tragedy*, pp. 135-36.
47. *Ibid.*, pp. 139-40.
48. *Ibid.*, p. 141.
49. Craven and Cate, *The Army Air Forces in World War II*, III, 316-17; Halle quotes a letter of Sir John Slessor, Commander of the RAF in Italy, which appeared in *The Observer*, August 16, 1964. See Louis Halle, *The Cold War As History* (New York: Harper & Row, Publishers, 1967), p. 64, footnote 2.

206 EAGLES EAST

Polish morale than material strength. Finally on September 10, the Soviets dramatically changed their position: Moscow was prepared to act with London and Washington in a concerted plan of assistance.[50] What prompted the Soviets to alter their course cannot definitely be known. Allied pressures combined with the bad press the Russians received from their refusals to cooperate may have convinced Stalin of the wisdom of making a concession that would rekindle the Soviet liberation image which had been all but destroyed by the stance at the Vistula. And the price was not great since the destruction of the Polish Underground Army was almost complete. Stalin could have his cake and eat it too: destroy the one force capable of opposition to the Soviet and Polish communists and pose as a liberator of the Polish nation. As Churchill put it, the Russians "wished to have the non-Communist Poles destroyed to the full, but also to keep alive the idea that they were going to their rescue."[51]

Despite Soviet insistence upon working out a coordinated plan with the AAF and RAF, the Russians began dropping supplies without parachutes on September 13—ironically, the contents were American canned food and ammunition. In view of this development, the AAF was free to execute its own supply drop to the Poles which was cleared by the Soviets but delayed due to bad weather until September 18.[52] The AAF's 110 Flying Fortresses, escorted by 150 Mustangs, took off on that date for Warsaw. Three bombers returned early and two were lost. One of the three fighter groups escorted the heavies all the way to Russia with only one loss. But the mission was not very successful. Out of more than 1,200 containers of food, ammunition and arms, less than 300 got into Polish hands. If the mission had been flown a few weeks earlier, when the Poles held a far wider area, they would have retrieved most of the supplies, and this could have made the crucial difference before the Russians finally entered the city.[53] If the Poles had succeeded against the Germans, it is difficult to see how the Russians could have done anything but reach a *modus vivendi* with the Warsaw

50. Msg., Harriman to Hull, September 10, 1944, *Foreign Relations*, 1944, III, 1396.
51. Churchill, *Triumph and Tragedy*, p. 144.
52. "History of Eastern Command," I, Ch. 5, para. 45-46; Bor - Komorowski, *The Secret Army*, pp. 342-43.
53. Allied Expeditionary Air Force, Daily Int/Tops Summary No. 243 (File: 520.332, in USAF/HA); Bor - Komorowski, *The Secret Army*, pp. 349-50.

Eastern Command 1944-45   207

Poles, provided western policy was firmer than it was during the agonizing efforts to get approval for the use of Soviet bases.

The Poles were jubilant over the American supply effort and appealed for additional help. The 8th Air Force scheduled another mission, but the Soviets on October 2 opposed further flights, claiming that the insurgents had been squelched by the Nazis. This was not entirely true. Although Warsaw surrendered on October 2, the insurgents elsewhere, such as in the area of Radom, continued to fight.[54]

One cannot help speculating on the implications of the opposing positions of Britain and the United States on the one hand and the Soviet Union. Ambassador Harriman's reports from Moscow dramatically revealed his profound disillusionment with Russian leaders whom he described as men "bloated with power [who] expect that they can force their will on us and all countries to accept their decisions without questions."[55] Harriman's advice of presenting strong representations of American displeasure with the Russians was milder than George Kennan's who advised "a full-fledged and realistic political showdown with the Soviet leaders."[56] Well might Kennan view with despair the progress of subsequent negotiations with the Russians after the failure of the first genuine test of political and military collaboration on a major wartime problem.

C. End of Operations

The AAF expected to continue and even expand operations from Soviet bases during the winter months. Arnold wanted the bases moved to Poland or Rumania to continue the strategic bombing offensive against the Nazis during the winter and thus deprive the enemy of an opportunity to recuperate. "Without such bases," Arnold declared, "our bombing offensive will suffer what I feel to be a most unnecessary and unforgivable lapse." Betraying

54. "History of Eastern Command," I, Ch. 5, para. 48; McFarland, "Air Power and the Warsaw Uprising," pp. 192-93. The RAF continued to fly missions until the middle of October. See Craven and Cate, *The Army Air Forces in World War II*, III, 316-17. Later attempts to get Soviet agreement to AAF plans which involved flights over Russian controlled territory to help small groups of Polish partisans failed. See msg., Deane to Hq., MAAF, November 21, 1944 (File: 622.311-1, in USAF/HA).
55. *Foreign Relations*, 1944, III, 1389, footnote 11.
56. George F. Kennan, *Memoirs: 1925-1950* (Boston: Little, Brown & Co., 1967), p. 211.

208 EAGLES EAST

an exaggerated optimism concerning the role of air power in forcing a Nazi surrender, Arnold suggested that "The Allied air forces are capable of inflicting the final death blow on Germany in the next few months." Russia, he implied, should not "deny the combined Allied efforts this assurance of an early victory."[57] During the summer of 1944 AAF officers discussed plans to base a permanent force of three bombardment groups and one fighter group on Soviet territory, flying 2,500 sorties a month. Expansion plans called for an increase of Eastern Command strength to 18,500 men.[58]

Meanwhile, the United States Military Mission in Moscow contributed its share to the planning by recommending that the Eastern Command be increased to 8,900 men and that after winterizing existing bases, four new airdromes be developed in the Vinnitsa area for operations in the spring of 1945. Deane's group, exaggerating the relationship of *Frantic* operations to later AAF flights from Siberia, believed that bases in Vinnitsa could be linked in a logistical network extending from the Black Sea to supply depots in Siberia.[59] It was at the Yalta conference that the United States submitted a proposal for the establishment of shuttle bases in Budapest. Although the Russians approved "in principle," they delayed in responding favorably to a request for a survey of the area. After the survey was made and the United States expressed a desire to initiate operations promptly, the Soviet Union replied that it still was not certain whether to allow the project to continue. In the face of these harassing delays and the approaching end of the war, the Joint Chiefs of Staff abandoned the plan.[60]

Expansion plans met with a chilly response from Moscow. The Soviets, already rapidly overruning eastern Europe, were not pleased to see more Americans in Russia. In fact the Kremlin

57. "History of Eastern Command," I, Ch. 2, para. 8.
58. *Ibid.*, II, Part 2.
59. *Ibid.* Vinnitsa was located approximately 270 miles west of Poltava. Mass graves of Stalin's purges were discovered there in 1943.
60. Report, Spaatz to Arnold, n.d., TAB D (File: MAAF, 0403/11/884, in WWIIRD/NA); memo, Roosevelt for Stalin, February 7, 1945, Ministry of Foreign Affairs of the U.S.S.R., *Stalin's Correspondence*, II, 189; msg., Marshall to Olson, Eisenhower, Spaatz, and McNarney, April 19, 1945 (File: 519. 1612-1942-45, in USAF/HA). At one point the movement of the entire 15th Air Force from Italy to Budapest was seriously contemplated. Air planners in Washington even speculated that there might be as many as 50,000 troops in Russia some day. R & R, AC/AS, Plans to AC/AS, Intelligence, September 5, 1944 (File: 145.95, in USAF/HA).

Eastern Command 1944-45 209

was not at all enthusiastic about a continuation of Eastern Command. It made this clear by urging the evacuation of Poltava, Mirgorod, and Piryatin by September 15. Faced with the collapse of the existing project, the AAF sought to salvage something—at least to hold Poltava with a reduced contingent of 200-300 men. A six-weeks delay in replying to the American request clearly showed that when Russian official approval finally came, it was a concession reluctantly made.[61] In view of the tense situation arising from the Warsaw uprising and the difficult political question of Poland in Allied diplomacy, the Kremlin's decision might have been a sop to clear the official air between Moscow and the capitals of the West.

Since the advance of the Soviet armies rapidly eliminated the number of strategic targets in eastern Europe, it must have been difficult for the Russians to understand why the United States was so persistent in urging not only a continuation but an expansion of operations from Soviet bases that were no longer crucial to the air power offensive. Suspicion, almost a congenital Soviet trait, tempered with a realistic assessment of Russian efforts in the war and ambitions for the future, chilled the desires of the Kremlin to foster further the Russo-American military collaboration on the eastern front. This was no more than a reflection of Soviet political policy which aimed at limiting, and wherever possible, eliminating non-Russian activities in eastern Europe.

Before Eastern Command hibernated for the winter of 1944, it had explored other aspects of military collaboration with the Russians with varying degrees of success. Perhaps the most productive area of a genuine exchange of information was in the field of weather forecasting. So successful was the cooperation in this non-sensitive area that the Joint Chiefs of Staff urged an expansion of the program to include weather data on the north Pacific—of obvious value to the United States if and when AAF units operated from Siberian bases.[62]

But *quid pro quo* was not the norm of the AAF-SAF relationship when it involved sharing intelligence information. As was to be expected, the AAF was far more generous in providing military information than the Russians. Eastern Command provided the Soviets with daily and weekly intelligence bulletins of SHAEF

61. "History of Eastern Command," I, Ch. 3, para. 31-32.
62. *Ibid.*, I, Ch. 5, para. 29.

210 EAGLES EAST

and USSTAF, allowed them to attend briefings of missions and to accompany AAF missions, offered regular and extensive information on aerial reconnaissance, and permitted Soviet personnel to work directly with specialized AAF units to learn and observe techniques and operations. On their part, the Russians were chary in providing intelligence bulletins, disapproved of foreign personnel accompanying Soviet air force missions, reciprocated little in the way of providing photographs of areas prohibited to the AAF, and were usually reluctant and evasive when confronted by specific questions respecting their military equipment, techniques and operations.

Characteristically, the Russians were more liberal in sharing technical information on German than Soviet equipment. The Russians permitted AAF observers to study Nazi launching sites for pilotless aircraft in Poland; yet they disapproved a request to inspect Soviet gas defenses. Even a request to see a Russian gas mask was ignored. On the other hand, the AAF agreed to comply with Russian requests for the Norden Bombsight and the C-1 Automatic Pilot, both of which were in operational use by the AAF.[63]

Considering the security practices of the Kremlin, the information the AAF did receive was a significant breach in a heretofore ironclad wall of silence. Moscow, forced by wartime exigencies, could not always demur or refuse American requests for a joint military project. Often lower echelon American officers mistook vague or delinquent replies to their questions as unwillingness of Soviet officers to cooperate. This was true in many cases, but often the explanation lay in a genuine lack of information by the Russians themselves who were part of a regimented hierarchal system which placed greater premium on secrecy than efficiency. An accurate assessment of this phase of AAF relationships with the Soviets was made by the perceptive historian of Eastern Command:

the tendency to be completely closemouthed about their own general and technical equipment, while expecting the Ameri-

63. *Ibid.*, para. 2-27. Approval came in May, 1944. See ltr., Giles to Rudenko, May 21, 1944 (File: H. H. Arnold, Box 129, in MD/LC). A small group of men was sent to offer a 72 hour condensed course to Russian pilots. The shortened course, given at Russian request, greatly displeased Arnold who felt that results would be poor. "Deane Report," II, 290-92. Generally speaking, the Russian pilot was technically inferior to his American counterpart but the Russian tried to make up for it in derring-do.

cans to be bountiful with their secret data and equipment, can only be attributed to the pervasive and persistent influence of their own internal security policy, a continued mistrust of foreigners and especially of foreign military intelligence, a habituation to past American generosity, a hard-headed self-interest, and a realistic sense of bargaining in war and post-war international relations.[64]

The temporary end of the shuttle missions in September, 1944, proved to be permanent, although the AAF hoped combat operations from Soviet bases would be resumed in the spring. Eastern Command, reduced now to a few hundred men, restricted its activities to the more prosaic but still important chores of maintaining liaison with the Russians and continuing exchanges of information. Troop dispositions on the eastern front were regularly forwarded to MAAF to enable delineations of the bomb line between the American and Soviet forces operating in close proximity. On its part, the Signal Section of Eastern Command handled 3,000 groups of weather traffic daily during the winter months.[65]

In contrast to the efficiency and cooperation the Soviets gave in evacuating American airmen who had been downed in Siberia during missions against the Japanese, the Russians were disinterested in helping Eastern Command to evacuate American combat crews from eastern Europe. Major General Edmund W. Hill who headed AAF matters in Deane's mission—late in February, 1945—came to an understanding with Marshal S. A. Khudyakov regarding the salvage of American aircraft and the evacuation of flyers from Russian occupied territory. This was in accord with the repatriation agreement signed by both sides at Yalta. Ostensibly, Eastern Command would handle salvage and evacuation matters north of the Carpathians, and the American mission in Bucharest would handle the matter south of the mountain chain. No sooner was the agreement made than Hill accused the Soviets of blocking American efforts. Reports of Soviet cannibalization of planes forced to land in eastern Europe and Soviet delays in informing AAF authorities at Poltava or Moscow about the downed aircraft raised serious doubts about the earlier assurances, always freely given, to cooperate.[66] Despite Soviet harassments, Eastern Com-

64. "History of Eastern Command," Ch. 5, para. 57.
65. "History of Eastern Command: October 1944-April 1945," p. 49 (File: 522.01-3, in USAF/HA).
66. Msg., Hill to MAAF, Feb. 26, 1945 (File: RG 334, Box 57, in WWIIRD).

212   EAGLES EAST

mand personnel, usually accompanied by Russian airmen, flew several missions to Poland to evacuate American airmen who had been forced down on missions as well as former prisoners of war. Between October, 1944, and March, 1945, almost 550 Americans made it to Poltava.[67]

The cycle of tension and misunderstanding concerning the evacuation of Americans from Russia reached a crescendo early in April when 88 men arrived in Bucharest where a MAAF detachment was to evacuate them to Italy. General Hill's earlier agreement with Khudyakov was either not known to local Soviet authorities at Bucharest or was vitiated by higher authorities. In either case, General Susaikov, in command at Bucharest, insisted that the eighty-eight Americans be dispatched to Odessa. General Schuyler, representing MAAF, objected but over his protests allowed sixty of the men to be dispatched to Odessa. The remaining twenty-eight, Schuyler argued, were too sick to sustain the trip from Bucharest to Odessa. When Hill sought to get Khudyakov to adhere to their earlier agreement, the general denied that there was one! The upshot was Soviet insistence on a policy they maintained until the end of the war—namely, that all American flyers be evacuated only through Odessa, forcing Schuyler to require almost all of the sick flyers to entrain for the Russian port.[68]

Other incidents contributed to chilling Soviet relations with Eastern Command. In March, an American pilot, temporarily detained by damage to his plane, attempted to fly out a Polish stowaway. When the Russians learned about the Pole, they prevented the American from leaving their jurisdiction. He was later turned over to American authorities who tried him by court-martial. He was fined. The American pilot was clearly wrong in what he attempted to do but the Soviets ascribed more to the

67. "History of Eastern Command: October 1944-April 1945," pp. 11-12.
68. "History of Mediterranean Allied Air Forces," pp. 406-09. There had been a similar incident earlier at Poltava where Eastern Command wanted to fly out eleven former American prisoners of war. Russian officials at Poltava, headed by Gen. Kovalev, refused, saying that all American evacuees were to be concentrated at Odessa. The degree to which AAF-Soviet relations had deteriorated was illustrated when Col. Thomas K. Hampton, the Commanding Officer at the time of Eastern Command, was ordered by Deane "not to allow these prisoners of war to proceed to Odessa unless General Kovalev threatens to use force." See "History of Eastern Command: October 1944-April, 1945," pp. 38-45. After VE Day former American prisoners of war were repatriated westward and overland rather than through Odessa. Msg., Deane to Marshall, May 31, 1945 (File: RG 334, Box 60, in WWIIRD/NA).

affair than was justified.[69] While the stowaway affair brought embarrassment to the United States and anger from Moscow, the sending of an unauthorized Eastern Command detachment of fourteen men to Lodz, Poland, to engage in rescue and repair work added another incident to the plethora of clashes which were now becoming the norm in AAF-Soviet military relations.[70]

The dispatch of the Americans to Lodz followed two failures on the part of President Roosevelt to get Stalin to agree to AAF contact teams to find, help, and evacuate hundreds of American ex-prisoners of war and stranded airmen. Stalin claimed that the whole affair was being well handled by the Russians themselves who, he alleged, were giving better treatment to Americans than United States officials were giving to Russian soldiers freed by the West. In the sternest note he sent to Stalin during the war, the President bemoaned: "This government has done everything to meet each of your requests. I cannot, in all frankness, understand your reluctance to permit American contact officers, with the necessary means, to assist their own people in this matter."[71]

It is significant that several incidents involved contacts between Americans and Poles at a time when the Russians were entrenching themselves in Poland. American crews, evacuated later from the area by Eastern Command, had a rare opportunity to acquire firsthand reports from Polish citizens of their treatment by the Soviet liberators. The Eastern Command detachment in Poland confirmed many of the earlier interrogations of AAF airmen. The Kremlin, suspicious of these contacts which compromised the image of the Soviets and provoked a paranoiac fear of a vast American intelligence network in collusion with the Polish underground,[72] boldly exploited the incidents to serve Russian

69. "History of Eastern Command: April-June 1945," pp. 6-7 (File: 522.01-4, in USAF/HA). See Chapter XII for the stowaway incident.
70. "History of Eastern Command: October 1944-April 1945," pp. 35-36. The group was ordered out of Lodz, confined under guard and evacuated by train. A British mission, sent to Poland in December, 1944, had the same fate. The five-man British group was arrested, sent to Moscow and later returned to Italy. See Jedrzejewicz, *Poland*, p. 602.
71. Msg., Roosevelt to Stalin, March 4, 1945; msg., Stalin to Roosevelt, March 5, 1945; msg., Roosevelt to Stalin, March 18, 1945; msg., Stalin to Roosevelt, March 22, 1945, Ministry of Foreign Affairs of the U.S.S.R., *Stalin's Correspondence*, II, 194-97. The Soviets earlier agreed to allow American contact teams at four or five points of concentration but later demurred.
72. After an interview with Stalin during which he explained the reason for the embargo on AAF flights from Soviet bases, Harriman wrote: "Stalin said

214 EAGLES EAST

political interests. Finally, on March 28, 1945, the Russians grounded American planes and personnel, excepting a few ATC supply and emergency flights from Tehran.[73]

The pervasive gloom affecting American military men in Russia at this stage in the war contrasted sharply with earlier enthusiastic pictures of camaraderie between the Russians and the Americans—fostered unduly by earlier commanders of Eastern Command. The historian of Eastern Command commented glumly in the last installment of his chronicle:

> It is hard to draw a true picture of the feelings that pervaded through the base through this painful, frustrating and sad period in the history of this command. It changed from apathy to despair, from disgust to shrot [sheer] hopelessness, from trying to forget the outbursts of angry accusations of the Soviets and higher headquarters. . . .[74]

Thus, long before the war's end, Russo-American military relations in the Soviet Union had deteriorated to a point little short of complete rupture. The always delicate military connection had undergone an erosion that anticipated the political cleavage, latent for so long during the war, that came to the fore at the Potsdam Conference.

The final evacuation of Eastern Command occurred on June 23, 1945, thus ending the longest sustained contact between American and Russian soldiers during World War II. Besides the 1,300 men based in Russia, almost 5,000 crew members and temporary AAF personnel saw duty in Russia for short periods of time. Equipment and supplies not needed elsewhere were turned over to the Russians.[75]

---

our planes had been landing in Poland for ulterior purposes in connection with the Polish underground." See msg., Roberts to Deane, April 16, 1945 (File: RG 334, Box 59, in WWIIRD/NA).
73. "History of Eastern Command: October 1944-April 1945," p. 26. The embargo lasted almost a month—22 days—before the Russians cleared the aircraft under rigid controls for air flight. See msg., Roberts to Deane, April 22, 1945 (File: RG 334, Box 59, in WWIIRD/NA).
74. "History of Eastern Command: April-June, 1945," p. 2. There were other factors that contributed to Russo-American strain at Poltava—the transfer of popular officers because of Soviet complaints and the periodic harassments of ATC planes by Soviet fighters.
75. *Ibid.*; "History of Eastern Command," I, Ch. 12, para. 1.

CHAPTER XIV

The Last Phase: Problems and Portents

THE LAST YEAR of the war witnessed serious negotiations over the final supply protocol and two items of crucial importance to Washington—namely, improving the fragile air link between the two states and inaugurating definitive plans to install the AAF on Siberian airdromes.

A. The Fourth Protocol

Negotiations over the Fourth Protocol revealed the extent to which doubt had crept into official thinking concerning the wisdom of continuing Lend-Lease without the Russians being required to advance some reasonable justifications for their requests. The desire to institute a relationship based upon a *quid pro quo* by which the Russians would be forced to collaborate, particularly on military matters of mutual interest, was a major concern of those who urged a sterner line toward Moscow.

Harriman and Deane saw eye to eye, arguing that "the time for blind accession to requests of the Russians for items in short supply is now past." Deane persuasively argued that there was bound "to be unnecessary wastage to the detriment of the overall war effort unless we insist on receiving information which will bear [out] the demands of the Russians for critical items."[1] On his part Harriman saw no reason why the Russians should not be required to submit supporting information on their requests. There was no excuse, the ambassador argued, for America to be deprived of urgent items without reasonable assurance that they

1. Msg., Deane to Wesson, January 14, 1944 (File: Soviet Protocol Committee Records, Box 18, in FDR/L).

215

216 EAGLES EAST

were being put to good use by the Russians. And besides, said Harriman, the government was vulnerable to public criticism at home unless it knew what recipients did with Lend-Lease.[2]

The embassy in Moscow had a strong case. There had been persistent rumors since the beginning of the Third Protocol about dubious Soviet practices involving Lend-Lease materiel. There were conflicting reports concerning shipments of aluminum which one observer said was used not for the purpose of building planes but filling holes in the concrete surfaces of wharves and warehouse floors.[3] An authenticated report told of the deterioration in open storage of scores of diesel engines which were then in short supply for *Overlord*.[4] Sales to Iran of cotton piece goods and sugar, both furnished under Lend-Lease to Russia, further bolstered the arguments of the critics.[5] Although a provision in the Master Agreement forbade the transfer of Lend-Lease goods to third parties, no limitation existed concerning the transfer of goods similar to Lend-Lease items. Despite several efforts to arrive at an agreement to cover these situations, the Russians demurred.[6]

Planes and tanks were also the subject of serious negotiation between the Russians and the Iranians. The aircraft deal apparently fell through because of lack of agreement on their use and the training of men to operate them.[7] But the fact that the Soviets were considering selling aircraft to another nation at a time when they submitted a request for 4,190 planes under the Fourth Protocol showed the need for a re-evaluation of the aid program.

The President's Soviet Protocol Committee, a rubber stamp agency which coordinated Lend-Lease to Moscow, opposed pro-

2. Msg., Harriman to Hopkins, January 15, 1944; msg., Harriman to Protocol Committee, March 2, 1944 (File: Soviet Protocol Committee Records, Box 18, in FDR/L).
3. Msg., Standley to Secretary of State, June 12, 1943 (File: 861.24/1523, in DS/NA); msg., Faymonville to Stettinius, June 30, 1943 (File: 861.24/1554, in DS/NA).
4. Msg., Harriman to Batt and Hopkins, January 6, 1944; msg., Marshall to Deane, January 18, 1944 (File: Soviet Protocol Committee Records, Box 18, in FDR/L).
5. Memo for files, initialled "ME," November 23, 1944 (File: 861.24/11-2344, in DS/NA). There was a report of Russian sales of Lend-Lease tires to the Persians but the amounts were so small that they did not justify the concern some officials attached to the matter.
6. Msg., Grew to Harriman, June 9, 1945 (File: Soviet Protocol Committee Records, Box 22, in FDR/L).
7. Memo for files, initialled "ME," November 23, 1944.

The Last Phase 217

posals which called for a firmer policy of distributing aid. The advice of the embassy in Moscow made General J. H. Burns, the ailing Executive of the committee, "heartsick."[8] General John York, who succeeded Hopkins as Acting Chairman of the committee, opposed the new course because it would injure "the steady improvement of our relations with the U.S.S.R." To require proof that they needed what they asked for, York argued, "could be interpreted as representing [the] U.S. belief that Russia's military effort no longer requires the present scale of aid." Even if Washington moved toward a different policy, York argued casuistically that it did not insure the desired result; besides he thought "it is rather late" to be changing policy.[9]

The improvement in Russo-American relations that York was talking about referred to the Tehran meeting which had ended in late 1943. Although the results of this first "Big Three" meeting were indecisive, there was an atmosphere of euphoria in official circles through the early months of 1944. Changing policy when a mood of optimism and expectancy gripped Washington was the last thing the White House wanted to do, especially in view of Stalin's promise to enter the Pacific conflict after the defeat of Germany and to begin conversations between American and Soviet military leaders. All of this held great promise for a critical theater that American war planners believed required Soviet involvement. Moreover, the spirit of Tehran seemed to pay special dividends when Stalin agreed to AAF operations against the Reich from Soviet bases.

The White House believed that it was better to continue the prevailing policy of aid, and hope that Moscow would respond to the generosity by establishing military collaboration with the United States in Siberia and on the eastern front than to use Lend-Lease aid as leverage to prod the Kremlin to respond on a reciprocal basis to American requests.

That is why when the Russians submitted their requests under the last protocol late in April, 1944, no effort was made to submit their claims to a scrutiny along the lines suggested by Harriman and Deane. Soviet aircraft requests were the lowest of the war, only 4,190. Except the request for 540 heavy bombers

8. Memo, York for Leahy, January 21, 1944 (File: Soviet Protocol Committee Records, Box 18, FDR/L).
9. *Ibid.*

218 EAGLES EAST

(300 B-24's and 240 B-17's), which was treated separately in connection with AAF bases in Siberia, the United States came close to meeting the Soviet list by offering 2,450 P-39/63's, 240 C-47's, 300 B-25's, and 30 Flying Boats.[10] These planes, plus additional allotments and left-overs from the Third Protocol, added up to 3,597 deliveries to the Russians at Fairbanks, Alaska, from the beginning of the Fourth Protocol to V-J Day.[11]

Soviet pressures for more fighters than those offered under the protocol prompted Arnold to suggest that the Russians take as many used P-39's and P-63's as were in the United States. The Russians, obviously in no critical need for planes, were incensed by the suggestion. Only 65 out of 481 planes inspected by them met their criteria.[12] Later, in March, 1945, the question of used aircraft arose in connection with a Soviet claim for swift delivery of 600 AT-6's and 500 AT-11's. The AAF could allocate 200-300 AT-6's but no AT-11's; it suggested that the Russians transfer their pilots directly from the AT-6 to the B-25 without transition in the AT-11 which the AAF was doing. The AAF offer of used B-25's and A-20's for training purposes did not impress the Soviets.[13]

The most disturbing incident involving aircraft during the last protocol concerned Soviet dissatisfaction with the P-63, the Kingcobra, which was an improved version of the P-39. Soviet experts contended that the plane was weak and submitted specifications which the AAF believed exceeded those of all American fighters then in combat. The AAF proceeded to modify the planes in accordance with its own standards, notwithstanding recriminations from the Russians.[14]

10. "Program of Requirements for Armaments, Equipment and Materials for Supply to the U.S.S.R. by the Government of the United Kingdom, United States, and Canada during the Period July 1, 1944 to June 30, 1945" (File: Soviet Protocol Committee Records, Box 3, in FDR/L); Minutes of meeting, protocol subcommittee on supplies, June 27, 1944 (File: RG 18, Box 206, in WWIIRD/NA).
11. Carr, "Great Falls to Nome," p. 201.
12. Ltr., Arnold to Rudenko, August 15, 1944 (File: H. H. Arnold, Box 129, in MD/LC); ltr., Kramarenko to Goodman, September 2, 1944; R & R, ACAS, M & S, to ACAS, Plans, September 7, 1944 (File: 145.95, Bk. 2, in USAF/HA).
13. Ltr., Giles to York, March 24, 1945 (File: H. H. Arnold, Box 130, in MD/LC). MAB allocated 225 AT-6's, 100 A-20's and 50 B-25's.
14. Carr, "Great Falls to Nome," pp. 203-06; ltr., Timberlake to Piskounov, February 4, 1945 (File: H. H. Arnold, Box 130, in MD/LC); ltr., Repin to Spalding, April 17, 1945; ltr., Spalding to Repin, April 24, 1945 (File: Lend-Lease Records, Box 83, in FRC). F. J. Ziombeck, a Bell aircraft expert, had

The Last Phase   219

As the Fourth Protocol drew to an end discussion concerning a Fifth began. But the uncertainty of Russia's role in the Pacific war precluded formulation of a new protocol. As far as aircraft was concerned, it was decided to reduce AT-6 allocations from an earlier level of 225 to 55 and that for the remainder of 1945, 40 C-47's each month would be supplied.[15] Moreover, under the Annex III Program, addressed specifically to Russia's preparations for entry in the Pacific war, the United States promised delivery of 50 PBY's, 30 of which were scheduled for flight delivery by the end of the protocol.[16] On May 28, 1945, the Russians submitted another list of supplies for Pacific use that included 120 B-29's and 80 PBY's. The bombers were disapproved; but the navy patrol ships were approved on the basis of known Soviet shortages and needs for this model.[17]

The tally of air force planes accepted by Russia during the war reached 14,018 (14,203 if one includes 185 naval patrol aircraft). Alsib compiled the most impressive record—7,925 planes to 993 for the South Atlantic ferry route, 3,868 for the water route to Iran and 1,232 for the North Russia run.[18]

B. Air communications

The air communications imbroglio saw the United States proposing improvements in mail and courier contact with Moscow while the Kremlin disposed of suggestions that would allow regularly scheduled flights to and from the Soviet Union.

It will be recalled that when the United States entered the war, the War Department urged the extension of air services via Tehran and Alsib. In 1942, when Ambassador Standley assumed his diplomatic post in Moscow, he particularly pressed Arnold's plan to develop the air route across Alaska and Siberia for com-

---

been in the group of engineers who taught the Russians how to use the P-39. He later returned to do the same with the P-63 but with less successful results.

15. Carr, "Great Falls to Nome," p. 207.

16. Annex III (File: Soviet Protocol Committee Records, Box 3, in FDR/L).

17. "May 28, 1945 Program" (File: RG 18, Box 203, in WWIIRD/NA); msg., Deane to Arnold, June 9, 1945 (File: RG 334, Box 60, in WWIIRD/NA). The Russians were quite sensitive to new American models, such as the P-59, P-80, and B-29, and asked for them as soon as they appeared. The American response was usually the same—refusal on the grounds that production was insufficient to meet needs.

18. See Appendix A.

220   EAGLES EAST

munication and transport purposes. The Soviets were consistent in
their opposition to flights of American planes into the Soviet Union.
This meant that mail and personnel destined for Russia were
delayed at Tehran as much as two or three weeks before Soviet
aircraft arrived to continue the flight to Moscow. There was some
improvement in the situation by the summer of 1942 but an
unscheduled flight every two weeks between Moscow and Tehran
could hardly be labelled efficient air transit.[19]

In the middle of 1943 Standley revived the subject of
improved air services. For the first time the Russians appeared
interested but they showed their skill in avoiding implementation
of the idea by suggesting the establishment of a joint company
similar to Deruluft, which flew before the war between Germany
and Russia, to operate between the two countries via Tehran. The
enormous political and economic problems involved made the
proposal quite unrealistic. Even if these problems had been worked
out it was difficult to see how the Russians, operating over the
entire route, could add to what the Air Transport Command was
already doing.[20]

Standley pressed the matter of air communications with
enthusiasm, hoping to offset the negative results of his famous
interview which earlier rocked Moscow and Washington. He suggested that the Tehran-Moscow link be improved by bi-monthly
scheduled flights and urged that a similar air service over Alsib be
instituted as well. To encourage acceptance of the proposal, Standley suggested a little frosting on the cake by offering the Russians
extra transports to operate over their sectors of both routes.[21]
From the American point of view the entire question of improved
air communications between the two countries was tied up with
the need to develop a cargo system to expedite materiel to China.
The Joint Chiefs hoped to pull a *quid pro quo*—American-operated
transport services as far as Irkutsk or Chita, and Soviet services to
Seattle on a weekly basis.[22]

During the Tehran meeting the Russians expressed their

19. See Chapter VI and VII.
20. AWPD, "Summary of Russian Situation," TAB F; msg., Secretary of State
to American Embassy in Moscow, June 28, 1943 (File: 145.95, in USAF/HA).
21. Msg., Standley to Secretary of State, June 12, 1943 (File: 145.95, in USAF/
HA).
22. AWPD, "Summary of Russian Situation," TAB F; msg., Hull to American
Embassy in Moscow, August 5, 1943.

The Last Phase 221

agreement in principle to the improvement of air communications between the two countries. When Molotov later made it known that the Russians were ready to talk seriously about the matter, Deane met Marshal Astakhov, Chief of Soviet Civilian Aviation, and proposed that the United States be authorized to make one round trip each week from Tehran to Moscow in a C-87. When the Soviets disapproved, Deane coordinated his efforts with his British counterparts who also were instructed to develop a Soviet-British air link. Deane offered four C-87's to the Russians for a Soviet-American communications system by way of Stockholm; an equal number of C-87's would be given to the Russians if the British were allowed to start a Soviet-British system through Turkey. The Kremlin never replied.[23]

It was not until late in 1944 that the Russians initiated a serious proposal on the matter. On September 19, 1944, Deputy Foreign Minister Andrei Vyshinsky proposed that a connecting point between the two air services be established at Cairo and in return generously agreed to guarantee 5,000 pounds of personnel and equipment each week on the Tehran-Moscow run, provided the United States gave ten C-47's above protocol commitments for this purpose. The shorter route through Stockholm was preferred by Washington, but Deane accepted the Soviet offer, provided the northern route eventually displaced the one through Cairo. Implementation of the arrangement was contingent on Russian transit rights to Egypt.[24] Either they had difficulty securing these rights or they did not try to get them because nothing came of the scheme.

While the matter was pending in Moscow, General Spaatz proposed delivery of 180 tons of ball bearings from London to Russia by the AAF. The Soviets reacted suspiciously because previous shipments had been sent from Sweden to England and from there by sea. Spaatz's proposal was a not-too-subtle effort to nudge the Russians to begin air operations through Stockholm. It did not work.[25] To the Russians there already were too many AAF planes flying over their territory. Moreover, the White House along with Whitehall was involved in the tensest dialogue of the

23. "Deane Report," Part II, 158-59.
24. *Ibid.*
25. Msg., Harriman to Secretary of State, August 11, 1944; msg., Harriman to Secretary of State, August 23, 1944, U. S. Department of State, *Foreign Relations of the United States: Diplomatic Papers, 1944*, Vol. IV: *Europe* (Washington: United States Government Printing Office, 1966), 1114, 1122.

222   EAGLES EAST

war with the Kremlin to get the use of Soviet bases for the AAF and RAF to aid the Polish Underground Army.

Meanwhile, the ten C-47's for the improvement of the Tehran-Moscow line that had been promised the Russians were delivered. And on January 11, 1945, the Russians, Deane wrote, inaugurated "a slightly improved service for the United States, which never reached [the] proportions agreed." That constituted the high point of improved air communications between the two countries. A subsequent effort after the Yalta conference to reopen discussion on the Stockholm route with the United States providing the necessary aircraft for the Russian leg of it, met with no response.[26]

Military and political relations had deteriorated so much by the time the Potsdam Conference convened that all President Truman could accomplish in improving air services was to propose a Soviet-American connection at Berlin to which the Air Transport Command had begun a twice daily service from London. The connection in Berlin was clearly in line with the new realities of the day, obviating the need to continue the long cumbersome nexus at Tehran. This did not require formal negotiation since each government operated flights into their own terminals: all that was required was a shuttle between the two.[27]

The negotiations over air communications as in so many other projects of military importance saw the United States cast in the role of proponent while the Soviet Union was the opponent. Byzantine subtlety melded with Muscovite candidness to extend negotiations. It is not difficult to find an explanation for the lack of Soviet enthusiasm to American proposals—ever since the fall of 1942 the Russians used Alsib regularly. To them there was simply no need to deal any differently with the Americans. Even if they genuinely wanted to develop more efficient air contacts, the Russians would not have been able to develop and sustain the kind of sophisticated service, complete with transports and facilities, that the United States was able to offer.

C. America's Siberian project

Throughout 1942 American policy was based on the assump-

26. "Deane Report," Part II, 160-61.
27. Memo, Gates for CG, AAF, July 7, 1945; memo for Arnold signed "Dean," July 8, 1945 (File: H. H. Arnold, Box 38, in MD/LC); ltr., Truman to Stalin, July 20, 1945, Ministry of Foreign Affairs of the U.S.S.R., *Stalin's Correspondence*, II, 252.

The Last Phase 223

tion that Japan would attack Siberia, thus forcing the Soviets into the Pacific conflict. Although this possibility was not entirely ruled out later, American planners increasingly talked about Soviet entry into the war against Japan when the military situation on the Russo-German front permitted. But this position had a hollow ring: the Soviet government continued to observe a policy of cautious neutrality toward the Japanese and did not reveal its intentions to the United States.

It was not until late in 1943, when the Russians captured the initiative from the Germans on the eastern front and the United States and Great Britain prepared to launch the cross-Channel invasion, that Stalin gave substance to the American assumption of Soviet willingness to enter the Pacific war. During a session of the Foreign Ministers Conference in Moscow in October, 1943, Stalin informed Secretary of State Hull that the Soviet Union would join its allies in the war against Japan after the defeat of Germany.[28] A month later he reiterated this to the President at the Tehran meeting. There the President used the opportunity to press once again for combined planning and a survey of Siberian installations before the Soviets entered the war.[29] The Combined Staff Planners dramatized the importance of AAF operations from the Soviet Far East when they stated early in December, 1943, that the overall objective of the allies in the Pacific was to obtain sites "from which we can conduct air bombardment and establish air and sea blockades against Japan, and from which to invade Japan proper if this should prove to be necessary." Meanwhile, AAF staffers prepared a study which called for the operation of an American force of 672 planes with a fifty per cent reserve for operations from the Maritimes.[30]

Soviet willingness to enter the Pacific war did not imply readiness to initiate detailed planning regarding AAF bases in Siberia. For months after the Tehran Conference the Soviets did nothing to facilitate meetings with Major General Deane, whose principal objective was to further Russo-American military collaboration in

28. Hull, *The Memoirs of Cordell Hull*, II, 1309.
29. U. S., Department of State, *Foreign Relations of the United States, Diplomatic Papers: The Conferences at Cairo and Tehran, 1943* (Washington: United States Government Printing Office, 1961), pp. 489, 529-30, 618-19.
30. Report of the Combined Staff Planners, with Annex I and III, December 2, 1943, *ibid.*, pp. 765-72; R & R, OPD to ACAS/Plans, January 20, 1944 (File: 145.95, in USAF/HA).

224 EAGLES EAST

the Pacific. At one point Ambassador Harriman despaired: "we still have a fight ahead to get the cooperation which we are entitled."[31]

The first hopeful follow-up to Stalin's Tehran revelations did not come until June, 1944, when the Soviet leader told Harriman that the United States could have six or seven air bases in the Maritimes. Stalin asked for heavy bombers and expressed interest in Harriman's offer that the AAF train Russian crews. During the next month Deane met the Chief of Staff of the Red Army, General Alexei Antonov, and presented an elaborate agenda for advanced Soviet-American planning on air force matters. Deane pointed out that the United States would provide the Soviets with enough planes to build four heavy bombardment groups and four fighter units—the nucleus of a strategic air force—for service in a Soviet-Japanese conflict. Thanks to Deane delivery of these planes was made contingent upon agreements providing for AAF operations from Siberia.[32] The need to conclude arrangements on the Siberian bases and the supply requirements for them was underscored by Anglo-American strategy decisions which *now* called for an invasion of Japan.[33]

After the Russians agreed to have AAF personnel train their flyers in heavy bombers, 26 officers and men—pared down from 126 at Soviet insistence—were organized as a combat crew training group. Commanded by Colonel Herbert Morgan, Jr., and known as the "Morgan Project," the group assembled at Topeka Army Air Field where they received six B-24's for training operations in Russia. But the Soviets, who originally urged that a training school be established at Abadan, were reluctant to accept Morgan's group. The AAF warned that the group would be disbanded if the Russians did not want its services. No reply came and so the ill-fated project was cancelled.[34]

31. Msg., Harriman to Sec. of State, 1/9/44, *Foreign Relations*, 1944, IV, 803.
32. "Deane Report," Part II, 187-88; msg., Harriman to Roosevelt, June 11, 1944, *Foreign Relations*, 1944, IV, 965-67. If it materialized the strategic air force organized for the Russians by the United States would have consisted of 300 bombers and 450 fighters. Memo of conversation, October 17, 1944 (File: H. H. Arnold, Box 25, in MD/LC).
33. Maurice Matloff, *Strategic Planning for Coalition Warfare, 1943-1944* (Washington: Department of the Army, 1959), pp. 486-89; 512.
34. Memo, Morgan for CG, 2d AF, November 3, 1944 (File: RG 18, Box 199, in WWIIRD/NA); msg., Deane to Harriman, August 13, 1944 (File: Lend-Lease Records, Box 83, in FRC).

The Last Phase   225

The Soviet government remained apathetic toward furthering collaborative efforts until the middle of October, 1944, when Stalin finally began to yield to pressures. During a series of meetings with Deane and Harriman, he announced that military conversations would be initiated in order to study broad strategic matters. Now he was willing to build and train a Russian strategic air force in the Far East with American help and to provide air bases for the AAF in the Maritimes and Kamchatka. The tone and emphasis of his remarks, however, indicated that he placed top priority upon strengthened ground and tactical air forces rather than upon the development and operation of Soviet and American strategic air forces in the Far East. Generously, Stalin said he would accept twenty heavies and the American instructors as the first step in building a Soviet strategic air force.[35]

Stalin's remarks seemed so promising that Deane asked Washington to send planning experts to capitalize on the new expansive mood in Moscow. The planning group, headed by Brigadier General Frank N. Roberts, arrived in Moscow in December, 1944, but accomplished little in the way of joint planning with its Soviet counterpart. Moreover, the Soviets dampened American expectations of using bases in the Maritimes, though the possibility of air force operations from Kamchatka was still held out. Even Soviet interest in a strategic air force, provided and trained by the United States, had waned considerably.[36]

The sagging hopes and expectations for American air force operations from the Soviet Far East received a boost at the Yalta Conference. Stalin promised that his country would enter the war against Japan within three months after the defeat of Germany. In reply to requests from the President, Stalin stated that he had no objection to AAF bases in the Maritimes, either at Komsomolsk or Nikolaevsk. But American bases on Kamchatka, he said, had to

---

35. "File for Use of General Arnold in Connection with his forthcoming Discussions with Ambassador Harriman," TABS B and E (File: 381 Russia, Case 1, Sec. 4, OPD, in WWIIRD/NA). The AAF strategic air force in the Soviet Union was to include 6 heavy bombardment groups, 4 long range fighter groups, 1 photo reconnaissance group, 1 troop carrier group and, if the Soviets were unable to provide them, 2 night fighter squadrons and 1 air sea rescue squadron. Study, "Russian Participation in the War Against Japan" (File: 381 Russia, Case 1, Sec. 4, OPD, in WWIIRD/NA).
36. "Deane Report," Part II, 190-91; Deane, *The Strange Alliance*, pp. 230-35, 259.

226 EAGLES EAST

be deferred due to the presence there of a Japanese consul.[37] Staff conversations between American and Soviet officers at Yalta further amplified the subject. Major General Laurence S. Kuter, representing the AAF, voiced requirements for two bases in the Komsomolsk-Nikolaevsk area, each capable of accommodating one group of Superfortresses. Kuter also asked for bases near Vladivostok from which B-17 or B-24 aircraft could greatly expand the air offensive against the Japanese. Soviet officers were most agreeable to these requests and suggested that an American survey party proceed "without delay" to the Komsomolsk-Nikolaevsk area.[38]

The spirit of Yalta was not translated into genuine action. The American survey team was not allowed to enter Siberia, and the staff conversations which Stalin had endorsed at Yalta proved to be an exercise in verbal obstructionism. The meetings, Deane commented, "never got beyond discussing organizational procedures."[39] Soviet inactivity and lack of genuine interest in America's Siberian project after the Yalta meeting negated earlier Russian displays of apparent willingness to cooperate.

By the end of March, 1945, the American planning group under General Roberts came to a realistic conclusion: Unless the Soviet Union gave immediate and complete support, the United States could not undertake strategic air force operations from Siberia in 1945. Even if the Soviets dramatically reversed their pattern of blocking joint cooperation on this question, the planning group seriously questioned the military benefits of American bases in Siberia. The logistical burden involved in such an undertaking, the group observed, "was not commensurate with the increased bomb tonnage on Japan that would result." In view of the swift movement of United States air, ground, and naval forces in the Pacific, which placed them by the spring of 1945 well within striking distance of Japan, the Siberian project no longer was a crucial one. In April, the Joint Chiefs of Staff abandoned attempts to secure the bases, thus reversing a major wartime policy toward the Soviet Union.[40]

Abandonment of the project did not mean, however, that

37. U. S., Department of State, *Foreign Relations of the United States, Diplomatic Papers: The Conferences at Malta and Yalta, 1945* (Washington: United States Government Printing Office, 1955), p. 767.
38. *Ibid.*, pp. 835, 837-41.
39. "Deane Report," Part II, 192-93.
40. *Ibid.*, pp. 194-95.

American policy respecting Soviet involvement in the Pacific war had altered. At the Potsdam Conference in July, 1945, American officials still regarded Soviet intervention against Japan as an important factor in contributing to the unconditional surrender of the Japanese government.[41] As is well known, Soviet action against the Japanese came five days before the war was over in the Pacific.

The American effort to secure bases in Siberia was not a hopeful one from the outset. Stalin had shown restrained interest, not enthusiasm, for American plans which called for basing the AAF on Russian soil. Even when Soviet military fortunes were so bleak late in 1942, Stalin refused to accept the offer of an Anglo-American air force in the Caucasus. Only after substantial western pressure did he allow AAF bombers to use bases in the Ukraine for the famous shuttle missions during the summer of 1944.

The American offer to build a Soviet strategic air force in return for bases in Siberia may have briefly attracted Stalin. But the advantages of such assistance for the strategic-bomber-starved Russians apparently did not override the disadvantages of having American military contingents on Soviet territory. Moreover, the development of a Soviet strategic air arm that late in the war would have been a belated and abrupt reversal of Soviet wartime conceptions of air power. Stalin was well aware that United States air force strikes against Japan would continue from other installations in the Pacific even if he refused to implement his promise of American bases in Siberia. Stalin's assurance of allowing the AAF to operate from Siberia emerges more as a political ploy to foster the image of a co-operative ally than a serious intention to assist the military operations of his ally from the Soviet Far East.

D. Epilogue

The story of the AAF and the Soviet Union during World War II has revealed a series of relationships which were determined essentially by the policy of the White House to keep Russia in the war. Whether or not White House fears of a separate Russo-German peace were justified is academic. The fact is the fear existed, especially during the first two years of the conflict. When

41. U. S., Department of State, *Foreign Relations of the United States, Diplomatic Papers: The Conference of Berlin (The Potsdam Conference), 1945* (Washington: United States Government Printing Office, 1960), II, 1462-63.

this is considered in the light of the massive engagement on the eastern front where most of the Wehrmacht was being contained, one can understand how policy makers in the White House and No. 10 Downing Street came to the conclusion that their bargaining power was considerably less than that of the Kremlin. No sooner did the fear of the Russians leaving the war in Europe abate than it was displaced by the urgency to get them involved in the Pacific. Again political policy was determined by military expediency.

Perhaps no one could predict with accuracy what would happen to the substance of an alliance in which Washington and London dealt with Russia not as equals but as inferiors. But as early as 1942 there were a few perceptive individuals who prophesied that the relationship was too one-sided and boded ill for the future. The number of voices who urged a reassessment of a policy which so distorted American perspectives increased in proportion to the appearance of new military and political facts which convinced them that 1943 or 1944 was not the same as 1941 or 1942.

The consequence of American policy was that the AAF represented a part, though an important one, of a massive effort of demonstrating unstinting cooperation with the Kremlin. The provision of aircraft and other critical items, it was hoped, would allay Soviet suspicions about the West and keep the Russians fighting. The implications of this policy made the American air force establishment a kind of sacrificial lamb, but before it was all over, not as bloody as it might have been.

To be sure, this policy was never agreeable to the AAF. From the outset the latter sought to minimize or at least to stabilize aircraft commitments while the White House urged increases to unrealistic levels. The compromises that were worked out in arriving at commitments under each protocol involved some hardships and difficulties, but thanks largely to Arnold, Marshall, and Stimson, at no time was irreparable damage done to the AAF's domestic training and equipment programs.

The policy of the White House meant that each time there was either an ominous silence or a sudden outburst of criticism from the Kremlin, the AAF was expected to find aircraft as the quickest and best means to placate the sullen Soviet chief. Even the Velvet project revealed that the combined air force was to serve essentially diplomatic objectives.

The Last Phase 229

None of this was lost on the Russians who were encouraged to manifest a stern, demanding, and critical bearing—not too difficult for the naturally suspicious leaders of the Kremlin. Little wonder that American efforts to collaborate with the Russians in delineating a bomb line in eastern Europe, establishing bases for the AAF in the Ukraine, planning joint air force operations from Siberia, and inaugurating improved air flights between the two nations met with delays, criticisms, and in most cases, refusals. When they did make a concession—as in the case of American bases in the Ukraine in 1944—the Russians did so with a sharp eye to political realities.

Somewhere along the line, it seems that it should have been necessary to introduce measures which would have forced the Russians, who were historically unaccustomed to collaboration, to retreat from these undesirable posturings and to adapt to the necessities of fighting a coalition war instead of allocating military responsibilities between two separate halves of the alliance.

The Lend-Lease phase of the relationship, which particularly dominated the attention of the AAF until 1943, saw the United States initially unprepared for the gigantic task of producing and delivering so many planes to the Russians. In time American know-how and commitment improved the situation, but by then the Russians no longer really needed the planes they asked for. During the last two protocols the Russians raised their acceptance criteria, refusing to accept used or imperfect planes and often delayed in flying away those that had been accepted. Though there was no strong evidence of Soviet stockpiling, critics were correct in asking if wastage of aircraft at the expense of American operations could be justified any longer.

Continuation of a policy that made every aspect of the AAF's relations with the Russians a subject for long, gruelling, and usually frustrating negotiations, makes one seriously wonder how the White House expected to negotiate from a position of strength with the Kremlin the political questions which were decided during the latter part of the war. The experience of the AAF substantiates the oft-voiced claim that the diplomacy of Washington was based upon the attainment of goals which were unrealistic from the outset and not seriously reappraised by policy-makers in the light of the failures and frustrations in air force collaboration with the Russians.

230   EAGLES EAST

More than other Americans, AAF personnel had the longest systematic exposure to Russian negotiators. They quickly learned that their counterparts were hard bargainers whose agreement "in principle" did not really mean what it implied. If disinterested in a proposal, the Russians usually preferred not to take any action at all, thus giving them two options—they were spared the charge of killing a proposal outright while at the same time they had the freedom of resurrecting it at a later date if they chose to do so. More often than not, however, Russian military men were extremely circumscribed in the latitude given to them by civilian authorities. Anyone who has followed the diplomatic and military history of this period must be struck by the abrupt shifts of the Soviet Union from accord to dissension, usually without any warning. These flights into Muscovite silence or rancor usually reflected the displeasure of the Kremlin with some action or inaction of Washington, often unrelated to the question under negotiation.

The AAF's relations with the Russians were not all one dirge of disappointment. Largely owing to the persistence of the War Department and the AAF in particular, a few chips in the wall of Soviet opposition were made. American internees were evacuated from the Soviet Far East with an amazing degree of cooperation. The Russians did share some military information of value with their AAF colleagues. But the most striking concession of the Russians concerned a project which is not likely ever to be repeated: the operation of AAF units from Soviet territory during the summer of 1944 involving some 6,000 Americans. This was indeed a precedent in Russo-American relations, but it was not one which paid the dividends that the AAF hoped for later in the Pacific.

In completing this inquiry into the air force aspects of Russo-American relations, one should consider the value of the planes the AAF delivered to the Soviets. Unfortunately, Russian writings on this subject are so limited by the party line that they are almost worthless. It serves no purpose from Moscow's point of view to evaluate objectively the value of American aid. This might give the impression that the mother of world communism was dependent in some way upon the bastion of world capitalism. Allied wartime aid is, therefore, shrouded behind propaganda. Although Soviet writers acknowledge the existence of aid from the West, they emphasize that it was insignificant in comparison with the

The Last Phase 231

assistance which Russia gave by fighting most of the German war machine.[42] When Russian writers mention American aircraft, the value of the planes is deprecated by criticisms of their quality and condition.[43] Ideology provides the framework for the assessment of foreign aid: Lend-Lease was merely a western tool to further imperialistic ambitions.[44]

In contrast to this picture, the following contemporary accounts, taken largely from intelligence reports, tell a different story concerning the quality and usage of American planes on the eastern front:

> Commander in Chief of S.A.F., Stalingrad area, remarked that the U.S.A. Boston bomber was an excellent airplane . . . there was absolutely no criticism of the Airacobra but they had too few of them.[45]

> Use of the A-20 on the Russian front as far back as 1942 has been brought to attention by Russian sources in Alaska. At the climax of the German offensive in Russia in 1942, the Russian town of Voronezh fell under German control. One large airport was immediately organized by the Germans who brought in 150 combat planes. Because of an immediate lack of gasoline, the planes were grounded and fell victims to dispatched squadrons of A-20's, who came to strafe and bomb. More than two-thirds of the planes were destroyed in a two day fight despite strong German fighter opposition.[46]

> Col. Machin said during his brief stay in Russia that it was determined by him that the performance of American planes on the Russian front was most satisfactory.[47]

42. A. Zheltov, "Vsemirno-Istoricheskaia Pobeda Sovetskogo Naroda," *Kommunist*, XXXII (1955), 52-54; Deborin, *Vtoraia Mirovaia Voina*, p. 139; A. Alexeyev, "Lend-Lease—Weapon of Aggressive American Imperialism, *"The Current Digest of the Soviet Press*, III (September 8, 1951), 9.
43. Israelian, *Diplomatischeskaia Istoriia*, p. 37; B. P. Surikov, "Po Povody Odnoi Falshivki Voennykh Prislushnikov Imperializma," *Vestnik Vozdushnogo Flota*, No. 6 (June, 1959), 89-92.
44. Alexeyev, *The Current Digest of the Soviet Press*, p. 8; Deborin, *Vtoraia Mirovaia Voina*, pp. 143-44; M. Popov, "Nachalo Agressii S Sh A v Gody Vtoroi Mirovoi Voiny," *Voprosy Istorii*, No. 11 (1949), 37-43, 64.
45. Extracts of communications concerned with "Soviet Opinion of USA and British Aircraft" (File: 9185, ACS, G-2, in WWIIRD/NA).
46. Annex 7, to G-2 periodic report, January 8-15, 1944 (File: 9510-9560, ACS, G-2, in WWIIRD/NA).
47. Extracts of communications concerned with "Soviet Opinion of USA and British Aircraft." Col. Michael G. Machin headed the Russian Military Mission which arrived at Fairbanks, Alaska, in September, 1942.

232   EAGLES EAST

Major Michael Kobin, Nome Russian Commandant, has
reported informally that 5 squadrons of American planes—
3 squadrons of P-39's and 2 of A-20's—all under the command
of Lt. Col. Nedosekin, played a prominent role in the Red
Army's capture of Smolensk. Lt. Col. Nedosekin formerly
commanded the Russian station complement at Nome.[48]
American fighters, the Tomahawk, Kittyhawk, and Airacobra are defending some of the most important points of
the Soviet Union, including Moscow, Leningrad and Murmansk. Crack pilots, many of them wearers of the highest
decoration, Hero of the Soviet Union, are flying them. Unanimously, they like them.[49]

By the end of 1942 the United States had exported more than
2,500 planes to the Russians. Of these, about 1,550-1,650 were in
Russia by the end of the year, far more than the Russians deployed
at Stalingrad for their counter-offensive. The aircraft sent in 1941-
1942 was absolutely crucial to the Russians during those dark days.
After that, Soviet industrial recovery was substantial enough to
satisfy needs in aircraft and in other munitions. But under the
preponderant impact of political considerations in determining
aircraft aid, approximately 11,500 planes were sent to the Russians
during 1943-1945, a period when the military urgency for these
deliveries had ceased to exist. These machines simply contributed
to the enormous capacity of over kill that the SAF enjoyed with
respect to the Luftwaffe.

The inescapable conclusion is that in the field of aerial affairs
the United States played the role of the eager, generous, rich and
often bumbling suitor whose attentions were met by a reluctant,
capricious and suspicious Soviet Union. What is ultimately significant is that these roles epitomized the whole of the contacts
between the two powers during World War II.

48. *Ibid.*
49. *New York Times*, March 6, 1943.

Appendix A

AIRCRAFT EXPORTS TO THE U.S.S.R.

June 22, 1941 to September 20, 1945[1]

	Delivered at Factories	Lost in North America		Departed North America	Lost After Departure	Diverted to Others	Arrived at Destination	Delivered to U.S.S.R. at Destination
		In U.S.	In Canada and Alaska					
BY ROUTE								
Alaskan-Siberian Ferry Route	8,058	74	59(4)*	7,925	0	0	7,925	7,925
South Atlantic Ferry Route to Abadan	1,055	17	0	1,038	43	1	994	993
Water to North Russia	1,543	0	0	1,543	310	1	1,232	1,232
Water to Persian Gulf Assembly at Abadan	4,142	0	0	4,142	231	0	3,911	(17)† 3,868
Total	14,798a	91	59(4)*	14,648	584	2	14,062	(17)†14,018
BY TYPE OF PLANE								
Pursuit Planes								
P-40 Alsib	50	0	2(1)	48	0	0	48	48
P-40 North Russia, Water	1,159	0	0	1,159	248	1	910	910
P-40 North Russia, Water, U.K. Acct.	49	0	0	49	0	0	49	49
P-40 Persian Gulf, Water	872	0	0	872	54	0	818	(6)†
P-40 Persian Gulf, Water, U.K. Acct.	300	0	0	300	0	0	300	1,090
P-39 Alsib	1,022	9	14(1)*	999	0	0	999	999
P-39 Alsib, U.K. Acct.	1,637	28	17	1,592	0	0	1,592	1,592
P-39 Alsib, Reimbursement Account	30	0	3	27	0	0	50	27
P-39 North Russia, Water	57	0	0	57	7	0	30	50
P-39 North Russia, Water, U.K. Acct.	35	0	0	35	5	0	30	30
P-39 North Russia, Water, Reim. Acct.	28	0	0	28	0	0	28	28
P-39 Persian Gulf, Water	1,101	0	0	1,101	38	0	1,063	(1)†
P-39 Persian Gulf, Water, U.K. Acct.	893	0	0	893	53	0	840	(1)† 2,020
P-39 Persian Gulf, Water, Reim. Acct.	121	0	0	121	0	0	121	(1)†
P-47 Alsib	3	0	0	3	0	0	3	3
P-47 North Russia, Water	4	0	0	4	0	0	4	4
P-47 Persian Gulf, Water	196	0	0	196	7	0	189	188
P-63 North Russia, Water	3	0	0	3	0	0	3	3
P-63 Alsib, U.K. Account	85	0	0	85	0	0	85	85
P-63 Alsib	2,333	10	11(2)*	2,312	0	0	2,312	2,312
Total Pursuit Planes	9,978	47	47(4)*	9,884	412	1	9,471	(9)† 9,438

	Delivered at Factories	Lost in North America		Departed North America	Lost After Departure	Diverted to Others	Arrived at Destination	Delivered to U.S.S.R. at Destination	
		In U.S.	In Canada and Alaska						
Light Bombers									
A-20 Alsib	1,396	24	9	1,363	0	0	1,363		1,363
A-20 South Atlantic	927	17	0	910	39	1	870		869
A-20 North Russia, Water	165	0	0	165	39	0	126		126
A-20 Persian Gulf, Water	637	0	0	637	79	0	558	(7)†	550
Total Light Bombers	**3,125**	**41**	**9**	**3,075**	**157**	**1**	**2,917**	**(7)†**	**2,908**
Medium Bombers									
B-25 Alsib	737	1	3	733	0	0	733		733
B-25 South Atlantic	128	0	0	128	4	0	124		124
B-25 North Russia, Water	5	0	0	5	0	0	5		5
Total Medium Bombers	**870**	**1**	**3**	**866**	**4**	**0**	**862**		**862**
Heavy Bombers									
B-24 Alsib	1b	0	0	1	0	0	1		1
Cargo Planes									
C-46 Alsib	1	0	0	1	0	0	1		1
C-47 Alsib	709	2	0	707	0	0	707		707
Total Cargo Planes	**710**	**2**	**0**	**708**	**0**	**0**	**708**		**708**
Observation Planes									
O-52 North Russia, Water	30	0	0	30	11	0	19		19
Advanced Trainers									
AT6-C North Russia, Water	8	0	0	8	0	0	8		8
AT6-C Persian Gulf Water	22	0	0	22	0	0	22	(1)†	20
AT6-F Alsib	54	0	0	54	0	0	54		54
Total Advanced Trainers	**84**	**0**	**0**	**84**	**0**	**0**	**84**	**(1)†**	**82**
PBN Navy Patrol Planes	138	1	0	137c	----	----	----		----
PBY-6A Navy Patrol Planes	48	----	----	48d	----	----	----		----
Total Navy Aircraft	**186**	**1**	----	**185**	----	----	----		----

†Water shipments received at Abadan washed out before delivery to U.S.S.R. pilots.
*At Fairbanks.
aDoes not include 186 PBN and PBY Patrol Planes.
bOne heavy bomber carrying a U.S. mission became stranded in Siberia and was transferred to the Soviet government.
cDeparted Elizabeth City, N.C.
dFifteen departed Kodiak, Alaska, 33 departed Elizabeth City, North Carolina.

Item	Lend-Lease Exports	Other Exports	Total Exports	Arrived	Lost Enroute	Diverted Enroute	Enroute on Sept. 20, 1945
Aircraft (For U.S. Protocol Account)							
AIRCRAFT AND EQUIPMENT							
Pursuit Planes	6,744	0	6,744				
Light Bombers	3,075	0	3,075				
Medium Bombers	866	0	866				
Heavy Bombers	1	0	1				
Transport Planes	708	0	708				
Flying Boats, PBN	137	0	137				
Flying Boats, PBY	48	0	48				
Observation Planes	30	0	30				
Advanced Trainers	84	0	84				
Aircraft (For U.K. Protocol Account)							
(Under Reciprocal Agreement)							
Pursuit Planes	2,915	49	2,964				
Aircraft (For Reimbursement Account)							
Pursuit Planes	176	0	176				
Link Trainers	11	0	11	11	0	0	0
Aircraft Landing Mats (1000 sq. ft.)	55,927	0	55,927	49,408	0	0	0

[1]Office of Foreign Liquidation, Department of State, *Report on War Air Furnished by the United States to the USSR* (Washington: Department of State, 1945).

According to T. H. Vail Motter the 14,018 figure was superseded by a larger one—14,834—which was given to the Russians in 1947 for the settlement of the Lend-Lease account. See Motter, *The Persian Corridor*, p. 125. This writer, not having access to Department of State and Foreign Economic Administration records after 1945, could not verify the new figure.

Appendix B

GLOSSARY OF ABBREVIATIONS AND TERMS

A-1—Assistant Chief of the Air Staff, Personnel.
A-2—Assistant Chief of the Air Staff, Intelligence.
A-3—Assistant Chief of the Air Staff, Training.
A-4—Assistant Chief of the Air Staff, Supply.
A-20—twin-engine attack or light bomber.
A-29—an observation and patrol bomber developed by Lockheed. Popularly known as the Hudson.
AAF—Army Air Forces.
AAG—Air Adjutant General.
ABC—American-British Conversations (January-March, 1941).
ABDA—American-British-Dutch-Australian.
ACAS/MS—Assistant Chief of the Air Staff, Materiel and Services.
AC/AS, Plans—Assistant Chief of the Air Staff, Plans.
ACS—Assistant Chief of Staff.
AFABI—Assistant Chief of the Air Staff, Intelligence.
AFADS—Assistant Chief of the Air Staff, Supply.
AFAEP—Assistant Chief of the Air Staff, Plans.
AFAFC—Ferrying Command.
AFASC—Air Service Command.
AFATC—Air Transport Command.
AFB—Air Force Base.
AFCAS—Chief of the Air Staff.
AFDAS—Deputy Chief of the Air Staff.
AFMAG—Air Adjutant General.
AG—Adjutant General.
AGP—Aircraft grounded for lack of parts.
Agwar—Adjutant General, War Department.
Airacobra—popular name for the P-39.
Amrus—American Military Mission to the U. S. S. R. and its home office in Washington.
Amsir—American Military Mission to Iran and its home office in Washington.
Arcadia—Washington Conference, December 1941-January 1942.
ASF—Army Service Forces.
ASW—Assistant Secretary of War.

236

Appendix B

ASWA—Assistant Secretary of War for Air.
AT-6—Single-engine advanced trainer.
ATC—Air Transport Command.
AUL—Air University Library.
AWPD—Air War Plans Division.
B-17—four-engine bomber, popularly known as the Flying Fortress.
B-24—four-engine bomber, popularly called the Liberator.
B-25—twin-engine bomber, known as the Mitchell.
B-26—twin-engine bomber, called the Marauder.
B-29—four-engine bomber, known as the Superfortress, which saw extensive service in the Pacific.
B-32—four-engine bomber which saw limited service in the Pacific.
Barbarossa—code name for the German invasion of Russia.
Bazaar—code name for the American survey of air facilities in Siberia. Also the name for the plan which provided for American air force assistance to the U. S. S. R. in the Pacific.
Bolero—code name for the build up of American armed forces in Great Britain.
Boston—a British designation for the A-20.
C-47—twin-engine military transport version of the DC-3.
C-53—modified version of the DC-3 designed for troop and hospital transport.
C-87—converted B-24 designed to carry cargo.
CAS—Chief of the Air Staff.
CG—Commanding General.
DB-7—early version of the A-20.
DS—Department of State.
DC-3—commercial designation of the C-47.
FDR/L—Franklin D. Roosevelt Library, Hyde Park, New York.
Frantic—code name for shuttle missions to and from Soviet Union.
FRC—Federal Records Center, Suitland, Maryland.
G-2—Military Intelligence Section.
Hq.—Headquarters.
Hurricane—British low-wing fighter. Sometimes called the Hurribomber when equipped to carry bombs.
ID—International Division.
JCS—Joint Chiefs of Staff.
Kittyhawk—British name for the late model series of the P-40.
Liberator—See B-24.
Lockheed-Hudson—See A-29.
Ltr.—Letter.
MAB—Munitions Assignments Board.
MAC—Munitions Assignments Committee (Air).
MD/LC—Manuscript Division, Library of Congress.
Milid—Military Intelligence Division.
Msg.—Message.
MS—Materiel and Services.
NA—National Archives.
O-52—observation plane, popularly known as the Owl.
OCAC—Office of the Chief of the Air Corps.
OCS—Office of the Chief of Staff.
OLLA—Office of Lend-Lease Administration.
OPD—Operations Division.
PBN—a modification of the PBY-5 (Catalina).
PBY-5—twin-engine patrol bomber flying boat, popularly called the Catalina.

238 APPENDIX B

PE-2—Russian twin-engine bomber.

P-39—single-engine fighter known as the Airacobra.

P-40—single-engine fighter known as the Kittyhawk and Tomahawk.

P-51—a fast single-engine fighter, popularly called the Mustang, which was superior to anything in the Luftwaffe.

PQ—designation given to convoys sailing to northern Russia.

R & R—Routing and Record Sheet.

SAF—Soviet Air Force.

SHAEF—Supreme Headquarters Allied Expeditionary Forces.

Spitfire—British single-engine fighter which was one of the finest aircraft used during World War II.

SPOBS—Special Observer Group, United States Army.

Stormovik—Name for the IL-2 which along with the PE-2 formed the primary equipment of Soviet tactical bomber units during the earliest part of World War II.

Tomahawk—British name applied to the A, B, and C models of the P-40.

Torch—code name for the Allied invasion of North Africa in November, 1942.

U.K.—United Kingdom.

USAF/HA—United States Air Force Historical Archives.

USSTAF—United States Strategic Air Forces.

Velvet—code name for the plan to place an Anglo-American air force in the Caucasus in 1942.

WD—War Department.

WDGS—War Department General Staff.

WPB—War Production Board.

WPD—War Plans Division.

WWIRB—World War I Records Branch. This section is now combined with the World War II Records Division and called the Modern Military Records Division of the National Archives. Most of the research in this study was compiled before this merger; therefore, separate designations are used throughout.

WWIIRD—World War II Records Division.

Bibliography

Unpublished Official Records

Arnold, Gen. H. H. Manuscript Collection. Library of Congress, Washington, D. C.

This collection was a concentrated source of valuable correspondence. Most of this correspondence was also found in the files of War Department agencies referred to below. Some pertinent documents were found, however, that were not located elsewhere. References are identifiable by the notation MD/LC for Manuscript Division, Library of Congress. Since this material was consulted on two occasions over a period of years, there are some variations in classification, reflecting recent changes in cataloging by the Library of Congress.

U. S. Department of State. Official Papers. National Archives, Washington, D. C.

Unpublished correspondence was available to the author. These papers added much to the information which was obtained from War Department papers and published documents. References thereto are cited as DS.

U. S. Foreign Broadcast Intelligence Service. Official Records. National Archives, Washington, D. C.

The records consulted were helpful in indicating Soviet reactions to Allied assistance.

U. S. Lend-Lease Records. Federal Records Center, Suitland, Maryland.

Limited but useful information was derived from this source. When cited, references are FRC.

U. S. Military Personnel Records Center, St. Louis, Missouri. Air Materiel Command, "Special One-Time Report of Deliveries of AAF Aircraft to USSR." 1947.

U. S. Soviet Protocol Committee Records. Franklin D. Roosevelt Library, Hyde Park, New York.

Much material not acquired elsewhere was found in these records. References are designated FDR/L.

U. S. War Department. Official Papers. National Archives, Washington, D. C.

The papers of War Department agencies proved to be the most fruitful source of material for this study. The questions of policy, strategy, supply and operations with respect to the air force aspects of American aid to Russia were reflected in the files of the following military agencies: The Adjutant

240 BIBLIOGRAPHY

General (AG), Assistant Chief of the Air Staff, Intelligence (ACAS/I), Assistant Chief of the Air Staff, Materiel and Services (ACAS/MS), Assistant Chief of Staff, G-2 (ACS, G-2), Assistant Secretary of War (ASW), Assistant Secretary of War for Air (ASWA), International Division, Army Service Forces (ID, ASF), Office of the Chief of Staff (OCS), Operations Division, War Department General Staff (OPD, WDGS), and the War Plans Division, War Department General Staff (WPD, WDGS).

The abbreviations cited above are the notations by which these agencies can be identified in the footnotes of this study. These papers are located in the World War II Records Division, referred to as WWIIRD/NA. The records of the Army Air Forces and Headquarters, Army Service Forces were also consulted. These are located in the World War I Records Branch, referred to as WWIRB/NA. This agency has recently been combined with the World War II Records Division into the Modern Military Records Division, National Archives.

——————. Official Papers. United States Air Force Historical Archives, Aerospace Studies Institute, Air University, Maxwell Air Force Base, Alabama.

Valuable information was obtained from the files of the Air Transport Command, Army Air Corps, Assistant Chief of the Air Staff (Intelligence), Assistant Chief of the Air Staff (Plans), British Air Ministry, Combined Chiefs of Staff, Joint Army-Navy Intelligence Service, Ninth Air Force, Special Observer Group, United States Army (Miscellaneous records), and the United States Strategic Air Forces. References to these sources are identifiable by file numbers, followed by USAF/HA for United States Air Force Historical Archives. A few sources were also consulted at the Air University Library, referred to as AUL.

U. S. War Production Board. Official Papers. National Archives, Washington, D. C.

These papers provided helpful information with respect to some of the broader aspects of American aid to the Soviet Union. References thereto are cited as WPB.

Correspondence and Interviews

Letter, Maj. Gen. Elmer E. Adler, Retired, to writer, September 4, 1962.
Letter, Lt. Gen. H. A. Craig, Retired, to writer, February 20, 1963.
Letter, Generalleutnant a. D. Walter Schwabedissen to writer, May 22, 1962.
Letter, Col. Hubert Zemke to writer, January 28, 1963.
Memo, Patrick K. Truesdell to writer, February 2, 1969.
Personal Interview with Maj. Gen. T. J. Hanley, Jr., Retired, December 27, 1962.

Government Publications and Printed Documents

Army Air Forces. *Army Air Forces Statistical Digest: World War II.* Washington: Office of Statistical Control, 1945.
——————. *Army Air Forces Statistical Digest: 1946.* Washington: Statistical Control Division, 1947.
Embassy of U. S. S. R. *Soviet War Documents: June 1941-November 1943.* Washington: 1943.
Jedrzejewicz, Waclaw (comp. and ed.). *Poland in the British Parliament, 1939-1945.* 3 Vols. New York: Jozef Pilsudski Institute of America, 1946-62.
Ministry of Foreign Affairs of the U. S. S. R. *Stalin's Correspondence with Churchill, Attlee, Roosevelt and Truman: 1941-1945.* 2 vols. London: Lawrence and Wishart, 1958.

Bibliography 241

Reports to Congress on Lend-Lease Operations. 1941-1946.

Roosevelt, Elliott (ed.). *F. D. R.: His Personal Letters, 1928-1945.* Vol. II. New York: Duell, Sloan and Pearce, 1950.

Rosenman, Samuel I. (comp.) *The Public Papers and Addresses of Franklin D. Roosevelt.* Vol. 1941: *The Call to Battle Stations.* Vol. 1942: *Humanity on the Defensive.* New York: Harper and Brothers Publishers, 1950.

U. S. Air Force. *United States Air Force Statistical Digest: 1947.* Washington: Director of Statistical Services, 1948.

U. S. Civilian Production Administration. *Minutes of the Council of the Office of Production Management, December 21, 1940 to January 14, 1942.* Washington: U. S. Government Printing Office, 1946.

_____. *Minutes of the Supply Priorities and Allocation Board, September 2, 1941 to January 15, 1942.* Washington: U. S. Government Printing Office, 1946.

U. S. Congress, Joint Committee on the Investigation of the Pearl Harbor Attack. *Hearings Pursuant to S. Con. Res. 27 and 49, Authorizing an Investigation of the Attack on Pearl Harbor on December 7, 1941 and Events and Circumstances Related Thereto.* Parts 1-39, 79th Cong., 1st and 2d Sess., 1946.

U. S. Department of State. *The Department of State Bulletin.* Vols. IV-VII, 1941-42.

_____. *Foreign Relations of the United States: Diplomatic Papers, 1941.* Vol. I: *General, The Soviet Union.* Washington: United States Government Printing Office, 1958.

_____. *Foreign Relations of the United States: Diplomatic Papers, 1941.* Vol. III: *The British Commonwealth, The Near East and Africa.* Washington: United States Government Printing Office, 1959.

_____. *Foreign Relations of the United States: Diplomatic Papers, 1941.* Vol. IV: *The Far East.* Washington: United States Government Printing Office, 1956.

_____. *Foreign Relations of the United States: Diplomatic Papers, 1942.* Vol.: *China.* Washington: United States Government Printing Office, 1956.

_____. *Foreign Relations of the United States: Diplomatic Papers, 1942.* Vol. III: *Europe.* Washington: United States Government Printing Office, 1961.

_____. *Foreign Relations of the United States: Diplomatic Papers, 1943.* Vol. III: *The British Commonwealth, Eastern Europe, The Far East.* Washington: United States Government Printing Office, 1963.

_____. *Foreign Relations of the United States: Diplomatic Papers. The Conferences at Cairo and Tehran, 1943.* Washington: United States Government Printing Office, 1961.

_____. *Foreign Relations of the United States: Diplomatic Papers, 1944.* Vol. III: *The British Commonwealth and Europe.* Washington: United States Government Printing Office, 1965.

_____. *Foreign Relations of the United States: Diplomatic Papers, 1944.* Vol. IV: *Europe.* Washington: United States Government Printing Office, 1966.

_____. *Foreign Relations of the United States: Diplomatic Papers, 1945.* Vol. II: *The Conference of Berlin.* Washington: United States Government Printing Office, 1960.

_____. *Foreign Relations of the United States: Diplomatic Papers, 1945. The Conferences at Malta and Yalta.* Washington: United States Government Printing Office, 1955.

_____. *Peace and War: United States Foreign Policy, 1931-1941.* Washington: United States Government Printing Office, 1943.

_____. *President's Forty-Second Report to Congress on Lend-Lease Operations, 1960.* Washington: United States Government Printing Office, 1961.

242   BIBLIOGRAPHY

————. *Report on War Aid Furnished by the United States to the U. S. S. R.: June 22, 1941-September 20, 1945.* Washington: 1945.

————. *Wartime International Agreements: Soviet Supply Protocols.* Washington: United States Government Printing Office, n.d.

U. S. House of Representatives. *Appendix to Committee Report on Communist Takeover and Occupation of Poland: Polish Documents Report of the Select Committee on Communist Aggression.* 83d Cong., 2d Sess., 1954.

U. S. Senate. *Hearings Before a Subcommittee of the Committee on Foreign Relations.* 77th Cong., 2d Sess., 1942.

U. S. War Department, International Branch, Army Service Forces. *International Aid Statistics, World War II: A Summary of War Department Lend-Lease Activities Reported through 31 December 1945.* Washington: 1946.

————, International Division, Army Service Forces. *A Guide to International Supply.* Washington: 1945.

————, Office of Chief of Finance. *Quantities of Lend-Lease Shipments: A Summary of Important Items Furnished Foreign Governments by the War Department during World War II.* Washington: 1946.

The War Reports of General of the Army George C. Marshall, General of the Army H. H. Arnold, Fleet Admiral Ernest J. King. Philadelphia: J. B. Lippincott Co., 1947.

Unpublished Official Studies

Army Air Forces. Air Transport Command (Prepared in 1945 and 1946).
"Alaskan Division, Air Transport Command, Historical Record Report."
"History of the Air Transport Command: Administrative History of the Ferrying Command, May 29, 1941-June 30, 1942."
"History of the Air Transport Command in Central Africa and the Middle East." Part I: "History of the Ferrying Command in Africa and the Middle East, May 1941-June 1942."
"History of the Air Transport Command, Ferrying Command Operations, December 7, 1941-June 30, 1942."
"History of the Northwest Air Route to Alaska: 1942-1945."
"History, 7th Ferrying Group, Ferrying Division, Air Transport Command, January 1942-December 1944."
"The Northwest Route under the Ferrying Division: Air Transport Command, June 16, 1942-November 1, 1942."

Army Air Forces, Assistant Chief of the Air Staff, Intelligence. "The AAF in the Middle East: A Study of the Origin of the Ninth Air Force." 1945.

Army Air Forces, United States Strategic Air Forces. "History, Eastern Command, USSTAF, 1941-44."

————. "History, Eastern Command, USSTAF, 1 October 1944 to 1 April 1945."

————. "History, Eastern Command, USSTAF, April-June, 1945."

Fennemore, George M. "The Role of the Department of State in Connection with the Lend-Lease Program." Washington: Department of State, 1943.

Great Britain, Air Ministry. "The Anglo-American Air Contribution to the War on Germany's Eastern Front." n. d.

Historical Section, European Theater of Operations. "The Special Observer Group Prior to the Activation of the European Theater of Operations." 1944.

Lepawsky, Col. Albert. "History, Eastern Command, USSTAF, 1941-1945." n. d.

Office of Foreign Liquidation Commissioner. "History of Lend-Lease." n.d.

Whiting, Theodore E. "Lend-Lease." Washington: Department of the Army, 1952.

Bibliography 243

Other Unpublished Sources

Allen, Betty Sue. "United States Lend-Lease to Russia, 1941-1945." Unpublished Master's thesis, Tennessee Technological University, 1968.

Carr, Edwin R. "Great Falls to Nome: The Inland Air Route to Alaska, 1940-1945." Unpublished Ph.D. dissertation, University of Minnesota, 1946.

Cross, Cecil C. "Lend-Lease to the U. S. S. R. vs. Its Possible Effects Upon the AAF." Unpublished Master's thesis, Air University, 1947.

Plocher, Generalleutnant a. D. Hermann. "The German Air Force Versus Russia on the Eastern Front." (unedited version of three volume study, GAF Monograph Studies 153-55. Air University.)

Published Official Histories

Behrens, C. B. A. *Merchant Shipping and the Demands of War.* London: Her Majesty's Stationery Office, 1955.

Cline, Ray S. *Washington Command Post: The Operations Division.* Washington: Department of the Army, 1951.

Craven, Wesley Frank and Cate, James Lea (eds.). *The Army Air Forces in World War II.* 7 vols. Chicago: The University of Chicago Press, 1948-58.

Great Britain, Air Ministry. *The Rise and Fall of the German Air Force (1933 to 1945).* Air Ministry Pamphlet No. 248, 1948.

Hall, H. Duncan. *North American Supply.* London: Her Majesty's Stationery Office, 1955.

Hall, H. Duncan and Wrigly, C. C. *Studies of Overseas Supply.* London: Her Majesty's Stationery Office, 1956.

Leighton, Richard M. and Coakley, Robert W. *Global Logistics and Strategy, 1940-1943.* Washington: Department of the Army, 1955.

Matloff, Maurice and Edwin M. Snell. *Strategic Planning for Coalition Warfare, 1941-1942.* Washington: Department of the Army, 1953.

Matloff, Maurice. *Strategic Planning for Coalition Warfare, 1943-1944.* Washington: Department of the Army, 1959.

Morison, Samuel E. *History of United States Naval Operations in World War II.* Vol. I: *The Battle of the Atlantic, September 1939 - May 1943.* Boston: Little, Brown & Co., 1950.

Motter, T. H. Vail. *The Persian Corridor and Aid to Russia.* Washington: Department of the Army, 1952.

Postan, M. M. *British War Production.* London: Her Majesty's Stationery Office, 1952.

Richards, Denis and Saunders, Hilary St. George. *Royal Air Force, 1939-1945.* 3 vols. London: Her Majesty's Stationery Office, 1953-54.

U. S. Civilian Production Administration. *Aircraft Production Policies Under the National Defense Advisory Commission and Office of Production Management: May 1940 to December 1941.* Historical Reports on War Administration. Special Study no. 21, 1946.

————. *Industrial Mobilization for War: History of the War Production Board and Predecessor Agencies, 1940-1945.* Vol. I: *Program and Administration.* Washington: United States Government Printing Office, 1947.

U. S. Department of the Army. *Command Decisions.* New York: Harcourt, Brace and Co., 1959.

————. *The German Campaign in Russia: Planning and Operations, 1940-1942.* Department of the Army Pamphlet No. 20-261a, 1955.

————. *Russian Combat Methods in World War II.* Department of the Army Pamphlet No. 20-230, 1950.

244 BIBLIOGRAPHY

U. S. Department of Defense. *The Entry of the Soviet Union Into the War Against Japan: Military Plans, 1941-1945*. Washington, 1955.

Watson, Mark Skinner. *Chief of Staff: Prewar Plans and Preparations*. Washington: Department of the Army, 1950.

Ziemke, Earl F. *The German Northern Theater of Operations, 1940-1945*. Department of the Army Pamphlet No. 20-271, 1959.

Memoirs, Autobiographies and Recollections

Anders, Gen. Wladyslaw. *Hitler's Defeat in Russia*. Chicago: Henry Regnery Co., 1953.

Arnold, Gen. Henry H. *Global Mission*. New York: Harper and Brothers, Publishers, 1949.

Bor-Komorowski, T. *The Secret Army*. New York: The Macmillan Co., 1951.

Brereton, Lt. Gen. Lewis H. *The Brereton Diaries: The War in the Air in the Pacific, Middle East and Europe*. New York: William Morrow and Co., 1946.

Cassidy, Henry C. *Moscow Dateline, 1941-1943*. Boston: Houghton Mifflin Co., 1943.

Churchill, Winston S. *The Grand Alliance*. Boston: Houghton Mifflin Co., 1950.

————. *The Hinge of Fate*. Boston: Houghton Mifflin Co., 1950.

————. *Their Finest Hour*. Boston: Houghton Mifflin Co., 1949.

————. *Triumph and Tragedy*. Boston: Houghton Mifflin Co., 1953.

Ciechanowski, Jan. *Defeat in Victory*. Garden City, New York: Doubleday and Co., Inc., 1947.

Davies, Joseph E. *Mission to Moscow*. New York: Simon and Schuster, 1941.

Deane, John R. *The Strange Alliance: The Story of American Efforts at Wartime Co-operation with Russia*. London: John Murray, 1947.

Ehrenburg, Ilya. *The Tempering of Russia*. Translated by Alexander Kaun. New York: Alfred A. Knopf, 1944.

Eisenhower, Dwight D. *Crusade in Europe*. New York: Doubleday & Co., Inc., 1949.

Galland, Adolf. *The First and the Last: The Rise and Fall of the German Fighter Forces, 1938-1945*. Translated by Mervyn Savill. New York: Henry Holt & Co., 1954.

Hull, Cordell. *The Memoirs of Cordell Hull*. 2 vols. New York: The Macmillan Co., 1948.

Ickes, Harold L. *The Secret Diary of Harold L. Ickes*. Vol. III: *The Lowering Clouds, 1939-1941*. New York: Simon and Schuster, 1954.

Ismay, Hastings L. *The Memoirs of General Lord Ismay*. New York: The Viking Press, 1960.

Jordan, George Racey with Stokes, Richard L. *From Major Jordan's Diaries*. New York: Harcourt, Brace & Co., 1952.

Kalinov, Cyrille Dimitrievich. *Les Marechaux Sovietiques Vous Parlent*. Paris: Stock, Delamain et Boutelleau, 1950.

Kennan, George F. *Memoirs: 1925-1950*. Boston: Little, Brown, & Co., 1967.

Kerr, Walter. *The Russian Army: Its Men, Its Leaders, and Its Battles*. New York: Alfred A. Knopf, 1944.

Krylov, Ivan. *Soviet Staff Officer*. Translated by Edward Fitzgerald. New York: Philosophical Library, 1951.

Leahy, Adm. William D. *I Was There: The Personal Story of the Chief of Staff to Presidents Roosevelt and Truman Based on His Notes and Diaries Made at the Time*. New York: McGraw Hill Book Co., Inc., 1950.

Nelson, Donald M. *Arsenal of Democracy: The Story of American War Production*. New York: Harcourt, Brace & Co., 1946.

Bibliography   245

Sherwood, Robert E. *Roosevelt and Hopkins: An Intimate History.* New York: Harper and Brothers, 1948.

Stalin, Joseph. *The Great Patriotic War of the Soviet Union.* New York: International Publishers, 1945.

Standley, William H. and Ageton, Arthur A. *Admiral Ambassador to Russia.* Chicago: Henry Regnery Co., 1955.

Stettinius, Edward R. Jr. *Lend-Lease: Weapon For Victory.* New York: The Macmillan Co., 1944.

Stimson, Henry L. and Bundy, McGeorge. *On Active Service in Peace and War.* New York: Harper and Brothers, Publishers, 1947.

Welles, Sumner. *The Time for Decision.* New York: Harper and Brothers, Publishers, 1944.

Monographs and General Works

Akademiia Nauk SSSR, Institut Istorii. *Ocherki Istorii Velikoi Otechestvennoi Voiny, 1941-1945.* Moskva: Izdatelstvo Akademii Nauk SSSR, 1955.

Allen, William Edward and Muratoff, Paul. *The Russian Campaigns of 1941-1943.* New York: Penguin Books, 1944.

Brown, William A. Jr. and Redevers, Opie. *American Foreign Assistance.* Washington: The Brookings Institution, 1953.

Clark, Alan. *Barbarossa: The Russian-German Conflict, 1941-45.* New York: The New American Library, 1965.

Cole, Wayne S. *America First: The Battle Against Intervention, 1940-1941.* Madison: University of Wisconsin Press, 1953.

Conquest, Robert. *The Great Terror: Stalin's Purge of the Thirties.* London: The Macmillan Co., 1968.

Dawson, Raymond H. *The Decision to Aid Russia, 1941: Foreign Policy and Domestic Politics.* Chapel Hill: The University of North Carolina Press, 1959.

Deborin, G. A. *O Kharaktere Vtoroi Mirovoi Voiny.* Moskva: Voennoe Izdatelstvo Ministerstva Oborony SSSR, 1960.

————. *The Second World War: A Politico—Military Survey.* Moscow: Progress Publishers, n. d.

————. *Vtoraia Mirovaia Voina.* Moskva: Voennoe Izdatelstvo Ministerstva Oborony SSSR, 1958.

Dennett, Raymond and Johnson, Joseph E. *Negotiating with the Russians.* Boston: World Peace Foundation, 1951.

Deutscher, Isaac. *Stalin: A Political Biography.* New York: Vintage Books, 1960.

Dulles, Foster Rhea. *Road to Teheran: The Story of Russia and America, 1781-1943.* Princeton: Princeton University Press, 1944.

Emme, Eugene M. (ed.). *The Impact of Air Power: National Security and World Politics.* Princeton: D. Van Nostrand Co., Inc., 1959.

Feis, Herbert. *Churchill, Roosevelt, Stalin: The War They Waged and the Peace They Sought.* Princeton: Princeton University Press, 1957.

Fuller, Maj. Gen. J. F. C. *A Military History of the Western World.* Vol. III: *From the Seven Days Battle, 1862 to the Battle of Leyte Gulf, 1944.* New York: Funk and Wagnalls Co., 1956.

Guillaume, Gen. Augustin L. *Soviet Arms and Soviet Power: The Secrets of Russia's Might.* Washington: Infantry Journal Press. 1949.

Halle, Louis J. *The Cold War As History.* New York: Harper & Row, 1967.

Institut Marksizma-Leninizma. *Istoriia Velikoi Otechestvennoi Voiny Sovetskogo Soiuza, 1941-1945 v Shesti Tomakh.* Vol. II: *Otrazhenie Sovetskim Narodom*

246 BIBLIOGRAPHY

Verolomnogo Napadeniia Fashistskoi Germanii na SSSR. Sozdanie Uslovii Ilia Korennogo Pereloma v. Voine, iiun 1941 g.-noiabr 1942g. Moskva: Voennoe Izdatelstvo Ministerstva Oborony SSSR, 1961.

Institute for Research in Social Science. *The Soviet Aircraft Industry.* Chapel Hill: University of North Carolina, 1955.

Israelian, V. L. *Diplomatischeskaia Istoriia Velikoi Otechestvennoi Voiny, 1941-1945.* Moskva: Izdatelstvo Ministerstva Oborony SSSR, 1958.

Ivanov, Lev N. *Ocherki Mezhdunarodnykh Otnoshenii v Period Vtoroi Mirovoi Voiny.* Moskva: Izdatelstvo Akademii Nauk SSSR, 1958.

Kilmarx, Robert A. *A History of Soviet Air Power.* New York: Frederick A. Praeger, 1962.

Langer, William L. and Gleason, S. Everett. *The Challenge to Isolation, 1937-1940.* New York: Harper and Brothers, Publishers, 1952.

_____. *The Undeclared War, 1940-1941.* New York: Harper and Brothers, Publishers, 1953.

Lee, Asher. *The Soviet Air Force.* 2d ed. London: Gerald Duckworth & Co., Ltd., 1952.

_____. (ed.). *The Soviet Air and Rocket Forces.* New York: Frederick A Praeger, Publishers, 1959.

Lohbeck, Don. *Patrick J. Hurley.* Chicago: Henry Regnery Co., 1956.

Liddell Hart, B. H. (ed.). *The Red Army.* New York: Harcourt, Brace and Co., 1956.

McNeill, William H. *America, Britain and Russia: Their Cooperation and Conflict, 1941-1946.* London: Oxford University Press, 1953.

Moskovskii, V. P. *Voenno-Vozdushnye Sily SSSR, 1918-1948: Kratkii Ocherk.* Moskva: Voennoe Izdatelstvo Ministerstva Vooruzhennykh Sil Soiuza SSR, 1948.

Plocher, Generalleutnant a. D. Hermann. *The German Air Force Versus Russia, 1941.* USAF Historical Studies No. 153. USAF Historical Division, Research Studies Institute, Air University, 1965.

Schroeder, Paul W. *The Axis Alliance and Japanese-American Relations.* New York: Cornell University Press, 1958.

Schwabedissen, Generalleutnant a. D. Walter. *The Russian Air Force in the Eyes of German Commanders.* USAF Historical Studies No. 175. USAF Historical Division, Research Studies Institute, Air University, 1960.

Snyder, Richard C. and Furniss, Edgar S. Jr. *American Foreign Policy: Formulation, Principles and Programs.* New York: Rinehart and Co., Inc., 1954.

Soviet Information Bureau (Moscow). *Falsificators of History: An Historical Note.* Washington: Information Bulletin of the Embassy of the Union of Soviet Socialist Republics, 1948.

Stockwell, Richard. *Soviet Air Power.* New York: Pageant Press, Inc., 1956.

Suchenwirth, Richard. *Historical Turning Points in the German War Effort.* USAF Historical Studies No. 189. USAF Historical Division, Research Studies Institute, Air University, 1959.

Telpukhovskii, B. S. *Velikaia Otechestvennaia Voina Sovetskogo Soiuza, 1941-1945: Kratkii Ocherk.* Moskva: Gosudarstvennoe Izdatelstvo Politicheskoi Literatury, 1959.

Voznesensky, Nikolai A. *The Economy of the USSR During World War II.* Washington: Public Affairs Press, 1948.

Wilmot, Chester. *The Struggle for Europe.* London: Collins, 1952.

Articles in Periodicals and Learned Journals

Alexeyev, A. "Lend-Lease—Weapon of Aggressive American Imperialism," *The Current Digest of the Soviet Press,* III, No. 30 (September 8, 1951), 8-10.

Bibliography

"ATC Operates a Skyway to Siberia," *Impact*, II, No. 8 (August, 1944), 30-36.

"ATC Serves Lend-Lease," *Impact*, I, No. 7 (October, 1943), 34-37.

Coy, Wayne. "Get Things Moving—FDR," *New Republic*, CXLIV, No. 15 (April 15, 1946), 546-47.

Fischer, George. "Genesis of U. S.-Soviet Relations in World War II," *The Review of Politics*, XII, No. 3 (July, 1950), 363-78.

Krayev, L. "On the Soviet-American Lend-Lease Negotiations," *The Current Digest of the Soviet Press*, III, No. 10 (April 21, 1951), 21-22.

Kühn, Arthur. "Die Endlose Strasse: Anglo-Amerikanische Kraftfahrzeuglieferungen für die UdSSR," *Osteuropa*, V (June, 1955), 169-75.

Lapin, N. "Anglo-Amerikanskie Falsifikatory Istorii Vtoroi Mirovoi Voiny," *Voprosy Istorii*, No. 5 (May, 1950), 37-50.

Lukas, Richard C. "Escape . . . American Internees in the Soviet Union: From General Deane's Report," *Aerospace Historian*, XVI (Spring, 1969), 14-17.

————. "Soviet Stalling Tactics in the Forties," *Aerospace Historian*, XIV (Spring, 1967), 51-56.

————. "The Impact of Barbarossa on the Soviet Air Force and the Resulting Commitment of United States Aircraft, June-October, 1941," *The Historian: A Journal of History*, XXIX (November, 1966), 60-80.

————. "The Velvet Project: Hope and Frustration," *Military Affairs*, XXVIII (Winter, 1964-65), 145-62.

Markoff, Gen. Alexei. "How Russia Almost Lost the War," *The Saturday Evening Post* (May 13, 1950), 31, 175-78.

Maurer, Maurer (ed.). "Notes on Velvet: General Adler's Mission to Moscow, 1942," *The Airpower Historian*, IX, No. 3 (July, 1962), 141-50.

May, Ernest R. "The United States, the Soviet Union, and the Far Eastern War, 1941-1945," *Pacific Historical Review*, XXIV (May, 1955), 153-74.

McFarland, Marvin W. "Air Power and the Warsaw Uprising, August-September, 1944," *The Airpower Historian*, III, (October, 1956), 186-94.

Morgenthau, Henry Jr. "The Morgenthau Diaries: IV—The Story Behind Lend-Lease," *Collier's*, XX (October 18, 1947), 16-17, 71-75.

Morton, Louis. "Soviet Intervention in The War With Japan," *Foreign Affairs*, XL (July, 1962), 653-62.

Pinkowski, Edward. "Soviet Trainees in U. S. A. in World War II," *The Russian Review*, VI, No. 1 (Autumn, 1946), 11-15.

Popov, M. "Nachalo Agressii S Sh A v Irane v Gody Vtoroi Mirovoi Voiny," *Voprosy Istorii*, No. 11 (1949), 37-64.

Potts, Ramsay D. Jr. "The Foundations of Soviet Air Power: A Historical and Managerial Interpretation," *The Annals of the American Academy of Political and Social Science*, CCXCIX (May, 1955), 38-47.

Rieckhoff, Herbert J. "A German View of the Soviet Air Force," *Military Review*, XXIX, No. 1 (April, 1949), 73-78.

Ringold, Herbert. "Lifeline to the U. S. S. R.," *Air Force*, XXVII (November, 1944), 24-27, 46.

Samsonov, A. "Velikoe Stalingradskoe Srazhenie," *Voprosy Istorii*, No. 5 (May, 1950), 16-36.

Standley, W. H. "Stalin and World Unity," *Collier's* (June 30, 1945), 17, 75-76.

Surikov, Maj. B. P. "Po Povody Odnoi Falshivki Voennykh Prislushnikov Imperializma," *Vestnik Vozdushnogo Flota*, No. 6 (June, 1959), 89-92.

Telpukhovskii, B. S. "Kommunisticheskaia Partiia—Vdokhnovitel i Organizator Pobedy Voine," *Voprosy Istorii KPSS*, II (1958), 34-56.

Whidden, Howard P. "Reaching a Lend-Lease Settlement," *Foreign Policy Reports*, XX (April 15, 1944), 22-32.

248 BIBLIOGRAPHY

"Who is Thwarting a Settlement of the Lend-Lease Account?," *The Current Digest of the Soviet Press*, III, No. 4 (March 10, 1951), 21-23.

Zheltov, Col. Gen. A. "Vsemirno-Istoricheskaia Pobeda Sovetskogo Naroda," *Kommunist*, XXXII, No. 7 (May, 1955), 44-57.

Miscellaneous

Heflin, Woodford Agee (ed.). *The United States Air Force Dictionary*. Air University Press, 1956.

Institute for the Study of the USSR, Munich, Germany (comp.). *Biographic Directory of the USSR*. New York: Scarecrow Press, Inc., 1958.

Keesing's Contemporary Archives. 1941-1945.

Maurer, Maurer (ed.). *Air Force Combat Units of World War II*. Washington: United States Government Printing Office, 1961.

Newspapers

New York Times. 1941-1945.

The Times (London). 1941-1945.

Index

Abadan, 83, 84, 87, 92, 169, 171, 179, 179n, 180n, 224

ABC-2, 3

Acheson, Dean, 58

Adler, Elmer E.: and Caucasus, 136; and erection facility at Abadan, 83; ferried B-25's to Iran, 92; mentioned, 163n; and Velvet, 153–63 *passim*

Africa, 56, 106

Afrika Korps, 141

Airacobra. *See* P-39

Air communications, 219–22

Aircraft: American production of, 4, 48, 49; deliveries to Air Corps, 4–5; foreign purchases of, 2–3; political overtones surrounding, 124

Air Service Command, 117, 169

Air Transport Command, 169, 190, 214, 214n, 220, 222

Air War Plans Division, 40, 42

AK. *See* Polish Home Army

Aleppo, 159n

Aleutian Islands, 106, 178n

Alison, John R., 29, 30, 31, 31n, 53, 69, 70, 73

Allied Control Commission, 194n

Allison Company, 72

Alsib: 56, 81, 219, 222; air route and bases, 98-108 *passim*; delivery record, 179, 180n, 219; discussed at Moscow Conference, 49, 50; feasibility of, 21; ferrying operations over, 125–38 *passim*; mentioned, 56, 81, 219, 222; opening of, 124

American Permanent Supply Mission, 73

Amirabad, 103

Amtorg Trading Corporation, 62, 62n, 72

Amur, 187n

Anderson, F. L., 203

Annex III Program, 219

Antonov, Alexei, 184, 224

Archangel, 23, 29, 33, 39, 49, 53, 56, 64, 64n, 65, 66, 69, 75, 102, 121, 139, 140, 196

Army-Navy Munitions Board Priorities Committee, 17

Arnold, Henry H.: aircraft allocations in Moscow Protocol, 54; air route to Russia, 96–105 *passim*; backlog of planes, 58, 166, 170-71; defective P-40's, 77; dealings with Gromov, 24-25; finding fifteen planes for Russia, 124; liaison, 184; needs of AAF, 2, 3, 5, 39, 115, 117, 119, 228; opposes heavies to Russia, 46; routes to Russia, 80, 81, 82; Second Protocol, 112–14, 165–66; and Soviet air strength, 32; spare parts for Russian planes, 27; Third Protocol, 176, 178-79; used fighters, 218; Velvet, 151, 152

Arnold-Towers-Portal Agreement, 113

Ashkhabad, 82

Astakhov, Marshal, 221

AT-6, 166n, 218

AT-11, 218

A-20: in backlog, 170n; delivery via

249

250   INDEX

Alsib, 128, 134, 167; delivery via Iran, 82n, 87, 92-93, 169; mentioned, 19n, 49, 54, 61; in Moscow Protocol, 46, 54, 120–21, 121n, 174; personnel needed to fly, 129n; in Second Protocol, 15, 175; spare parts for, 79; in Third Protocol, 177; used, 218; value to Russians, 231–32

A-29, 20, 46, 49, 53, 53n

Aurand, Henry S., 58, 59, 77, 117

Australasia, 61

Austria, 185

AWPD/1, 40

AWPD/2, 42, 43, 44, 54

AWPD/4, 99

B-17: in AAF, 22, 25; destroyed and damaged in Russia, 199; production shortage of, 178; requested in Fourth Protocol, 218; requested by Russians, 22, 24, 25; and Siberian bases, 226

B-24: in AAF, 22; Bradley's, 137; flying Harriman–Beaverbrook mission, 47; in Halverson Detachment, 141; in Morgan project, 224; requested in Fourth Protocol, 217; requested by Russians, 22, 177n; and Siberian bases, 127, 226; and Velvet, 151

B-25: delivery via Alsib, 128, 167; delivery via Iran, 82n, 87, 92–93, 169; in Moscow Protocol, 46, 54, 120–21, 121n; personnel needed to fly, 129n; for Russians, 19n, 23–27, 49, 54, 54n, 61; in Second Protocol, 115, 175; spare parts for, 79; for survey of Siberia, 127; in Third Protocol, 174–76; used, 218

B-26, 22, 26–27

B-29, 96, 177n, 219, 219n

B-32, 96

Baikal, Lake, 106

Baku, 82, 151

Balfour, H. H., 48, 49

Balkans, 186, 189n, 191

Ballard, Richard H., 169-70

Baltic, 186

Barbarossa, 1, 5, 6, 8, 9, 12, 111

Bari, 194n

Barr, P. M., 183

Baseball. *See* Eastern Command

Basra, 81, 82, 83, 84, 87, 88, 92

Bathurst, 87

Batjer, John F., 183, 183n, 187, 190

Battle of Britain, 2, 43

Battle of Stalingrad, 174

Batum, 151

Bazaar, 137, 138

Beaverbrook, William: and Moscow Conference, 39, 43, 47, 50, 51; mentioned, 34, 61, 140

Bell Company, 175

Belyaev, Alexander I., 104–5, 126, 128, 128n, 132, 133, 165n, 177n

Berlin, 188, 189, 222

Biryusov, S. T., 187

Black Sea, 151, 197, 208

Blechhammer, 185, 186

Bock, Fedor von, 11

Bolero, 135

Bolling Field, 26, 74n

Bomb line, 181–91 *passim*, 211, 229

Bor-Komorowski, Thaddeus, 202, 202n

Boston bomber, 49, 92–93, 115, 231

Bradley, Follett: Alsib, 152n; direct aid on eastern front, 144n; mission to Moscow, 125-38 *passim*; Velvet, 152, 161

Braov, 182n

Brereton, L. H., 141, 151

Bridge, Donald, 190n

British Air Commission, 84

British Air Ministry, 110n

British Commonwealth of Nations, 112

British Purchasing Commission, 3

Brooke, Alan, 144

Brown, Douglas, 73

Bucharest, 182, 182n, 183, 183n, 184, 187, 190, 211, 212

Budapest, 182, 182n, 188, 208, 208n

Bulgaria, 181n, 185

Bureau of Aeronautics, 118

Burns, James H.: Division of Defense Aid Reports, 16, 17; heavies for Russia, 46; mentioned, 117; Moscow Conference, 44; Russian aircraft requests, 18; Soviet Protocol Committee, 217

C-1 Automatic Pilot, 198n, 210

C-46, 174

C-47: for air service with Russia, 221, 222; approved for Russia, 117; delivered via Alsib, 170; in Fourth Protocol, 218; in Second Protocol, 175; in Third Protocol, 174, 175

INDEX

251

C-53, 117
C-87, 165n, 221
Cabell, C. P., 183
Cairo, 87, 153, 160, 221
Canada, 102
Cape of Good Hope, 56, 169
Caspian Sea, 151
Cassidy, Henry, 148
Cate, James L., 198n
Caucasus: air force in, 139–63 passim; mentioned, 136, 227
Central-Aero-Hydro-Dynamic Institute, 6
Chaney, James E., 42, 44, 46, 48, 49, 50, 53, 71, 96
China, 104, 105, 105n, 126, 175
Chita, 193, 220
Churchill, Winston S.: Argentia Conference, 34; convoys to Russia, 67, 68, 122–24; Hopkins, 55; Maisky, 37, 38; transportation of supplies to Russians, 57; Velvet, 139–63 passim; visit to Stalin, 142, 143, 144; Warsaw uprising, 202–7 passim
Chuvakhin, Dmitri S., 74
Civil Aeronautics Board, 89
Clark, Alan, 203
Combined Bomber Offensive Plan, 193
Combined Chiefs of Staff: bomb line liaison with Russians, 184–89 passim; mentioned, 118, 158, 160, 181, 185
Combined Staff Planners, 223
Connally, Thomas T., 172
Connolly, Donald H., 170
Constanta, 182, 182n
Convoys to Russia, 56, 57, 58, 63–68, 121–22, 142, 143, 146, 149
Co-Prosperity Sphere, 95
Coy, Wayne, 22
Cracow, 182n
Craig, H. A., 104
Craven, Wesley F., 198n
Curtis, Charles P., Jr., 16
Curtiss-Wright Company, 72
Czechoslovakia, 185

DB-3, 9
DB-7, 121n
DC-3, 116, 127
Deane, John R.: air service to Russia, 221, 222; American policy toward Russia, 215, 217; bases in Siberia,

223–26; bomb line and liaison, 181, 184–87; Eastern Command, 193–214 passim
Debrecen, 182n, 197
Defense Aid, 42, 54, 58, 114
Deruluft, 220
Dill, John, 118
Director of Military Requirements, 102
Division of Defense Aid Reports, 16, 17
Doolittle, James H., 103
Douglas Aircraft Company, 92, 171
Dresden, 189
Drohobycz, 198
Drummond, R. M., 136, 153–63 passim, 163n

Eaker, Ira C., 182n, 183, 184, 185, 197
Eastern Command, United States Strategic Air Forces, 192–214 passim
Eden, 110n
Egypt, 104, 121, 146, 149, 153, 156
8th Air Force, 189n, 198, 200, 204
82d Air Depot Group, 171
82d Fighter Group, 183
Eisenhower, Dwight D., 103
El Alamein, 161
Elizabeth City, 178n
Embick, Stanley D., 44, 46
Evill, D. C. S., 151

Fairbanks, 102, 125, 127, 128, 132, 134, 135, 167, 168, 169, 170, 179, 180n, 218, 231n
Falalaev, Fedor, 153–56
Faymonville, Philip R.: aircraft technicians for Russia, 74, 74n, 75; assists Burns, 16; information on air routes, 96; mentioned, 21, 22, 68; and Standley, 91
Ferrying Command, 88, 117
15th Air Force, 183, 189n, 200, 208n
Fifth Protocol, 219
Fighters. See P-39; P-40
Flying Boats, 218
Foreign Ministers Conference, 223
4th Flying Corps, 198
Fourth Protocol, 215–19 passim
France: fall of, 2; invasion of, 192, 193, 204, 216, 223
Frankel, Samuel B., 65
Frantic, 182, 194n, 198n

Galati, 182, 182n

252 INDEX

Galatz. *See* Galati
Galland, Adolf, 198
German Air Force. *See* Luftwaffe
German High Command, 198
German Sixth Army, 162
Germany, 40, 43, 111, 111n, 112, 112n, 185, 193, 200
Gillies, John A., 93–94
Goebbels, Joseph P., 201
Goering, Hermann W., 122
Golikov, Philip I., 20, 21, 21n, 26n
Golitov, General, 50
Gormly, Samuel, Jr., 182
Great Britain. *See* Churchill
Great Falls, 168, 170
Greely, John N., 90–94
Griffiss, Townsend, 75, 96, 98
Gromov, Michael, 24, 25, 26
Gromyko, Andrei, 26, 116

Halverson Detachment, 141
Hamilton, Rear Admiral, 121
Hampton, Thomas K., 212n
Hanley, T. J., Jr., 40, 63
Harriman, Averell: American policy toward Russia, 215, 216, 217; bases in Russia, 193, 195, 224–25; defective P-40's, 71; mentioned, 34; Moscow Conference, 44, 46, 47, 49, 51, 52, 53; Moscow Protocol, 57, 58; shuttle service, 88; Velvet, 143; Warsaw uprising, 204, 207
Harvey, Alva L., 127, 131, 131n, 132n
Hauser, John N., 94
Hawaii, 5, 58
Heavy bombers: for Russia, 43, 44, 45, 165, 178; in shuttle missions, 197, 200, 206
Henderson, Loy, 74, 91
HE-111, 198
Hickam Field, 198
Hill, Edmund W., 211, 212
Hitler, 35, 52, 66, 107, 109, 124, 202
Hopkins, Harry: aircraft for Russia, 46, 117, 119; Alsib, 105–6, 105n; financing aid to Russia, 47; mission to Moscow, 28-36; ships for Russia, 61, 86; Soviet Protocol Committee, 217; technicians for Russia, 73, 74; Velvet, 142, 142n
Hull, Cordell: aid to Russia, 59; air service to Russia, 105n; bases in Siberia, 98–99; Iran, 83; war against Japan, 223

Hungary, 183, 200
Hurley, Patrick J., 162n
Hurricane, 49, 69, 121n, 139, 147

I-15, 9
I-16, 9
Iceland, 68, 102, 178n
India, 61, 104, 175
Invergordon, 29
Iran, 33, 56, 64, 68, 80–94 *passim*, 120, 121, 140, 159, 168, 169, 179, 216, 219
Iraq, 82
Irkutsk, 193, 220
Italy, 193, 194, 194n, 197, 198, 200, 201, 203, 205, 208n

Japan, 17n, 95-108 *passim*, 125, 173, 187n, 193, 205, 223, 225, 226
John Brown Club, 172
Joint Aircraft Committee, 3
Joint Board Estimate, 40, 41, 95, 96
Joint Chiefs of Staff: aircraft allocations to Russia, 165; air service with Russia, 220; American forces in Siberia, 101, 226; bases in Russia, 193, 195, 208; exchange of weather data with Russia, 209; mentioned, 190; Warsaw uprising, 204
Jokanga, 122
JU-88, 198

Kalinov, Cyrille, 10
Kamchatka, 98, 225
Kampinos, 203
Karachi, 82, 83
Karmilitsin, Ivan S., 93-94
Katyusha, 50, 50n
Kazan, 81, 82
Kazvin, 76, 84, 85
Keitel, Wilhelm, 198n
Kennan, George F., 207
Kesselring, Albert, 10
Kessler, Alfred, 193, 200
Khartoum, 87, 88
Khosrowabad, 83
Khudyakov, S. A., 211, 212
Kiev, 140
King, Ernest J., 118, 142
King, Myron, 190
Kittyhawk, *See* P-40
Kobin, Michael, 232
Kola Inlet. *See* Murmansk

INDEX

253

Komsomolsk, 225, 226
Konigsberg, 204
Kopets, General, 11
Korolenko, General, 137
Kotov, Lieutenant General, 183
Kovalev, General, 212n
Krasnoyarsk, 128, 130, 131
Kremlin. See Stalin
Krutikov, Alexei D., 65
Kuibyshev, 89, 90, 153
Kuter, Laurence S., 226

Land, Emory S., 63
Leeb, Wilhelm Ritter von, 11
Lend-Lease: Act, 4; Administration, 88, 89; aircraft, 95, 96, 97, 105, 107, 125, 132, 138, 194n; mentioned, 24, 47, 54, 59, 60, 61, 87, 108, 163n, 164, 169, 178, 192, 215, 216, 216n, 217, 229, 231; supplies, 143, 145, 148, 154, 159, 162, 196
Lenin, 6
Leningrad, 232
Levant, 159n
Liaison, 181–91 passim
Libya, 140
Light bomber. See A-20
Lightning. See P-38
Litvinov, Maxime, 98-99, 105–6
Lockheed-Hudson. See A-29
Lodz, 213
Lovett, Robert A.: aircraft allocations, 20, 26, 27, 46, 54, 117, 119n; delivery routes, 19, 20; spare parts for Russia, 78; stopgap aircraft aid to Russia, 19, 20
Luftwaffe: mentioned 2, 51, 66, 109, 110, 111, 144, 149, 168, 174, 193, 199, 232; strength of, 1, 9, 11, 13n, 32, 110n, 111n, 161, 162, 175n, 198n
Lukashev, Konstantin, 62

MacArthur, Douglas, 99
MacFarlane, Mason, 194n
Machin, Michael G., 231, 231n
McCloy, John J., 63
Maisky, Ivan, 38
McNarney, Joseph T., 29, 30, 31, 33, 96
Malinovsky, Rodion, 183
Manchuria, 136
Maritime Provinces, 98n, 107, 187, 223, 225

Marshall, George C.: air routes to Russia, 104, 105, 133; impact of Pearl Harbor on aid to Russia, 58, 59, 60, 61; impact of relations with Japan on Siberian project, 97n; needs of AAF in determining allocations, 40, 114, 115, 118-19, 228; spare parts for Russia, 28; stopgap aircraft aid to Russia, 18, 19, 22; Velvet, 142, 145, 146, 150, 155
Martin Company, 26
Materiel Command, 169
Maxwell, Russell L., 144n
Mediterranean Allied Air Forces, 182, 183, 211, 212
Medium bomber. See B-25
ME-109, 9
ME-110, 9
Meyers, B. E., 26, 77, 78
Miami, 87
Michela, Joseph A.: capacity of Archangel, 64n; defective P-40's, 71, 75, 76; information on air routes, 96, 97-98, 104; O-52's, 77; technicians for Russia, 73
Middle East. See Iran
Mielec, 182, 190n
MIG, 9
Mikolajczyk, Stanislaw, 202
Mirgorod, 195, 199, 209
Miskolc, 182n
Mitchell, Billy, 96
M-9 Norden Bombsight, 198n, 210
Molotov, Vyacheslav M.: 152; air routes to Russia, 90, 132, 136, 137; mentioned, 105, 105n, 152; Moscow Protocol, 51; pact with Ribbentrop, 2, 5; Second Protocol, 115; Standley's criticism, 172; Velvet, 159, 161
Moore, R. C., 117
Moravska Ostrava, 186
Morgan, Herbert, Jr., 224
Moscow. See Stalin
Moscow Conference, 37, 38, 54, 140
Moscow Protocol, 37, 46, 51, 55, 56, 57, 61, 71, 109, 114n, 120–21, 121n
Motter, T. H. Vail, 180n
Mozhaisky, Alexander F., 6
Munitions Assignment Board, 117, 178n
Murmansk, 56, 64, 65, 66, 121, 122, 196, 232
Mustang. See P-51

254 INDEX

Navy Bureau of Aeronautics, 3
Nedosekin, Lieutenant Colonel, 232
Nelson, Donald, 63
Newfoundland, 45
Nikolaevsk, 225, 226
9th Air Service Command, 153
Nome, 50, 102, 125, 126, 132, 134, 232
Normandy, 198
North Africa, invasion of, 146, 154, 161, 192
North American Company, 26

Odertal, 186
Odessa, 212, 212n
Office of Production Management, 17
O-52: deliveries under Moscow Protocol, 121n; lack of spare parts for, 77; for Russians, 46, 53, 53n, 54, 54n, 61
Oil fields: Caucasus, 140; Persian, 144; Rumanian, 139, 141, 159n
Oumansky, Constantine: Soviet requests for aid, 15, 16, 20, 21, 26n, 28, 30, 35
Overlord. See France, invasion of

P-38, 177, 177n, 183, 200
P-39: delivery of, 128, 167, 171n, 177, 179n; lack of spare parts for, 76; in Protocols, 121n, 174, 175, 176, 218; Russians taught to use, 218n; and Stalin, 147, 148, 149; value to Russians, 231–32
P-40: defective, 69-79, 90, 94; delivery of, 128, 134, 147, 167, 171n, 176, 177, 232; initial shipment of, 19, 19n, 20, 21, 22, 23, 29, 30, 31; in Moscow Protocol, 46, 49, 54, 61, 120–21, 121n
P-47, 177, 177n
P-51, 177, 197, 200, 206
P-59, 219n
P-63: Russians taught to use, 219n; in Third Protocol, 175, 176, 177, 177n; in Fourth Protocol, 218
P-80, 219n
Pacific. See Alsib; Japan; Siberia
Panama, 58
Pan American Airways, 86, 87, 88
Patterson Field, 26
PBN, 178n
PBY, 178n, 219
Pearl Harbor, 37, 57, 58, 59, 62, 86, 87, 95, 96, 98, 98n, 99, 107

Perminov, A. R., 198
Persian Gulf Service Command, 163n, 170
PE-2, 9, 48
Philippines, 5, 87, 107
Piryatin, 195, 199, 209
Ploesti, 182, 182n. See also Oil fields: Rumanian
Poland, government - in - exile, 186; Home Army, 202, 222; mentioned, 193, 198, 200, 207, 210, 213, 214n; partisans, 186
Poltava, 195, 198, 198n, 208n, 209, 211, 212n, 214n
Posevalk, 189
Potsdam Conference, 214, 222, 227
PQ. See Convoys
Pravda, 35, 36
President's Soviet Protocol Committee, 216
Prossen, P. J., 131
Pursuit planes. See P-39; P-40

Radom, 207
Rahmel, 200
Ramsbottom-Isherwood, H. N. G., 69
Red Air Force. See Soviet Air Force
Repin, Alexander K., 21
Riga, 182
Roberts, Frank N., 225, 226
Rommel, Erwin, 104, 143
Roosevelt, Elliott, 195
Roosevelt, Franklin D.: air route to Russia, 90, 105; Alsib, 125, 126, 137, 138; American internees, 213; American policy in Pacific, 100, 106; Argentia meeting, 34; bases in Russia, 101–7 passim, 193; cash and carry, 2–3; convoys to Russia, 67, 68, 123; heavies for Russia, 22, 23, 45; impact of Pearl Harbor on aid to Russia, 59, 60; invasion of North Africa, 123; priority of aid to Russia, 42, 63, 112, 113; shipment of planes to Russians, 14-27 passim, 61, 167, 176; technicians, 72; transports for Russia, 119; Velvet, 123–24, 139-63 passim; Warsaw uprising, 202–7 passim
Royal Air Force, 2, 3, 173, 183n, 203, 204, 222
Ruhland, 198
Rumania, 181n, 198, 200, 207

INDEX 255

Rundstedt, Gerd von, 11
Russian High Command, 151
Russian Military Mission (Alaska), 133
Rychagov, General, 11

Safety line. *See* Bomb line; Liaison
Sarajevo, 185
Schuyler, General, 212
Seattle, 220
Second Protocol, 109–24 *passim*, 164, 170, 180
Second Ukrainian Army, 183
Services of Supply, 176
7th Ferrying Group, 134
17th Depot Repair Squadron, 171
SHAEF, 209
Shakurin, Commissar, 48, 49
Shaposhnikov, Boris M., 144
Shuttle bombing. *See* Eastern Command
Siberia: project, 223–27 *passim*; survey of, 95–108 *passim*; 125, 126, 127, 130, 131, 137–38. *See also* Alsib
Sikorski, Wladyslaw, 140n
16-Liberator Project, 87. *See also* Velvet; Siberia
Slavin, General, 186
Smolensk, 232
Sofia, 183n
Somervell, Brehon, 176
Soviet aircraft industry, 6, 7, 7n, 8, 11, 12, 110, 111n, 174n
Soviet air force, 6, 9, 10, 11, 13n, 32, 51, 109, 110, 110n, 111, 111n, 148, 162, 184, 232
Soviet Military Mission to the United States, 20, 21, 29
Soviet pilots, 23, 24
Soviet Purchasing Commission, 104, 173
Soviet Union: inclusion under Lend-Lease, 4; policy toward American internees, 103, 103n; pre-1941 orders for planes, 8; requests for heavy industrial goods, 18; stopgap aircraft aid to, 14–36 *passim*; unfreezing Soviet assets in U.S., 15
Spaatz, Carl, 88, 197, 203, 221
Spalding, S. P., 173
Spare parts, 27, 28, 70, 75, 77-79
Sperry Company, 26
Spitfire, 49, 147, 149, 150, 166n
Spokane, 24, 26, 81

Stalin, Joseph V.: AAF plane landing in Siberia, 103, 103n; aircraft shipments to Russia, 48, 62; Alsib, 102, 107, 125, 134, 135; American internees, 213; bases in Siberia, 224–27 *passim*; Churchill, 38–41 *passim*; convoys to Russia, 68, 122–24; criticism of Western aid, 143, 148; direct military aid, 140; Eastern Command, 193, 195; German air strength, 8n, 32, 110n; Hopkins, 30, 31, 32, 33; invasion of North Africa, 143; Russian air strength, 8n, 32, 110n; second front, 143; shuttle line, 89; Velvet, 139–63 *passim*; war against Japan, 125, 135, 137, 138, 223, 225, 227; Warsaw uprising, 202–7 *passim*
Stalingrad, 13n, 111, 162, 162n, 231
Standley, William H.: air service to Russia, 89, 219–22 *passim*; Alsib, 102, 105n, 107, 126, 132; Greely mission, 91, 92; lack of Russian publicity to American aid, 171–72; second front, 147n
Steinhardt, Laurence, 30, 35, 52, 73
Sterligov, General, 127, 128, 133, 137
Stettin, 185, 188
Stettinius, Edward R., 26, 59, 62
Stimson, Henry L.: AAF needs, 40, 228; Alsib, 23, 125; deliveries of planes to Russians, 21n, 25, 45, 59, 60, 114; Greely mission, 90, 92; opposes political overtones of aid to Russia, 113; Oumansky, 23; routes to Russia, 82–83; Soviet Military Mission, 26; spare parts for Russia, 27, 28
Stockholm, 221, 222
Stormovik, 48, 50
Strategy and Policy Group, 187
Stratemeyer, George E., 124
Superfortresses, 226
Supplemental National Defense Appropriations Bill, 47
Susaikov, General, 212
Sweden, 221

Takoradi, 81
Tedder, Arthur, 188
Tehran, 82, 83, 84, 87, 90, 103, 151, 219, 220, 221, 222
Tehran Conference, 178, 192, 193, 194, 195, 214, 217, 221, 223

256 INDEX

Telpukhovskii, B. S., 10
10th Air Force, 141
Tenth Kilometer Airdrome, 69
Third Protocol: mentioned, 216, 218; negotiations over, 164, 172–80 *passim*
376th Bombardment Group, 151
Thurston, Walter, 75–76, 84
Tirpitz, 121
Tito, 194n
Tokyo, 17n, 155
Tokyo Raid. *See* Doolittle
Tomahawk. *See* P-40
Topeka Army Air Field, 224
Torch, 146, 149, 150
Towers, John H., 118
Transports: deliveries to Russia, 165–66; production of, 117; Russian requests for, 116–19, 128, 129, 130, 132, 135
Truesdell, Patrick K., 188n
Truman, Harry S., 222
Tupolev, Andrei N., 6
Turkey, 197, 221
205th RAF Group, 205

Ukraine, 140, 195, 227, 229
Uman, 140
Umm Qasr, 83
United Nations, 147
United States Military Mission to the USSR, 193–214 *passim*
United States Strategic Air Forces. *See* Eastern Command
United States Supply Mission in the USSR, 173
Urals, 12, 41

Varna, 182n
Velvet, 139–63 *passim*, 228
Vienna, 185, 188, 189
Vilna, 202
Vinnitsa, 208, 208n
Vistula, 203, 206
Vladivostok, 21, 33, 49, 50, 64, 98, 98n, 106, 155, 187n, 226

Volga, 41, 163n
Volhynia, 202
Vorobiev, General, 183
Voronezh, 231
Voroshilov, Kliment E., 144
Vyshinsky, Andrei Y., 221

Waldau, Otto von, 10
Walker, K. N., 46
War Department: general staff, 187; opposition to aiding Russia, 15, 22; Second Protocol, 109, 164; shuttle service, 89; Velvet, 140–63 *passim*
Warsaw: mentioned, 190, 204; uprising, 200, 202–7, 209
Washington Protocol. *See* Second Protocol
Wehrmacht, 203, 228
Welles, Sumner: Alsib, 20; Oumansky, 20; policy toward Russia, 15, 33, 34, 35; stopgap aircraft aid to Russia, 18, 19
Wheeler, Raymond A., 83, 91
White Sea, 64, 66, 122
Willkie, Wendell, 147
Wilson, Henry Maitland, 181, 181n, 185, 186, 194n
Wilson line. *See* Wilson, Henry Maitland
Winant, John G., 83

Yak, 9, 183
Yakoviev, General, 187
Yakovlev, N. D., 31
Yalta Conference, 188, 189, 189n, 208, 211, 222, 225, 226
York, Edward J., 103
York, John, 217
Yugoslavia, 183, 185

Zagreb, 188, 189, 189n
Zemke, Hubert, 31, 31n, 53, 69, 70, **73**
Zhukovsky, Nikolai Y., 6
Zhukovsky Air Academy, 6, 6n
Ziombeck, F. J., 218n